EQUALITY·FOR WOMEN

PROSPERITY FOR ALL

EQUALITY FOR WOMEN

PROSPERITY FOR ALL

THE DISASTROUS GLOBAL CRISIS OF GENDER INEQUALITY

AUGUSTO LÓPEZ-CLAROS
and BAHIYYIH NAKHJAVANI

ST. MARTIN'S PRESS ☘ NEW YORK

EQUALITY FOR WOMEN = PROSPERITY FOR ALL. Copyright © 2018 by
Augusto López-Claros and Bahiyyih Nakhjavani. All rights reserved.
Printed in the United States of America. For information, address
St. Martin's Press, 175 Fifth Avenue, New York, N.Y. 10010.

www.stmartins.com

Designed by Steven Seighman

Library of Congress Cataloging-in-Publication Data

Names: Lopez-Claros, Augusto, author. | Nakhjavani, Bahiyyih, author.
Title: Equality for women=prosperity for all : the disastrous global crisis of
    gender inequality / Augusto Lopez-Claros and Bahiyyih Nakhjavani.
Other titles: Equality for women equals prosperity for all
Description: First edition. | New York : St. Martin's Press, [2018] | Includes
    bibliographical references and index.
Identifiers: LCCN 2018017186 | ISBN 9781250051189 (hardcover) |
    ISBN 9781466852044 (ebook)
Subjects: LCSH: Sex discrimination. | Women's rights. | Equality. | Economic
    development.
Classification: LCC HQ1237 .L65 2018 | DDC 323.3/4—dc23
LC record available at https://lccn.loc.gov/2018017186

Our books may be purchased in bulk for promotional, educational, or business use.
Please contact your local bookseller or the Macmillan Corporate and Premium
Sales Department at 1-800-221-7945, extension 5442, or by email at
MacmillanSpecialMarkets@macmillan.com.

First Edition: October 2018

10 9 8 7 6 5 4 3 2 1

CONTENTS

ACKNOWLEDGMENTS

THIS BOOK COULD NOT have been written without the support and the insights of a large number of friends and colleagues, all of whom were patient enough to provide us with their feedback and observations, which did much to improve the final manuscript. We would like to acknowledge one colleague in particular, whose contributions were crucial to the writing of this book. Sarah Iqbal's research on the human rights dimension of gender equality was very much the starting point for the chapter "Rights and Wrongs." She also generously provided us with important data and valuable insights for the chapter on violence against women. This is a relatively new area of focus for the *Women, Business and the Law* report, a project that actually provided the initial inspiration for this book; the WBL project has been ably managed by Sarah in recent years.

It would be difficult to name all but equally impossible not to mention some readers whose insights, commentary, and encouragement helped to shape this book. Among these are Laurie Adams, Noorjahan Akbar, Veronika Bard, Kaushik Basu, Julia Berger, Nancy Birdsall, Maud de Boer Buquicchio, Erica Bosio, Diana Chacon, Monica Das Gupta, Bani Dugal, Amanda Ellis, Saba Ghori, Ruth Halperin-Kaddari, Coby Jones, Yasmeen Hassan, Ernesto Hernandez-Cata, Asif Islam (who brought to our attention key pieces of data and relevant dimensions of the literature and was one of our most committed readers), Melissa Johns, Jackie Jones, Khrystyna Kushnir, Nora Lankes, Hans Peter Lankes, Jannie Lilja, Mirta Tapia de Lopez, Cristina Manzano, Katherine Marshall, Yasmina Mata, Bahia Mitchell, Elena Mustakova, Moisés Naim, Lindsay Northover, Valeria Perotti (who co-authored with one of us a paper on the role of culture in economic development which was the starting point for the chapter "The Culture Question"), Rita Ramalho (who contributed several key ideas and material to the chapter on women and work), Anna Reva, Eduardo Rodriguez Veltze, Melanne Verveer, and Farbod Youssefi. We would like to express special appreciation to Laura Apperson, Marcia Markland, and Katherine Haigler at St. Martin's Press who provided constant encouragement and generous editorial support. We are grateful to Debra Manette for her excellent copy editing, and Nancy Ackerman from AmadeaEditing provided expert additional editorial support. Any limitations and imperfections in the book, however, are our own.

The views expressed in this book are the authors' own and do not necessarily reflect those of the organizations with which they are affiliated.

INTRODUCTION

*As long as women are prevented from attaining their
highest possibilities, so long will men be unable to
achieve the greatness which might be theirs.*
—'Abdu'l-Bahá, Paris, 1912

THE RIDDLE OF THE SPHINX

The disparity between the sexes and their supposed equality has
posed a riddle that has perplexed minds great and small, in one
culture or another across the planet, since the beginning of time.
We cannot quite resolve the conundrum. Men and women belong to
the same species; we are all members of the human race. And yet we
are clearly different. It is not merely skin deep, this difference; it is
not "just" a disparity of race and color. It seems to be a fundamental
difference of function, of biology, some would even say of neurology,
psyche, possibly soul.

So how can we be "equal"? We have puzzled over this paradox
for millennia.

At first glance there seems to be no solution to the enigma, no answer to the riddle. We stare at the sexless features of this weathered
Sphinx[1] and find no clue in its blank gaze, no key to the pitiless differences spawned by its enigmatic gender. Indeed, obsessive scrutiny

only complicates matters, for the multiple disparities between men and women can blind our eyes, like sand. And so we have concluded over time that the only way to lay the problem to rest and resolve the riddle is by avoiding it altogether. We have drawn clear demarcations round our separate genders and defined who we are in strict relation to what we are not, just to reassure ourselves of our existence. In other words, we have preferred sex segregation to equality if only to control the threat posed by our differences.

A strict separation between the sexes, of social and political roles, of public and private space, has been one way of resolving the conundrum for many societies and cultures over the ages. It is like nationalism, racism, even religion. Countries can ignore each "other" and feel no economic or cultural threat, as long as they are miles apart; we can convince ourselves that "East is East and West is West and never the twain shall meet,"[2] as long as there is no outsourcing of the labor force and no international competition over the market. Similarly we have imagined that sex segregation could lay the riddle of gender to rest. As long as men and women kept to their separate spheres, as long as their roles and responsibilities were strictly defined and rigidly regulated by gender-specific laws and customs, we could try to convince ourselves that the problem did not actually exist. The patriarchal order has resolved the dilemma by ignoring the conundrum, and keeping women in their place.

But the Sphinx is a subtle creature. Her riddles have a way of returning to haunt us.

When Sophocles wrote his tragedy *Oedipus Rex* in 429 BC, he conjured what it would be like to live in a city cursed by the Sphinx. The imaginary Thebes of classical antiquity was a place where a man could murder his father with impunity and marry his mother without a qualm. It was a place where a son, standing innocent at the crossroads of choice with his eyes wide open, could still be completely blind to his own and his parents' true identity. And in this city, the wells were poisoned and people were dying because they could not solve the Sphinx's riddle.

Sophocles' play dramatized the terrible price society would pay if sexual taboos were ignored, if paternity was not strictly controlled, and if women were not kept in their place. The answer to the riddle of what walks with four legs in the morning, two legs at noon, and three in the evening was "man"; it was also a warning against a world in which sisters could be daughters, in which women could rule over their murdered husbands and commit incest with their sons. Sophocles was, in effect, sounding the credo of the patriarchal order.

But perhaps the real curse of the Sphinx is our blindness to the fact that it contains multiple meanings. The curse of our times is no longer what poisoned our wells in the past. The riddle of our age can no longer be solved by the old answers. The plague that is poisoning our civilizations today, and undermining our cultures, is neither incest, nor the loss of paternal identity. It is the segregation of the sexes. We are living in a world today cursed by gender inequality.

No one has a monopoly on it either. The curse is everywhere: in the public as well as the private sphere, at the domestic as well as the international level. It controls our finances, our information technology, our laws in many a land. It exists in rich countries as well as poor, can characterize every race that calls itself human, and has manifest itself across virtually all cultural traditions. The whole planet, and not just Thebes, lies in its grip.

It is also protean, for gender inequality assumes myriad shapes, a thousand and one different forms and faces: the control of joint income and assets in the household; the violation of basic human rights through enforced female seclusion and domestic violence; the abuse of power in the buying, selling, and inheriting of property; obsolete laws and our inability to implement new ones. Some kinds of inequality can be as subtle as mere misinformation, as invisible as the suppression of essential knowledge, which cripples a person's autonomy.

Other kinds, especially in the private sphere, can masquerade more gracefully, as protection, as security, even as "love." The sheer pervasiveness of this curse is proof of its complex causes, its multiple consequences. The riddle of the Sphinx can only be resolved by its own disparities in our times.

Its answer lies in the equality of the sexes.

LOOKING FOR ANSWERS

For more than two centuries, the inequalities prevalent between men and women in the world have been defined in moral terms.[3] The debate for and against gender equality, which began in the late eighteenth century and which is still far from being over, has traditionally been grounded in notions of human dignity and social justice. Many have spoken about how the suppression of women's rights and freedoms is inconsistent with democratic values and international law. We have focused on how it is a violation of ethics, a denial of basic logic, and a subversion of moral philosophy. We have argued about gender equality in terms of rights and wrongs.

But the subject has been pushed beyond the boundaries of ethics in recent decades. It has raised questions about religion and culture, which have provoked intense emotional debate in our times. Gender inequality has brought people out on the streets. It has morphed into a political cause as well as a quasi-religion and mystique. The exposure of physical and psychological abuse, of domestic oppression and emotional violence, has lifted voices and raised banners across the world. Veils have been cast off and reimposed. Women have refused to wear bras and claimed control over their reproductive rights. Much breath and rhetoric have been expended on this subject, and not just ink, but tears and sometimes even blood, have been dangerously spilt.

Lately, however, the discussion has become less heated. Emotion has been overtaken, to some degree at least, by economics. This is a relatively new development. The tone is cooler now, but steelier.

Debates are becoming determinedly measured, in more ways than one. Arguments on the subject are drawing on a growing body of academic research, which claims that the price we are paying for inequality is too high, that "gender inequality in education and employment reduces economic growth."[4] We are starting to assess the costs of inequality to society as a whole and to define women's lack of opportunity on economic rather than ethical grounds. This is a very different approach to the subject.

It has taken millennia for us to admit to this fundamental reality: that gender inequality is a waste of human resources. It has taken centuries to look, fairly and squarely, at the bottom line of women's rights. Although sexual oppression has existed for much longer than the environmental crisis, we have estimated the costs arising from climate change much more quickly, have been willing to evaluate the damage resulting from our ruthless exploitation of natural resources much more readily than we have been able to bring ourselves to account for the losses sustained, the potential squandered, and the myriads of lives ruined on this planet as a result of the systematic repression and abuse of half the human race.

Now we are finally beginning to sum it all up. We are learning to read the equation differently. It is time to recognize that equality for women = prosperity for all.

This book will ask some critical questions about the misallocation of resources and the restrictive laws affecting women, about the relationship between failing economies and the legal status of women, about the long-term consequences for society of ignoring the culture of violence against women. Some of these questions are so complex that they have already resulted in a century of false answers, to the detriment of both sexes. Others are so troubling that we have found ways to sidestep them for millennia, to our mutual cost. But although many of these questions are still challenging, we can no longer elude the answers.

And there are two reasons why.

The first, as already indicated, is the blindingly obvious but until relatively recently unacknowledged fact that the subjugation of women has resulted in a whole range of social ills and possibly even political dysfunction across the world. What is more, these ills are becoming worse the longer they are allowed to prevail and are posing a threat to our collective security. The suppression of women is causing grave consequences across the generations; we can no longer ignore it. The dysfunction of civil society resulting from the denial of women's aspirations is a growing burden; we can no longer sustain it. Society as a whole is paying a heavy price for the limitations imposed on women, and the costs of inequality, economically as well as environmentally, individually as well as collectively, are just too high to pay any longer.

The second reason is that gender equality is not a zero-sum game; it does not imply any loss for men. Quite the reverse. It is of benefit to all and to the advantage of all, because the development of human potential is a collective necessity. We all pay the price when our legal systems curtail a woman's property rights, or reduce the number of jobs she can hold, or place restrictions on her ability to contribute to the "business of life," or subject her to a culture of violence, both physically and psychologically. The most competitive countries in the world, those that are prosperous, that have attained high levels of income per capita, and that are currently operating near the boundaries of what economists call the "technology frontier," are the very same countries where women have the greatest equality, where their rights are protected, their well-being is promoted, and their potential is increasingly enhanced. In other words, when men walk in partnership with women, it is to their own advantage. When they do not, economies fail.

WHY ECONOMIES FAIL

Of course, oversimplification will not serve; this subject, as the Sphinx well knows, is a complex and multifaceted one. There are many reasons why a country's economy may not flourish. For example, it may depend for its income on a handful of commodity exports, the prices for which are beyond its control. This happened in 2009, when the Russian economy contracted by 8 percent because it was entirely dependent on oil and a few other commodities, the prices of which collapsed as a result of the global financial crisis. A country's economy may also be unable to sustain improvements in living standards because of volatile conditions, such as bad weather, changes in taste, or other unexpected shocks. In the early 1980s, US monetary policy turned sharply contractionary to tackle double-digit inflation, and the subsequent rise in interest rates all over the developing world precipitated a debt crisis, which led to years of low growth. Frequently, authorities may simply fail to implement policies that are supportive of growth, through excessive borrowing, or by spending resources they do not have, or by wasting them on oversized military establishments and prestige projects instead of education and public health. Even when macroeconomic policies are focused on the so-called right things, such as improved productivity and competitiveness, a country can suffer from a range of institutional weaknesses—widespread corruption, excessive bureaucracy and red tape, an overly protective trade regime—all of which undermine private sector investment.

In addition, we do not fully understand the relative importance of all these factors—accumulation of savings, the declining role of agriculture, demography, government policy, migration, technological change, globalization, to name but a few. We do not entirely grasp their relative roles, either, in shaping the evolution of income inequality, particularly between men and women, and the links between this inequality and economic growth. Some of these factors are obviously more amenable to change than others through shifts in the content of policies. Others—technological innovations, for example—are more exogenous in nature, responding to a combination of factors, such as human creativity, the profit motive, and, to a lesser extent, government incentives. We also cannot ignore that the relative importance of such factors will naturally vary from country to country, depending on its stage of development; their significance also shifts over time, in response to structural changes in the global economy.

Economists have built successful careers on the strength of failures that cannot be ignored. Failed economies have been exhaustively analyzed, critically assessed, painstakingly compared, and laboriously studied over the past decades. Problems related to mindless regulation, rampant inflation, lack of policy implementation, and endemic corruption have kept experts busy since the early decades of the twentieth century, when it became lucrative to propose theories on how economies could improve. But the one factor that seldom enters the discussion when assessing the effectiveness of any particular economic policy concerns the role of women. The single subject that is systematically relegated to peripheral importance is gender. It is in this area that our failures have been the most glaring.

Perhaps we have ignored the gender issue because we have failed to see women as essential protagonists of successful economic development. And perhaps we have underestimated the importance of the role played by the law in influencing the lives of women and enhancing economic opportunities for them. This book will focus on the relationship among these three key factors—women, economic opportunity, and the law—in an attempt to come closer to solving the riddle of equal rights.

WOMEN, BUSINESS, AND THE LAW

For those who have examined gender inequalities from a legal perspective, it rapidly becomes clear that governments virtually everywhere use the law to abuse women's rights and discriminate against women. And it is equally clear that the first casualty of such discrimination is a woman's economic empowerment. In every legal system in the world that is in some way geared against gender equality, women suffer from an economic point of view. The Gordian knot between business practice and the laws of the land has effectively created a stranglehold for women everywhere. If they are to acquire those necessary rights that would make them equal partners with men in society, this stranglehold needs to be loosened.

Innumerable studies conducted in recent decades have exposed just how many forms of gender discrimination are embedded in the law and how these varying aspects of discrimination have dramatic economic consequences for the lives of women. The law can curtail job opportunities available to a woman, reducing meaningful recompense for her social contributions. It can impose limits on her working hours or on the types of industries in which she can be employed, excluding her from major sectors of the economy and, in particular, from better-paid jobs. The law can place a married woman at a disadvantage in terms of gender-differentiated property rights, giving control of household assets to her husband. Since banks almost always prefer to use land, buildings, and other physical assets as security for loans, moreover, the law can also prevent a man's wife from utilizing those assets as collateral to gain independent access to the financial system. The law can impose restrictions on a married woman's freedom of movement too, requiring that she have permission from her husband to work or to travel. In many countries, moreover, the law designates the husband as head of the household, which gives him control over key decisions, such as choosing the family residence, obtaining official documents necessary to start a business, and engaging in activities that boost entrepreneurship. In all these cases, the law is being used, consciously or not, to undermine the very conditions that would be conducive to the establishment of a more just and equitable society.

Since these facts have gradually become obvious to thinkers and analysts over the past few decades, increasing research has been undertaken to examine the causes and evaluate the consequences of the economic dimensions of gender discrimination sanctioned by laws around the world. One example of such a systematic examination is the Women, Business and the Law (WBL) project at the World Bank, and its findings will be drawn upon in this book as a means of analyzing the links between women, economics, and the law.

The WBL project monitors the relationship between gender equality and the law in 173 economies, accounting for 98 percent of world gross national product. It provides a close reading of the constitutions, the civil codes, the family law, and other legal instruments in these countries in order to assess their impact on women's lives. It asks a series of critical questions that highlight the possibility of restrictions on women's participation in the economy in order to reveal areas of gender discrimination within different dimensions of the law. It then analyzes the limits imposed on equality so as to show the impact of such discrimination on the broader economic life of the nation.[5]

Set in relation to one another and in conjunction with a close reading of the law in each of the economies analyzed, the answers to these questions offer a compelling dataset, a fascinating map outlining the legal impediments affecting women's participation in key areas of economic life. They also provide evidence of how these impediments can compromise the economic performance of the country as a whole. They show, at a glance, not only where the law is being used to abuse woman's rights but also which forms of abuse directly correlate to and have an impact on the economic health of a nation. The results, based on a cross section of countries, are effectively a clinical diagnosis of the current state of gender equality in the world.

The 2016 *Women, Business and the Law* report addresses some of the critical questions to be explored in this book. Its data illustrate how the interrelationships between restrictive laws, weakened economies, and women can be enlightening as well as surprising, disturbing but also difficult to ignore. It proves that, like most enduring riddles, the questions we ask often provide us with the best of answers.

These chapter summaries highlight some of those questions.

THE CHAPTERS

1: The People Problem

Where are the missing women of the world and how much are we paying for their disappearance? Who is killing the baby girls and what are the long-term consequences of "son preference"? In the past, we thought the "people problem" simply meant there were too many of us. Now we realize that the dangers posed by a population explosion may be less ominous than those we create when we leave half the population out of the definition of "us." Chapter 1 analyzes the relationship between gender equality and demographics and asks why men always come first.

2: The Virus of Violence

Why do the privileges of "son preference" invariably lead to violence against women? How do imbalanced demographic patterns impact the health and survival of women and girls, and what are the exclusively female forms of abuse to which they are subjected in various cultures and societies? Chapter 2 evaluates the root causes and endemic consequences of violence against women and assesses the costs of the physical, psychological, and economic discrimination against them, particularly under the so-called protective guise of provisions and prohibitions of family and labor law.

3: Women and Work

What is "woman's work"? Why are women sometimes kept out of the labor force and so often relegated to the least well paid or least prestigious jobs when they choose to join it? What happens to an economy when women who want to work outside the home are given few incentives or are actively discouraged from contributing their talents to society? Chapter 3 looks closely at the consequences of women's exclusion from the economy, at their underrepresentation in decision-making roles, and at whether or not quotas help address the problem of their diminished political and economic empowerment.

4: The Culture Question

What if outdated labor laws cannot be changed because of cultural taboos? What if women who try to improve their lot become victims of cultural crimes? Can legislation intervene when religion sanctifies certain interpretations of gender roles and rights and privileges the status quo that is resistant to change? Chapter 4 attempts to address one of the most complex, contentious, and ambiguous aspects of gender inequality: namely, how culture and "cultural exceptionalism" have dominated discussion about the universality of human rights.

5: Rights and Wrongs

Can universal rights really have an impact on gender equality? Can international conventions change age-old customs at the grass roots? And have female suffrage and the vote actually empowered women to legislate change over the course of the past century? Chapter 5 explores this history from the mid-nineteenth century until the present day and looks at the ways in which civil law, common law, and, increasingly, sharia as well as traditional Asian laws have influenced women's mobility, protected their marital and inheritance rights, and shielded them from "legal" abuse.

6: Education for Equality

Where does education fit into the equation? How does it influence gender equality and have a lasting impact on the economic health of a society? Is it really the ultimate barrier that could resolve the issue of gender inequality, or is it actually the ultimate threat to young girls who seek higher education in certain cultures? What kind of education can serve the goal of improving gender equality and how far can the fabric of civic society be enhanced and changed by it? In Chapter 6 we gauge the benefits of providing and evaluate the costs of denying education to girls.

7: The Costs of Inequality

This book begins by asking why economies fail and what women have to do with it. But it ends by looking at the costs of maintaining systems of governance that license injustice and privilege gender inequality. Chapter 7 looks closely at the data provided by the WBL project at the World Bank in order to assess which laws must change if women's rights are to be upheld, their security protected, their employment access improved, and their education enhanced. It asks whether gender equality can really bring prosperity to all.

1

THE PEOPLE PROBLEM

*Numbers tell us, quietly, a terrible story
of inequality and neglect.*
—AMARTYA SEN

*When we see extremely skewed demographics,
we have very good reason to suspect
that something is wrong.*
—ERIC RIES

GENDER GENOCIDE

Let us try to keep a measured tone and talk politely about this subject, if we can. The naked truth is that after centuries of denial, we are finally acknowledging what might be called a predilection for sons in certain societies. That is to say, we are now ready to admit that many people, from various cultural backgrounds and across a wide spectrum of ages, have preferred to have baby boys rather than girls. This is one of the most disturbing and age-old manifestations of gender discrimination in the world and is accompanied by its dark double, the rejection of daughters.

Where have all the women gone, and what has happened to our girls?

There are bound to be missing factors in any assessment of what are the drivers of human prosperity. It is difficult to analyze exhaustively how these factors can weaken the fabric of society, or in what ways, for instance, discriminatory labor laws can jeopardize economic growth. But of all the absent elements in this analysis, none is as significant as leaving women out of it altogether.

There was a time when leaving women out of the records was the norm in both East and West. Most women in history, unless they happened to be queens or empresses, notorious prostitutes or apostates, were not considered a significant part of any equation. We learn of the missing through paintings and through literature, through private letters and personal objects, like thimbles, spindles, spoons, and lace. But history rarely gave us the identities of the users. The triumphs and tragedies of half the human race were all too easily obliterated.

But we have become better at keeping track of the missing in our own times. It is possible to maintain records of our losses in undreamed-of ways today. Instead of writing elegies read by few or private diary entries intended for none, we now mourn the missing publicly, litter the window fronts of post offices with photos of lost cats and dogs, and stick the faces of our children on the lampposts of city streets, to advertise their disappearances. And there may be darker reasons too for remembering. Massacres have left their bloody traces on the pages of history. Holocausts and genocides must not be forgotten if they are not to be repeated, even after years of political amnesia and denial. And we have discovered that forensic science can pursue war crimes into their graves and bring their perpetrators to court at last. We have learned to memorialize the missing in order to bear witness to their rights as well as to recall their names.

The erasure of half the human race surpasses designation, however; it is beyond calculation. It was not until this century that the missing women of the world began to be evaluated by society.

Decades before the extremist group called Boko Haram kidnapped 276 girls in Chibouk, northern Nigeria, in April 2014, the Nobel Prize–winning economist and philosopher Amartya Sen brought the problem of missing girls to international attention. In his 1990 article in the *New York Review of Books* and a subsequent editorial he submitted to the *British Medical Journal* (1992), he noted that "son preference" may have resulted in as many as 100 million missing women worldwide. Sen arrived at this terrifying estimate by initially looking at the seemingly anodyne ratio of women to men in societies where both sexes received broadly equal health care and medical attention. He then assessed the number of extra women who ought to have been alive in a particular period in countries where women faced a number of disadvantages. Eleven years later, Sen (2003) reported that some reductions in female mortality worldwide had been "counterbalanced by a new female disadvantage . . . through sex specific abortions aimed against the female fetus" (p. 1297).[1] In other words, in certain countries, females were undergoing a kind of prenatal gendercide.

These are harsh terms, but they are, unfortunately, supported by the facts. A cursory glance at male/female ratios over the last century alone shows some disturbing trends in demographics. The United Nations' *World Population Prospects 2015* indicates that in 2015, 50.4 percent of the world's population was male, meaning there were some 101.8 males for every 100 females. In other words, there was a marked male advantage over the female population at this time, which means there are more men alive today than women. But the opposite should be true. It has been well established, in societies that provide broadly equal health care and nutrition to both sexes, that male mortality rates are usually higher than female ones,[2] and there is a natural female mortality advantage in all age groups across the globe. In other words, given half a chance and the same opportunities, the norm would be for women to live longer, survive better, and overcome crises more easily than men. If our current male/female ratios indicate the opposite, therefore, if statistics show a reverse trend in the population at this time, we have to wonder why.

It should be noted that the current masculinity ratio reflects a global average; it spans different parts of the world and disguises substantial regional differences. For example, there is currently a very low ratio of 88.8 males for every 100 females in Eastern Europe, but a higher ratio of 97.9 to 98.4 in North America and up to 104.8 men for every 100 women in Asia. These differences, in turn, reflect the variations of the male/female ratio at birth and contrasting mortality rates in different countries. Such ratios can also fluctuate according to a wide range of factors, from cultural differences to forced migration. Ansley J. Coale (1991), one of America's most distinguished demographers, pointed out, for instance, that in the late nineteenth and early part of the twentieth century, immigration to the United States was large and predominantly male. This had pushed the sex ratio up by 1910 to 1.06 males for every female. However, as the proportion of foreign-born citizens in the United States fell sharply in succeeding decades, the sex ratio also fell.

World wars as well as migration have created serious imbalances in populations too, and these also need to be taken into consideration. According to the 1897 census in Russia, for example, the male/female ratio was 1.001, but by 1946, under the burden of revolutions and world wars, there were only 77.3 men in the Soviet Union for every 100 women. Large declines in the male population were also observed in the aftermath of World War II in both Japan and Germany. But given these facts as well as the expected norms, what has led to the current predominance of men in the world? Why, despite recent anomalies caused by war and migration and the natural mortality advantage allowing for a higher ratio of women to men, are there more males than females on the planet today?

It is time to ask some serious questions about the missing women of the world. Where are they? What has happened to them? Are women in the early twenty-first century paying with their lives for the bloodletting on the battlefields of the twentieth century? Is the real Third World War being waged against women today? Even if "gendercide" is too strong a word to use, it may no longer be necessary to be quite so polite about "son preference."

CHINA AND INDIA

Before addressing the more chilling aspects of our collective response to these questions, it must be admitted, from the outset, that the numbers of missing women are particularly high in China and India. In a study published in the *British Medical Journal* in 2009, Wei Xing Zhu, Li Lu, and Therese Hesketh focused on China's excess males, noting that, historically, preference for sons has been manifest postnatally through female infanticide and the neglect and abandonment of girls. Where this persists, it is mainly due to lack of access to necessary medical care. However, since the early 1980s, it has become possible to select males prenatally with ultrasonographic sex determination, and as a result, sex-selective abortion has become possible. This technology is now widely available in many countries, contributing to the emergence of high sex ratios from birth. The highest sex ratios are found where there is a combination of preference for sons, easy access to sex-selective technology, and a low fertility rate due to government restrictions. In these countries, the birth of girls must be prevented to allow for the desired number of sons within the allotted family size.

Zhu, Lu, and Hesketh report that for Chinese children born during the period 2000 to 2004, the overall sex ratios clearly indicated "son preference" across all age groups; they were high across virtually all regions with the exception of Tibet. They were highest in the one- to four-year age group, with a ratio of 1.24 more boys than girls, rising to 1.26 in rural areas. The latest UN data for China (2015) shows a sex ratio in the zero to one year age group of 1.15 more boys than girls, compared to 1.08 in 1990 and 1.04 in 1970.

In India, the data show a similar upward trend. In the northwest of the subcontinent, in 1991, there was only one district where the sex ratio showing son preference was in excess of 1.25, but by 2001, the number of districts showing similarly disturbing imbalances had risen to forty-six. The overall national average, moreover, had risen to a ratio of almost 1.08 more men than women, the highest it had been since 1961. But the latest census data for 2011 show an even further rise in the national average to 1.09, with the states of Haryana (1.20), Punjab (1.18), and Delhi (1.15) still showing particularly high ratios. We can see worrying signs in these statistics. According to an article in *The Economist* (2015), the consequences of the gender imbalance in India and China are likely to last for decades and will probably become worse before getting any better: "It will take the two countries with their combined population of 2.6 billion—a third of humanity—into uncharted territory." Even a casual reader of such ominous warnings can recognize that something is very wrong. The drive to eradicate women and girls in certain countries will have devastating social consequences.

A 2010 study released by the Chinese Academy of Social Sciences noted that the shortage of young women threatens to become so critical that within a mere ten years, it is very probable that one in five young men in China will not be able to find a bride.

"If China had had a normal sex ratio at birth, there would have been 721 million girls and women living in 2010, according to a report in 2012 by the United Nations (UN) Population Fund. In fact, there were only 655 million women alive that year—a difference of 66 million, or 10 percent of the female population," is how *The Economist* puts it. In other words, according to researchers Ebenstein and Sharygin (2009, p. 402), China is on the cusp of a major social crisis due to the "dramatic deterioration in men's marital prospects."

According to this same study, there will be some 30 to 40 million more young Chinese men than women aged nineteen and under by the year 2020, and for every 100 marriageable women during the four years between 2050 and 2054, there could be as many as 186 single men. This extreme imbalance, in a population roughly twice as large as the entire young male population of Germany, France, and the United Kingdom *combined*, carries serious implications.

In India, the corresponding estimates, which are also very worrying, suggest an excess of some 28 million males. There was a 9.2 million rise in the number of Indian men aged twenty-five to twenty-nine between 2000 and 2010. The numbers of Indian women who could marry them, in their early twenties, rose by only 7.6 million, however.[3] According to *The Economist* (2015), "Even if India's sex ratio at birth were to return to normal and stay there, by 2050 the country would still have 30 percent more single men hoping to marry than single women," a dangerously high number. Christophe Guilmoto, senior fellow in demography at the French Institute for Development Research, claims that assuming no change in the sex ratio at birth, "the peak could be even higher" by 2060 to 2064, in fact almost double, with 191 men for every 100 women. Even if the sex ratio were to return to normal by 2020, Guilmoto believes "the marriage squeeze would still be severe, peaking at 160 in China in 2030, and at 164 in India 20 years later."[4]

The consequences for women in these countries could be appalling and the social implications of this imbalance will certainly affect the rest of the world as well. But although it has proven traditionally difficult to address the problem, its cause is absurdly easy to identify. It is due to what Amartya Sen has called "son preference" in certain societies, which in other, less politically correct terminology is simply a war against women.

The time has come to account for the missing in this war.

WHY PREFER SONS?

There is no simple answer to the question of why societies prefer sons. Many reasons have been given for why some cultures retain a preference for sons; many explanations have been put forward to show how this preference has brought about the phenomenon of missing women. But the most obvious and endemic of the reasons is the prevalence of patriarchal family systems in many countries. This age-old tradition has served to marginalize women for millennia and is at the root of the phenomenon of missing women in the world today.

When patriarchal values are embedded in religious traditions and sanctioned as divinely ordained, they are very hard to eradicate. Ebenstein (2006, p. 6) points to the possible role of Confucian values in Chinese society, which clearly relegated women to a secondary role even during the Communist era. These values, which are being specifically evoked by the leadership of the country today, are betrayed by the maxim "The perfect woman must obey her parents when a child, her husband when a wife, and her son when a widow." But China's ancient belief systems are not the only ones that convey this same idea. Similar statements have been exploited in Jewish, Islamic, and even Christian religions to maintain the patriarchal systems in the West, both in the past and in the present, leaving lasting traces of "son preference" even in the most seemingly advanced societies.[5]

Traditional Hindu laws, too, exemplify to what a degree patriarchy has economic implications in India, where there is a critical need to pay dowries for daughters in order to offset the fact that a woman cannot, according to religious beliefs, inherit property.[6] Sons in such cultures are valued as the source of wealth and long-term security, whereas daughters are naturally a liability, a potential for debt. Surveys in China and India also point to the perceived advantage of bringing sons into the world to do the backbreaking work on family farms and to provide old-age support to parents. This is particularly important in those countries with seriously inadequate levels of social protection for the elderly and the physical as well as financial dependence of older generations on the younger ones.

But patriarchy is manifest in political ideology as well as through religion and culture; it can have social as well as economic reasons, all of which play a role in the mystery of missing women in the world. Nor are the age-old traditions of infanticide the only ways in which "son preference" has been maintained. Programs such as China's rigorous one-child policy, first introduced in 1979, imposed a compulsory reduction in fertility on the population and provided powerful incentives, both medical and financial, for parents to engage in sex selection in order to ensure the birth of a son. Scientific progress does not erase our prejudices; it simply makes it easier for us to implement them.

The following pages will show how patriarchal customs and patrilineal lines of kinship play an important role in "son preference." They will also explore how ancestor worship has led certain cultures to believe that the fewer girls there are in a family, the better for its name, fame, wealth, and power, in both this world and the next. The reasons why there are far higher mortality rates for girls than boys during early childhood may underscore the causes for the missing women in the world.

THE MALE LINE

A key factor in explaining the preference for sons in certain societies is the rigidity of patrilineal kinship systems. In countries where this problem is most pronounced, the main assets that provide the foundation of the family's finances are passed through the male line only. This practice sharply limits the ability of women to sustain themselves outside the orbit of a man. In some instances, women do not have equal rights to inherit money; in others, they are unlikely to inherit land.[7] Whatever the circumstances, they invariably symbolize an economic burden to the family. Strenuous efforts will be made, therefore, to maintain the male line, by adopting sons from the father's male relatives, if necessary, or by the head of the household taking a second wife or concubine. Wherever patrilineal kinship is the norm, the negative consequence to a woman's quality of life is considered less significant than the perceived costs to the family.

A girl's primary responsibility, therefore, is to produce sons who would allow for the continuation of the family line and the stability of the patrilineal social order. In rural China, Korea, and parts of northwest India, the normal practice is for a girl to marry outside her village and to leave her own family in order to join that of her husband. This process, moreover, is nearly irreversible. In other words, it is very difficult—if the marriage fails—for a girl to return to her parental home. Her "place" in the family will have been taken and her notional land entitlement is likely to have been assigned to others, including incoming brides from other villages. Thus, a rigid, male-based social order has dire implications for the well-being of women and girls. Das Gupta et al. (2003, p. 11) note that "parents are under much social pressure to ensure that their daughters marry, as evidenced by the negligible proportions of women never married in their thirties in the censuses of these countries. Daughters must leave and make way for incoming daughters-in-law." This is the case even if it means marrying undesirable or otherwise unsuitable partners.

"Son preference" in some countries can manifest itself in even more extreme ways. In Afghanistan, for instance, families without sons often opt for dressing young girls as boys. This will enable the "boy" to enjoy some of the social benefits of being a man, such as greater mobility and easier access to the educational system and to employment opportunities. By giving the sham "son" these benefits, moreover, the family as a whole will acquire an improved social status. The existence of a son, even a fake one, will not only bring economic advantages but prevents the public shame of not being able to carry forward the family line.[8]

What this means to the disguised daughter herself has been less well documented. If the example of Iran is anything to go by, it could account for the rise in sex-change operations in recent years, which attempt to endorse homosexual practices under religious law;[9] it might also lead to an increasing dependence on artificial insemination in such cases, a further example of how scientific advance can be appropriated to support archaic patriarchal attitudes. Ultimately, it can only add to who is "missing," at least in terms of political and legal visibility. The World Health Organization (WHO) includes Iran among the twenty-seven countries in the world most notorious for the impact of "son preference."

To the extent that a young wife is able to deliver sons, moreover, she will see an enhanced status over her life cycle in a traditional patriarchal society. The relative power of Chinese grandmothers is proverbial, but it is a power base firmly anchored in the support of her sons. If she has none, she is more likely to lead a life of penury, humiliation, and marginalization, in which mistreatment and abuse are quite common and have been well documented.[10] In parts of northwest India, a woman who has no sons might well be replaced by a second wife and relegated to the status of a servant performing household work. "Son preference," therefore, has a direct impact on the social erasure of women.

ANCESTOR WORSHIP

There is a second reason for "son preference," which is possibly even more significant in China and Korea than in other countries. Male ancestor worship means that if there is no son to ensure the maintenance of the patrilineal family line, the position of the father in the afterlife is gravely at risk. Furthermore, the wrath of ancestors is also incurred, and the family is doomed to difficulty and bad luck in this earthly life. The situation is no less dire in northwest India, where, according to this tradition, failure to ensure the continuity of the (male) family line risks spiritual oblivion. Ancestor worship entails additional complications in Korea, similar to those afflicting wealthy families in eighteenth- and nineteenth-century Europe, where sons do not have equal status within the family hierarchy. Preference is given to the eldest, who then bears the main responsibility for caring for his parents and ensuring the continuation of the family line. Younger sons have different rights and roles in society; their privileges and burdens are fewer in the family, although they still wield far more power than their mothers, sisters, daughters, or wives.

Unlike in some parts of China and India, a father without sons in Korea cannot co-opt the son of a brother to perform ancestor worship on his behalf. This may also help to explain why in Korea—a country with a much higher level of per capita income than China or India and at a more advanced stage of development—"son preference," until relatively recently, has proved to be quite resilient to the advancement of education and overall modernization. In the survey work leading up to their 2003 study, Das Gupta et al. (p. 19) report that even among the highly educated classes in Korea, having girls only is perceived as "a terrible tragedy," since no one in the family will be able to tend to the soul of the departed father. A life of spiritual desolation awaits the hapless father of girls. One grandmother insisted that it was not that daughters were unproductive or expensive to marry. On the contrary, women perform much of the hard labor in the fields, and their marriage costs virtually nothing. Rather, she said, "people don't want daughters because they are not helpful to the family—they leave the family when they marry. Daughters are useless! It is *sons* who are able to inherit assets and keep the rituals of ancestor worship."

WHERE HAVE ALL THE WOMEN GONE?

The "missing women" phenomenon entails various kinds of discrimination, including the most violent, which can occur all through a woman's life. There is an analysis in the next chapter regarding the more obvious forms this can take, such as rape, sexual abuse, and physical assault against women. But the present chapter will identify how female mortality, which is frequently caused by violence, can skew the sex ratios through lack of health care and proper nutrition, through reproductive illnesses and maternal mortality, and as a result of female genital mutilation and cutting.

An important proviso should be borne in mind, however. This subject is notoriously difficult to evaluate, and there are still other causes of female mortality waiting to be researched, many of which may or may not be due to gender discrimination. In a recent contribution to the "missing women" literature, Siwan Anderson and Debraj Ray (2010), researchers at the University of British Columbia and New York University, respectively, undertook an interesting accounting exercise. They estimated how many women in India, China, and sub-Saharan Africa are "missing" across age groups and how they "disappear" due to different diseases. By comparing the relative death rates for males and females in these countries, the authors were able to calculate the number of excess female deaths by age and by disease in the year 2000. Some of their conclusions are startling: "(1) the vast majority of missing women in India and a significant proportion of those in China are of adult age; (2) as a proportion of the total female population, the number of missing women is largest in sub-Saharan Africa, and the absolute numbers are comparable to those for India and China." Most interestingly, "a comparable proportion of women was missing at the start of the twentieth century in the United States, just as they are in India, China, and sub-Saharan Africa today" (p. 1262). Thus, the data suggest that the problem may reflect not only "son preference" and discrimination against girls and women but also excess female mortality related to other factors, not all of which have yet been identified. The question of why women are missing in such large numbers still remains to be fully answered.

One fact, however, is known: murder begins early. The problem starts with sex-selective abortion and continues with infanticide. As Sen (1999, p. 106) has pointed out, "There is indeed considerable direct evidence that female children are neglected in terms of health care, hospitalization and even feeding."[11] Ebenstein[12] argues that among the millions born in China and India during the past four decades, the female deficit is largely explained by sex-selective abortion and neonatal infanticide, in that order.[13] In China, somewhere between 37 and 45 percent of women are missing due to prenatal factors. In other words, the war against women often begins before birth. The World Bank (2012), analyzing these deeply entrenched cultural habits, reports that "Chinese and Indians living in the United States show very similar patterns of sex selection in first and second births" (p. 123).

If girl children survive the early years, their circumstances only deteriorate in many countries as a result of ill health and lack of nutrition. Their condition from early adolescence onward can be further aggravated by sexual violence, genital mutilation, and abuse, which often culminates in maternal mortality, suicide, and murder. But of all the factors responsible for women dying, Amartya Sen (1999) believes that it is the neglect of female health and nutrition that is the most important. Since the "missing women" dilemma relates directly to the public health dimensions of this problem, it may be helpful to begin by looking at the different ways that women and men have access to the fundamental safety and integrity of their persons and to the differences in their nutrition and health care.

HEALTH CARE AND NUTRITION

Many factors contribute to the social inequalities experienced by women in the area of health care, particularly with regard to their reproductive well-being. As described earlier, the fundamental misogyny and misaligned power relationships implicit in patriarchal systems cause women to be frequently subjected to deprivation, chastisement, and abuse. Such treatment, in turn, leads to their urgent need of medical attention. But their plight becomes all the more desperate at such times because of lack of access to adequate health care services[14] or unfair practices sometimes used by providers of such services, from the use of expired medication, for example, to financially crippling hospital bills. Such biases operate not only within the individual household, where women and girls are not equally valued—and are sometimes even deprived of adequate basic nutrition—but are reinforced by community norms and values regarding women's sexuality, reproduction, and rights.[15] Women are most neglected in their hour of greatest need.

Bias also operates at the level of health legislation, policy, and education, where the widely differing requirements and capacities of men and women regarding sexual functioning and reproduction are not adequately recognized and where funding is so often manipulated for political or sectarian ends. Gita Sen et al. (2002) underline this distinction when they write:

> *A gender and health equity analysis insists that, although differences in health needs between women and men do exist in relation to biological and historical differences, this does not "naturally" lead [to] or justify different or unequal social status or rights in just societies.*[16]

Another aspect of bias is the way in which women are invariably exposed to greater health risks because of the nature of their traditional roles in certain societies. Where gender assigns to women the washing of clothes, the fetching of water, and the cooking of meals, they are exposed to much higher rates of infection and disease from contaminated water and indoor smoke,[17] compromising them further in areas of reproductive health. For example, malaria in a first pregnancy is an important cause of chronic anemia; it also leads to spontaneous abortion, stillbirth, and maternal mortality.[18] In addition to these factors, by far the most important cause for missing women in sub-Saharan Africa is HIV/AIDS. Biological differences combined with endemic poverty can therefore greatly affect the susceptibility of women to infection and disease, the severity of which can have serious consequences for society at large.

REPRODUCTIVE ILLNESSES

In their article on reproductive health, Cottingham and Myntti[19] describe the intricate complexities of mapping reproductive health worldwide. Even with the epidemiological data available, it is very difficult to measure, with any accuracy, the global burden of disease according to the disability-adjusted life year.[20] Much has been lost in translation and more always needs to be done to track the worsening condition of women in the world as a result of war, displacement, epidemics, and deteriorating environmental factors. The picture, grim as it is, could always become grimmer.

Based on the existing "map" of reproductive issues, such as sexually transmitted infections, maternal mortality and morbidity related to pregnancy and childbirth, perinatal conditions, congenital anomalies, HIV and AIDS, and the risks of unsafe sex, women account for fully 71 percent of the overall disease burden from unsafe sex. Furthermore, conditions related to unsafe sex account for 12 percent of women who die between fifteen and forty-four years of age, and of 15 percent of those who die of their disabilities, the highest numbers are in sub-Saharan Africa, India, Latin America, and the Caribbean.[21] The research, disaggregated for sex, indicates that women constitute 22 percent of the global burden of reproductive ill health compared with 3 percent for men. But even these figures do not present a complete picture. Cottingham and Myntti do not take into account problems such as fistula and incontinence, conditions brought about by female genital mutilation or cutting, by stillbirth and infertility, or the consequences of sexual abuse and other forms of violence against women. Nor are the mental health dimensions measured of reproductive diseases.[22] In other words, the truth is probably far worse than these figures might indicate.

Early and unwanted childbearing, HIV and other sexually transmitted infections, and pregnancy-related illnesses account for the greatest proportion of health problems experienced by women—especially those in low-income countries. It is estimated that about 225 million women do not have access to elementary family planning techniques enabling them to choose the number and the spacing of their children. This results in some 85 million unintended pregnancies per year in developing countries, with all their attendant consequences and complications.[23]

MATERNAL MORTALITY

The inferior status of women obviously adds to the numbers of female deaths and the most dramatic indicator of this inequity comes from the maternal mortality ratio. This ratio is defined as the number of maternal deaths in a given period per 100,000 live births during the same period. The WHO reports that 303,000 women die every year—over 800 daily—from problems related to pregnancy and childbirth alone. According to WHO statistics (compiled in the World Bank's World Development Indicators), the highest lifetime risk of dying in childbirth in 2015 was in Sierra Leone, where the probability that a fifteen-year-old female would die eventually from a maternal cause was 1 in 17. In India, it is 1 in 220; in China, it is 1 in 2,400; in the United States, 1 in 3,800; in Italy, 1 in 17,100. Numberless impoverished women in the world suffer obstructed childbirth[24] and are unable to access competent obstetrical care in time. They either die during labor or suffer permanent injuries, such as fistula, and are simply banished from their communities and left alone to perish.[25]

Unsafe abortion is another killer and accounts for 13 percent of global maternal mortality. This means that about eight deaths from abortion take place every hour. Of the 46 million abortions performed annually worldwide, some 20 million are performed by non-medical and untrained individuals, resulting in complications that lead to 68,000 to 70,000 deaths each year. In those cases where women survive, they are usually left with lifelong health problems.[26] Iqbal Shah and Elisabeth Ahman (2009, p. 1149) from the WHO report that maternal deaths due to such problems are higher in regions with restrictive abortion laws. Moreover, their study also confirms what has long been known, namely, that legal restrictions on safe abortion do not reduce its actual incidence: "[W]hile the numbers of legal and safe abortions have declined in recent years, unsafe abortions show no decline in numbers, despite being entirely preventable." They concluded that the Millennium Development Goal was unlikely to be achieved "without addressing unsafe abortion and associated mortality and morbidity."[27]

FEMALE GENITAL MUTILATION OR CUTTING

Female genital mutilation or cutting continues to be performed for nonmedical reasons on an estimated 2 to 4 million girls each year. Many of these girls are teenagers and not a few are below the age of eight. Dating back centuries and defended by its proponents, both Muslim and Christian, as ensuring the virginity and marriageability of girls, this practice has been reported in all parts of the world and is recognized internationally as an extreme form of discrimination against women. Usually performed by nonmedically trained women, it not only leads to severe trauma and excruciating pain but routinely results in such long-term complications as shock, ulceration, chronic infection, and bleeding as well as obstructed childbirth. Although most prevalent in Africa and the Middle East, the practice of some form of female genital mutilation or cutting occurs in immigrant communities in parts of Asia and the Pacific, North and South America, and Europe, according to reports by Amnesty International.

This subject, linked directly to the question of culture, will be discussed in Chapter 4, but it needs to be mentioned here because of its critical impact on female mortality and the sex ratio.

In fact, violence against women—to be discussed in the next chapter—is also critical to the sex ratio. In countries where the population balance is skewed and even where the sex ratio is falling, the incidents of violence against women invariably increase. The long-term effects of this anomaly, moreover, are likely to be felt for decades. This is particularly the case in China, where the problem of rising violence and a declining female population has acquired worrying proportions. The fact that a higher ratio of single men than women in society leads to antisocial behavior is a stark reality that is no longer possible to ignore.[28]

Columbia University's Lena Edlund and several of her colleagues at the University of Hong Kong (2008) argued that an increase in the sex ratio in China had a dramatic impact on crime. It accounted for a high percentage of urban violence and property destruction, offenses that almost doubled between 1988 and 2004.[29] Valerie Hudson and Andrea den Boer (2005), professors at Brigham Young University and the University of Kent, took this research one step further and made a strong case that large numbers of "unattached young adult males" posed serious security threats to society as a whole. They warned that according to the evidence, an imbalance in favor of males in the population definitely increases crime rates in cities, and in proportion to the rise in violent crime, there is a parallel upsurge in drug use, drug smuggling, and prostitution. The worst effect is the expansion of a thriving market in the kidnapping and the trafficking of women. These undesirable consequences, in turn, led governments to "favor more authoritarian approaches to internal governance and less benign international presences."

A recent example of this tendency can be found in the jailing of five young Chinese feminists who tried to display their indignation at the rise of sexual harassment by demonstrating on the streets of

Beijing on the eve of International Women's Day in 2015.[30] Following their summary arrest and detention, these women were subjected to incessant interrogation;[31] instead of listening to their warning message and taking heed of its seriousness, the Chinese government attempted to blame them for "picking quarrels and provoking troubles." Even though international attention led to their release on bail, their story illustrates how the devaluation of women places them under pressure as a result of sex ratios being skewed.

Ebenstein and Sharygin (2009, p. 400) argued that a rapidly rising population of single men in China "will affect the prevalence of commercial sex activity and the transmission of sexually transmitted infections, including HIV." They also provided some historical support for the thesis that imbalanced sex ratios could have a security dimension. In the eighteenth century, "the Qing dynasty government responded to the rising sex ratios brought about by high levels of female infanticide by encouraging single men to colonize Taiwan." A century later, when poor economic conditions in Shandong Province led to rampant female infanticide once again, a similar problem was created, and rebellion was the result. As the large numbers of males in the population matured, they "organized an uprising against the Qing dynasty."

Although we have developed new strategies as well as casualties in the deadly wars we wage these days, we seem to repeat the same mistakes again and again in the age-old war against women. No matter how sophisticated we think we are, we are still mired in the mud of that ancient battlefield.

RICH VERSUS POOR

One interesting dimension of the phenomenon of "missing" women and girls is its pervasiveness across various social strata and geographical regions. It does not matter how rich, how poor, how sophisticated, or how "primitive" we may be, this problem is endemic. It has appeared in countries at different stages of development and with different degrees of industrialization, with diverse levels of openness to the world, and with contrasting social and economic factors. In other words, the idea that the poor might show a greater proclivity than the rich when it comes to sacrificing their daughters is not borne out by the data.

In the northern states of India—as well as in Korea, where census data have picked up high juvenile sex ratios in the last several decades—evidence actually points to *higher* levels of discrimination among those who are better off. In fact, the worst sex ratios in India have been registered in Punjab and Haryana, which are among the richest states in the country. In China, the provinces with higher literacy rates tend to have higher sex ratios. However, the data also show that, beyond cross-group comparisons—for example, the rich versus the poor—it is also possible to detect a rise in discrimination against girls when the family is subject to some external stress that worsens its relative economic situation with respect to the recent past. Families that have become poorer as a result of crop failure or the closing down of traditional markets for their products will revert to increased "son preference." In China and Korea, war and famine in the mid-twentieth century resulted in more active discrimination against girls.

Nor is the problem concentrated only in China, India, and Korea. According to the UN, abnormally high sex ratios are also prevalent in several of the former Soviet republics, such as Armenia, Azerbaijan, and Georgia. The problem is also evident in some of the former Yugoslav republics, namely, Serbia and Bosnia. It exists in Egypt, in Bangladesh, and in Pakistan too and, perhaps not surprisingly, in other countries with a large mixed population, such as Singapore, which has sizable Chinese and Hindu minorities (see Figure 1.1). Declining fertility rates and the increasing availability of ultrasound technologies could well result in a broader dissemination of the war against girls, a war that, according to Amartya Sen (1999, p. 104), is

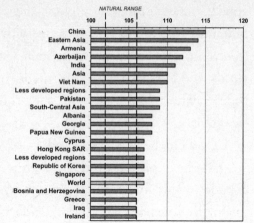

Figure 1.1: Sex ratios: An international perspective, 2015–2017 (sex ratios at birth per 100 female newborns)
Source: United Nations, World Population Prospects: The 2017 Revision, *Population Division*

one of the most "crude and sharply visible aspects of gender inequality." It is literally taking place on a global scale.

Although China is now taking steps to adjust its population policy, the impact on the current imbalance is still uncertain.[32] In India, the latest UN data show the sex ratio at close to a historically high level, but the ratio may be on its way to stabilizing or, in any event, may be peaking; this allows for the possibility that the growth rates of masculinization are decelerating in the population. This has already happened in Korea, where the sex ratio has actually fallen from its peak in 1995.[33] In an editorial titled "Too Many Single Men," *The Economist* notes that "the war on baby girls is winding down, but its effects will be felt for decades." The authors emphasize this point, adding, "But whatever policymakers do now, the sex imbalance will cause trouble for decades. The old preference for boys will hurt men and women alike."[34]

If we draw back from the close scrutiny of statistics for a moment and look at the larger picture of social development at the levels of education, of employment opportunities, and of careers available to women, we discover that these too have a significant impact on demographics. The aging populations of North America, Europe, and East Asia clearly indicate that fertility rates in these countries have dropped below the normal replacement levels. In other words, they show that when there has been a choice between career and reproduction, career has come first. Couples in these countries have put off having children during economic downturns. Although children may represent social security and care for the elderly in poor populations, they may be an economic liability for the middle classes or the upwardly mobile. A study in the United States found 49 percent of high-achieving women to be childless, as compared with only 19 percent of their male colleagues.[35] Many women who choose not to have children are not distressed about this choice, despite pressure from friends and family.[36] However, the career structure in these countries seldom allows for time out to have children; it does not encourage women to achieve a balance between work and family responsibilities and often forces them to choose one or the other. When they opt for raising a family, they frequently are penalized for it. Many women who stop working to have children find themselves in great difficulty when they attempt to return to their previous careers.

Consequently more and more women in certain countries prefer to have no children. The proportion of American women between ages forty and forty-four who have never given birth rose to 15 percent in 2014, which is up from 10 percent in 1976. Among the educated members of this population who have advanced degrees (M.D.s or Ph.D.s), the proportion of childless women is 20 percent, but this has been even higher in the past and is a decline from 35 percent in 1994.[37] The United States has maintained some population growth through immigration and higher birth rates among the poor, but in European countries (e.g., Italy), we see sharply declining birth rates among the educated and native-born middle classes. However, this is not due to the increase in working women, because Italy, which has the lowest fertility in Europe, also has the fewest women in the workforce. Only those countries with policies that help women both to work and to have children can maintain replacement levels and keep the population stable.[38]

One hidden dimension of gender bias is the different reactions to demographic imbalances. Although an excess of males is seen as socially destabilizing, as discussed earlier in this chapter, little concern has been expressed for the implications of an excess of women. What happens to women who are unable to find husbands, who are unable to have babies and raise families, especially in societies where women's opportunities and independence are constrained? Whether in relation to the plight of girls in Afghanistan who have to pretend to be boys in order to protect their family's honor, or the members of either sex in Iran who are forced to endure the complications of sex-change treatment in order to meet the strictures of sharia law, there are ways, as mentioned before, of sweeping women under the proverbial carpet that redefine the "missing" as those who have simply been made, in Ralph Ellison's famous term, "invisible."

QUESTIONING ASSUMPTIONS

Despite the overwhelming evidence that gender bias has led to cases of "missing women" in the world, there are nevertheless some curious examples that fly in the face of perceived patriarchal orthodoxy and challenge us to question our assumptions.

Although it is true that, in certain cultures, the majority of the old do, indeed, live with their married sons, this pattern is not universal. Evidence shows that in the Philippines, older parents are just as likely to live with the families of married daughters as with those of married sons, making daughters just as valuable as sons in performing this essential role of social protection. It is not surprising, then, that there is no evidence of pronounced "son preference" in the Philippines, where sex ratios are broadly normal—in fact, 1.05, close to the world average.

The extent to which the payment of dowries is a strong disincentive to have girls is not wholly convincing either. The data actually show that parents spend three to five times more on the wedding of a son than on that of a daughter, often providing the new couple with housing and many household items. However, the parents may see such expenses and the additional costs of providing a son with an early financial push in his new life as a worthy investment. They ensure his place within the patrilineal family line—akin to buying domestically produced goods—unlike the money spent on a daughter's wedding, the benefits of which will accrue to her husband's family and must therefore be perceived as a net loss of resources to the girl's own. In this case, the funds might be better saved for the wedding of a son. What is portrayed as the economic argument for "son preference"—the high cost of dowries—may, in fact, merely reflect the built-in cultural factors that justify "son preference" and are upheld by the rigidity of the social order and the primacy of males within it. The fear of dowry debts may not necessarily lead to female infanticide.

Equally suspect is the argument that sons are needed for the hard work of the family farm. An overwhelming body of data shows that women contribute a significant share to farm labor. However, the data on labor force participation tend not to pick up on the work performed by women. This is because it is perceived largely as an extension of women's domestic duties at home, which, of course, find no place in the statistics on the gross national product.[39] As noted by Das Gupta et al. (2003, p. 170), "[O]fficial statistics show that the State of Haryana in northwest India has an especially low rate of female labor force participation, but in fact women do almost all the manual labor on the fields through the whole crop cycle, while men spend short periods of time ploughing with tractors and operating tube wells." When surveys are done to measure labor force participation, men's contribution to the farm is duly noted, given male ownership and overall managerial control.[40] But the vital input of women is invisible.

It is also interesting to note that in the countries of Southeast Asia that have a less rigid social order and where girls are perceived by their parents as having a higher intrinsic value—as opposed to simply being an export to be sold out of the family and more or less struck from its genealogy—the sex ratio is also much closer to normal levels. In such cultures, daughters are able to sustain meaningful, stable relationships with their parents even after marriage, because they are the ones on whom the elderly increasingly depend.

In fact, there is overwhelming evidence worldwide to disprove the idea that sons are essential for the protection of the elderly. It has been estimated that over 60 million families in the United States are caring for an aging or disabled person at home, and according to one source, at least 66 percent, or two-thirds, of the caregivers are women.[41] Nor does this high percentage indicate an easy option, emotionally or financially. "As parents live longer, more women are feeling the crunch."[42] Over the next five years, it has also been estimated that one out of five workers, principally women, will have to quit their jobs in order to care for an elderly parent. The impact on their personal lives as well as on the economy will require further study.

Who will care for the elderly if there are fewer women in the world? Who will take on this role if the rising male ratio increases violence against women, and democratic values and social services are eroded as more and more of them experience rampant female abuse? How long will old people survive in societies suffering from such gender imbalances? Is it any wonder that euthanasia is increasingly an option, or that nine out of ten support its legalization in certain European countries today?[43] Are the armies of female carers of the elderly a sign of coming change, or do their numbers simply reveal a new set of casualties in the war on women?

It is certainly time to talk about peace. A number of options suggest themselves in thinking about the public policies that might be put in place to help mitigate discrimination against girls and bring an end to the numbers of "missing women." These include *protection for the aged, gender budgeting,* and changes through *civil society and grassroots initiatives.* These efforts may not end the war on women yet, but they could signal a much-needed and long-overdue truce.

SOCIAL PROTECTION FOR THE AGED

One of the options before us concerns the urgent need to protect the old and provide for their well-being in countries without adequate systems of social protection or where there are austere and extremely low levels of pension coverage. Public policies aimed at strengthening the systems of social protection in China and India would clearly allow a growing number of parents to feel less vulnerable and less inclined to see their sons as insurance policies against the liabilities of old age. Without the need to depend on sons financially, the "son preference" would gradually give way to a more balanced attitude toward daughters. This is a particularly important consideration in China, where rural peasants account for some 44 percent of the country's 1.4 billion people, the vast majority of whom have no access to social security or state-provided medical care and who therefore are traditionally reliant on the support of sons in old age.[44]

Studies comparing the savings behavior of households with sons and those with daughters have shown, moreover, that the former amass more than the latter in all parts of China. Shang-Jin Wei and Xiaobo Zhang (2009) estimate that half of the increase in savings in China during the period from 1990 to 2007 can be attributed to the increase in the sex ratio. Given the dearth of brides that is expected in the next decade in China, this is a curious development. Strange as it may seem, families with sons tend to respond to the scarcity of brides by increasing their savings; interestingly, this behavior then spills into the real estate market, so that regions with a higher sex ratio have shown rising housing prices.

To the extent that they might encourage people to spend more and hoard less, better social safety nets and pensions for the elderly would certainly be useful in a country like China. This could perhaps boost national consumption too and would certainly help reduce China's trade surplus, which at times has been a source of friction with trade partners. This is particularly the case with the United States and the European Union, but also other Asian countries as well. Such reforms might not have a direct impact on ancestor worship but would surely reduce the pressure on men to have sons. One can only hope that these reforms might also raise the value of daughters to some extent, at least above the rampant housing markets.

GENDER BUDGETING

A government's budget is also a powerful mechanism for implementing new priorities in society. Over the past twenty years—particularly in economic programs supported by international financial institutions—increased attention has been paid to ways in which a government may try to assess whether particular fiscal measures could adversely impact women and undermine the goal of gender equality. This is particularly important in the majority of countries where women are not represented during budget deliberations; it is urgent where distributional implications of particular budget formulations involve social dislocations and place an unfair portion of the burden of the economic adjustment on vulnerable groups. Gender budgeting could play a vital role in pursuing a variety of economic and social goals, such as a better-functioning tax system and increased spending on education and maternity care; this, in turn, would ensure an improved profile in public finances while also having an impact on the safety and health of women.

Needless to say, the overwhelming majority of finance ministers, chairs of parliamentary budget committees, and other senior officials working on draft budgets are men at this time. Experience shows that equity issues are seldom given the prominence they deserve in their deliberations. The reasons vary. In some cases, governments do

not have the administrative capacity to do the sort of budget target-
ing that is at the center of effective social policy. This is particularly
true in the developing world, as illustrated by the regressive energy
subsidies that governments often provide, the overwhelming share
of whose benefits go to the wealthy rather than the needy in their
populations. In other cases, a government's budget often becomes the
arena for negotiating compromises with the political opposition, in
which case the education of women or girls or indeed any other cause
with a strong gender dimension seldom is given high priority.

In fact, the historical deficit bias in fiscal policy making and the
levels of public debt in countries everywhere usually drown out such
concerns amid a rising tide of red ink. Sadly, what happens all too
often is that governments either just do not care or else are held to
ransom by privileged elites who distribute the spoils of the state as
they will. In this respect, the more transparent the budget process
and the more open it is to public scrutiny, the easier it will be to
monitor and analyze the gender effects of various policies. The more
likely, too, will it be possible to hold policy makers to account for
the effects of their decisions on the well-being, health, and lives of
women.

It may be worth exploring an additional dimension in this debate
by asking if governments do enough to deploy the state budget as an
instrument to promote gender equality. We live in a world of scarce
resources, and how effective a government is in its use of available
funds has a considerable bearing on its ability to promote or detract
from sustainable economic development. Unfortunately, there are far
too many examples of massive waste when it comes to state budgets.
Rather than utilizing resources to promote opportunity and shared
prosperity, many governments, particularly in the developing world,
use them to distort and deteriorate income distribution. An eloquent
example of this is provided by a 2015 International Monetary Fund
study that factors in the cost of negative externalities from energy
consumption according to which subsidies for petroleum products,

electricity, natural gas, and coal amount to some $5.3 trillion per year. This astronomical sum is the equivalent of about 6.3 percent of global gross domestic product, or 8 percent of total government revenues, the world over. However, the benefits of gasoline subsidies, as the study shows, are the most regressively distributed in the world, with over 60 percent of the total accruing to the richest 20 percent of households. For diesel and liquefied petroleum gas, 42 percent and 54 percent, respectively, of the benefits go to these higher-income groups. The removal of such subsidies, the authors of the International Monetary Fund study claim, could lead to "a 21 percent decline in CO_2 [carbon dioxide] emissions." It could also generate "positive spillover effects" by reducing global energy demand and thus have a tangible impact on mitigating the effects of climate change. Indeed, it would be difficult to come up with a public policy that is more socially and environmentally destructive than subsidizing energy consumption. And this is a policy that has been put into place and maintained for the most part by men.[45]

When we learn, therefore, that the latest data (2015) in India shows that there are 287 million people (two-thirds of them women) who cannot read and write—that is to say, who do not have access to the most important tool to escape from poverty in the twenty-first century—we have to be careful not to imply that the reason for this is because "India is a poor country." The reality is quite different. India spends dozens of billions of dollars on energy subsidies every year.[46] Like other governments that account for the $5.3 trillion in subsidies mentioned earlier, policy choices made, for the most part by men, are feeding the driving habits of the middle classes over the more urgent needs of hundreds of millions who do not have access to information and to knowledge today. While a minority in India and in dozens of other countries as well are driving around in their air-conditioned cars, the majority find the most important portals for poverty alleviation slammed shut in their faces.

NONGOVERNMENTAL ORGANIZATIONS
AND GRASSROOTS INITIATIVES

There is obviously a role for civil society, too, when it comes to changing public policy. Promoting healthier attitudes on issues of gender equality is already a broadly established discourse in much of the developing world. The relative influence of nongovernmental organizations and other civil society organizations in promoting equity has been considerably enhanced, moreover, by the arrival of the internet and other modern communication technologies. Governments intent on providing better incentives for families to see girls as equally valuable could work with nongovernmental organizations and the media to promote more egalitarian values from a gender perspective.

In this respect, the Chinese government's Care for Girls campaign—providing girls with free public education in some of the regions with the highest male sex ratios—is an encouraging sign of the increasing seriousness with which problems of gender inequity are being viewed. Further collaboration with the nongovernmental organization community could prove to be particularly fruitful, in light of the limited gains made as a result of other government-sponsored policies. In China, for instance, the family planning law of 2002 banned the use of ultrasound or other technologies to establish the sex of the fetus, but the policies—implemented at the local level—have run up against the tougher population targets imposed by China's one-child policy, which, since 2015, is finally being relaxed, for the first time in many years.

But even in the obdurate case of female genital mutilation and cutting, it has been found that although Western efforts to eradicate the practice have long been perceived as "interference," local, grassroots programs employing group efforts of mothers and daughters in neighboring villages are proving effective when they focus on the medical risks.[47]

One hopeful sign that a combination of sound public policies and the forces of globalization can help reverse the problem of "son preference" is provided by Korea, whose sex ratio over the past decade, as already mentioned, has gradually begun to return to more normal levels. Although still on the high side—1.05 in 2016, compared to nearly 1.15 in 1995—these reductions show that even deeply entrenched prejudices and cultural norms are not immune to education and modernization; they clearly indicate that the empowerment of women resulting from integration into the labor market is a force of change.

CONCLUSION

Gender equality is frustratingly slow to achieve. As sex ratios and underlying demographic imbalances indicate, it poses a challenge to one of the most profound of human prejudices. Despite all the intense efforts of agencies and organizations and the outspoken courage of individual leaders to reverse these trends, the picture is still grim. Too many women are still missing from the picture. However heartening it is to learn that Botswana lifted restrictions on the industries in which women may not work, that Finland, the Kyrgyz Republic, and Moldova now allow fathers to take extended parental leave, or that Morocco revised its contract law to give married women the right to start businesses and get jobs without their husband's permission, the war against women remains rampant. Rural women everywhere still represent more than two-thirds of the world's illiterate adults, and women only hold about 23 percent of elected parliamentary seats globally. Even where basic gender equality appears to have improved, we are still far from living in societies where men and women are in true partnership.

Clearly, it will take far more than demographics to achieve this. In addition to changes in the law and directions of policy in this regard, there needs to be a profound transformation in our values, our attitudes, and our understanding of equality as well as gender if we are to alter entrenched habits in the home, engrained customs in the community, and the moral environment at decision-making levels of society. The sad truth is that many of the barriers facing women still stand. The battlefront may have shifted but the war against them still rages.

And it takes place, increasingly, at the unprotected frontiers of their own bodies. Violence against women is on the rise. Rape is still not considered a crime in many countries and goes unpunished. Sexual enslavement and forced prostitution still devastate the lives of the poor and, like physical violation, continue to be routinely used as weapons. Female infants are still being buried alive, and prenatal testing is now being used as a subterfuge for aborting female fetuses.[48] As award-winning journalists Nicholas Kristof and Sheryl WuDunn have pointed out, forced marriage and bride burning are still common in South Asia, and a pregnant woman in Africa is 180 times more likely to die of complications than in Western Europe. Even in the United States, 90 percent of AIDS cases in people under twenty years of age are girls, and women everywhere are still at the mercy of the brutality and abuse, the wife beating and harassment that have oppressed them for millennia.

When will it end?

2

THE VIRUS OF VIOLENCE

[T]o say violence is a sickness that threatens
public health isn't just a figure of speech.
It spreads from person to person, a germ of
an idea that causes changes in the brain, thriving
in certain social conditions.
—BRANDON KEIM, *WIRED*

[M]en have greater permission from society to act
violently and impulsively than women do. They therefore
have less reason to control their aggressive impulses.
Women who act explosively, on the other hand,
would be considered unfeminine, unfriendly, dangerous.
—ENCYCLOPEDIA OF MENTAL DISORDERS

One thing that worries me about crime series these
days is just how violent they all are . . . they nearly
all start off with some young woman being
raped and murdered and cut up and thrown
in a dustbin.
—JOHN BANVILLE

ONE TOO MANY

On the evening of December 16, 2012, a twenty-three-year-old female physiotherapy student, Jyoti Singh Pandey, and her male friend, Awindra, boarded a bus to go home after watching a movie in a New Delhi mall. As the bus trundled around the city ignoring would-be passengers, several men on board took turns, over the next hour, in gang raping and beating up Jyoti after overpowering her friend. Then they threw them both off the bus. The young woman was in an appalling condition, suffering from serious internal injuries. She died in a hospital thirteen days later.[1]

This incident sparked massive uprisings throughout India. Voices of outrage rose up and down the land; indignation was deep, anger was loud. Protesters called for tougher laws against rape, harsher punishment for sexual offenses, legislative reform, and government recognition of the cultural impunity enjoyed by men who committed such crimes. Demands were made for swifter justice for the victims and stricter law enforcement against offenders. It was noted that many police officers often failed to file charges for such crimes and were frequently bribed to hush the matter up when they did. But for once, this story could not be hushed up. Jyoti's rape and murder made world headlines and its reverberations lasted for weeks, for months. It drew attention to the problem of violence against women in ways that had never been possible before. It was as if, after centuries of sexual aggression against women, millennia of violence against girls, this was one rape too many.

The New Delhi case catalyzed an ongoing debate in India about what the government could and should do to protect women. A thirty-day investigation was launched conducted by the Justice Verma Committee, whose findings, amounting to a 644-page report of great depth and detail, called for radical changes in government policy and legislation. The horrific death of the young woman heightened awareness and intensified sensitivities all over the country, not only about the pervasiveness of such extreme attacks but also about the ubiquity, the extent, and the dismal frequency of other types of sexual harassment in Indian society, including stalking, voyeurism, and so-called "eve-teasing." This term, which covers all sorts of public pestering, from catcalls and whistles on the streets, to nudging, groping, and unsolicited touching, is commonly used in India. It not only highlights the general acceptance of such harassment but adds insult to injury by understating it, by minimizing its implications, by defining it in hokey language that turns a blind eye to its impact on women's lives. After 2012, the dangerous inappropriateness of such language and behavior was finally admitted by many in India; "eve-teasing" has now been recognized as a contributing factor to sexual assault and conducive to instances of violence against women in that country. That rape and brutal murder in the New Delhi bus was a watershed case.

Even so, shockingly enough and despite the public uproar that ensued, there have been several other notorious incidents since that time. According to the statistics of the National Crime Record Bureau, reported rape in India has risen alarmingly by 35.2 percent between 2012 and 2013 alone.[2] In late 2014, five men were arrested for the kidnapping, extortion, and gang rape of a Japanese tourist who was allegedly held captive and repeatedly raped for nearly a month in the state of Bihar. Barely two weeks after her escape, four more men were arrested for the alleged raping of a Nigerian woman, kidnapped outside the same New Delhi mall where Jyoti watched her last film in 2012. The problem is deeply rooted.

But violence against women is not unique to India, of course.[3] And the "one too many" phenomenon has been repeated elsewhere in recent years. The burned and brutalized body of Ozgecan Aslan, a twenty-year-old female psychology student, found in the southern district of Mersin, for instance, created an uproar in Turkey in 2015.

A young woman from an underprivileged background but of outstanding promise and intelligence, Ozgecan was last seen catching a
minibus home from her university at the end of the day. According
to reports, as soon as she was the last person left on the bus, the driver
apparently diverted the route and tried to rape her. When she tried to
fight back and defend herself with pepper spray, he stabbed and beat
her to death with an iron bar. The driver's father and a friend helped
him attempt to cover up the crime. Her burned and mutilated body
was later found in a riverbed.[4] Although the driver may have con-
fessed to killing the young woman, he allegedly denied the rape at
first, claiming that the murder was the result of an argument. And
so it would have been: an argument over forced sexual intercourse,
otherwise known as rape.

The ensuing protests throughout the country in 2015 brought
the issue of violence against women to the forefront of attention
in Turkish society. Women were up in arms; men took to the streets
wearing skirts to show their solidarity. These protests not only
sharpened criticism against some senior government officials but
resulted in vocal disapproval of their misogynist language and overt
condemnation of gender discrimination. They even led to a symbolic defiance against the country's religious authorities. In spite of
clerical censure and the established practice of Islamic burial rites,
women claimed the right to carry Ozgecan's coffin to its final resting
place instead of walking at the back of the funeral procession. In
fact, they insisted on being alone to do it, and not a single man was
allowed to touch the young woman's coffin, although many thousands expressed their outrage at what had happened to her, and
dozens created a circle of defense around the women coffin-bearers
during the funeral procession. Such insubordination to the express
injunctions of religious leadership was unprecedented in Turkey.
The violation and death of that young student was clearly one rape
too many.

THE ROOTS OF VIOLENCE

Violence against women is ubiquitous. In the words of a 2010 UN report:

> *In all societies, to a greater or lesser degree, women and girls are subjected to physical, sexual and psychological abuse that cuts across lines of income, class and culture. The low social and economic status of women can be both a cause and a consequence of this violence. (p. 127)*

It also appears to be timeless. Rape, sexual assault, and aggression toward the so-called weaker sex has been endemic for millennia; it has occurred in all cultures, in all periods of history. And its traumatic consequences have simply been accepted as part of the human condition. It has even been abstracted, almost sanctified by art. Its impact on the Sabine women has been immortalized on canvas; its effect on a prepubescent girl has been aestheticized in literature; the death of maidens has even been transformed into a Romantic musical trope. And it has gone so far as to be justified and excused by the social sciences. Today's perpetrators of cyberstalking and sexual harassment have sometimes been cast as psychological victims themselves, rather than as responsible citizens. Our unwillingness to recognize that lack of physical safety, of so-called integrity of person, continues to constrain the lives of women and girls all over the world, and constitutes a fundamental aspect of the violence to which they are continuously subjected.

Unfortunately, despite growing outrage and indignation on the subject and all the attempts at legislation and increasing media attention it has received, the physical vulnerability of women continues to be the most obvious indicator of their inequality. As Leslee Udwin, the director of the documentary *India's Daughter*, states: "Gender-inequality is the primary tumour and rape, trafficking, child marriage, female foeticide, honour killings and so on, are the metastases. And . . . the problem is not lack of laws. The problem is implementation of them."[5] Her article about the two-year-long experience of filming Jyoti's rapists illustrates this.

In virtually all regions of the world, long-held customs and fundamental prejudices have resulted in unequal power relationships between the sexes, which, as we saw in Chapter 1, begins before birth and continues after death. Women's biological difference from men has been interpreted as a sign of their lesser worth; it has resulted over time in more aborted female fetuses, more girls molested, and more women victims of violence than men. The corollary to this notion, that women are the source of evil and temptation, has all too easily led to the belief that they themselves must be to blame for their ill treatment, that if they suffer violence, it is because they "asked for it." In the article she published a day before the airing of her documentary in every other country besides India, Udwin records the comments made by one of the perpetrators in the New Delhi rape case which illustrate this particular mind-set:

> *A decent girl won't roam around at nine o'clock at night. A girl is far more responsible for rape than a boy . . . About 20% of girls are good . . . People had a right to teach them a lesson . . . the woman should have put up with it.*

Udwin's fundamental point, however, is that such offences are only "a part of the story"; in her opinion "the full story starts with a girl not being as welcome as a boy, from birth . . . If a girl is accorded no value, if a girl is worth less than a boy, then it stands to reason there will be men who believe they can do what they like with them." In order to illustrate this, she lets the lawyers who defended the murderers of the twenty-three-year-old student speak for themselves. One of them claimed, in the course of the trial, that "in our society, we never allow our girls to come out from the house after 6:30 or

7:30 or 8:30 in the evening with any unknown person . . . Sorry, [friendship between men and women] doesn't have any place in our society. We have the best culture. There is no place for a woman . . ." The other echoed almost identical sentiments during a subsequent televised interview. To change such attitudes is a challenge indeed, and one which can only be faced if we understand its underlying cause.

FEAR OF WOMEN

Ironically enough, in spite of the comparative physical weakness, perceived inferiority, and imposed inequality of women, they have also been feared. They have been considered dangerous and a prime threat to men. So if violence against them is endemic, perhaps it may also be because of this ancient fear. As Karen Armstrong (2014), the writer, television personality, and scholar of religion, has concurred, "Mythology is not simply an inferior version of history; it speaks of timeless realities and often brings to light hidden anxieties. An unconscious fear of female power may be one of the reasons why men have needed to segregate and seclude their womenfolk in a hopeless attempt to keep this potency within manageable bounds."

But these acts of segregation may perhaps have been imposed in society not only to contain women but to prove men as superior. According to human rights lawyer and journalist Eric Berkowitz: "Since the dawn of humankind, men have not only feared women's sexuality, they have also, to a surprising extent, measured their power in terms of how effectively they could suppress the rights of women on a variety of fronts."[6] In other words, women have served to bolster men's egos, to show them that they can dominate the natural world and its wayward powers; they have provided men with the means to reassure themselves of their ability to maintain control over life and death.

As a result of these deep-seated fears, women have borne the brunt of violence for millennia. They have been accused of treachery and deceit, of fickleness and hypocrisy in almost every culture. They have been blamed for bad harvests, lost battles, aborted babies, and the evil eye all over the world. Feminist literature has pointed out, moreover, that since women are considered suspect at best and evil at worst, they can easily be perceived as deserving of every penance and punishment, from the pain of childbirth to physical assault, from social humiliation to gang rape and murder.

But although this fear has been sanctioned by both secular and religious authorities in the past, thinkers and analysts of our own times have traced its roots to nothing more nor less than psychological and sexual taboos and have begun to address and discuss these much more openly over the past century.[7] But intellectual discourse and reasoned argument, especially about such taboos, do not eradicate fear overnight. As will be shown in Chapter 4, the fear of the feminine is still being used to justify the worst gender crimes in the world.

GUILTY TILL PROVEN MORE GUILTY

No wonder, therefore, that women's default position is sometimes one of guilt. Why else would millions of wives submit to the age-old practice of beating and abuse? Why else would they bow their heads and accept to be battered and brutalized for such reasons as burning the food, going out of the house without permission, expressing an opinion, or laughing in public? Why would they consider it normal to be punished for responding too quickly or not soon enough, for refusing sex or simply arguing with their husbands? And worst of all, why would they punish their daughters for such behavior? The default pattern of submitting to violence appears to be passed from generation to generation. When children see their mother being beaten, they accept it as the norm. If they are boys they grow up to perpetuate violence on the women in their lives; if they are girls, they end up accepting or inflicting abuse in their turn. That is why such violence is so difficult to control.

It is also extremely difficult to measure with any accuracy. By making women complicit partners to the crime, violence becomes the most hidden, the most invisible of all offenses, whether it takes the form of rape, wife battering, deliberate injury or cutting, honor killings, sexual abuse, trafficking, or enslavement. Gender crimes, especially those perpetrated by intimate partners, are committed with impunity because of the silence imposed by the stigma of guilt, by individual shame and the pressures of family honor. As a result, the *majority* of incidents of violent crimes against women and girls go unreported because of the victims' own fear of disclosure.[8] Sexual assault is either considered too disgraceful to be mentioned or is treated as a "domestic matter" that should not be interfered with—even when laws prohibiting violence of any kind against women are unequivocal. Since victims of sexual violence are often ostracized and isolated, they prefer not to advertise their plight; they either bury "their" shame voluntarily, or accept "hush money" to stay quiet. They are even forced to marry their attackers at times, in order to keep the matter under cover, usually with devastating results.[9]

NOT TELLING

Only about one-quarter of all physical assaults, one-fifth of all rapes, and one-half of all stalkings in America are reported to the police. Even when statistics of violence against women are available in a given country, moreover, it is impossible to estimate precisely how many female victims there are in the world. Whatever we calculate is "the tip of the iceberg," therefore, because of what researchers Hoeffler and Fearon have defined as "the fundamental problem of underreporting." We should bear in mind that "the figures on sexual violence [offer] a very conservative estimate."[10]

A woman's ability to report domestic violence is limited for both psychological and physical reasons. Many women rationalize away their situation, as already indicated, when they are not inhibited by fear of reprisal or dread of social ostracism. According to the Harvard psychologist Craig Malkin, a relationship with an abusive partner is like a gambling addiction: "People wind up blaming themselves for the abusive behavior of their partners. They convince themselves if they approach the person differently, maybe they won't be abused . . . There's a psychological effect like gambling: the moments of tenderness and intimacy are unpredictable, but they are so intense and fulfilling that the victim winds up staying in the hopes that a moment like that will happen again."[11]

Unsympathetic and untrained police are also part of the problem in many countries; they not only blame women for "provoking" the violence of their assailants but even go so far as to advise them to take a shower and wash their hands after being raped, effectively erasing all evidence of the crime. It is hardly surprising, with such external as well as internal impediments, to find that the task of gathering statistics about incidents of violence is not easy.

The intimate and domestic nature of this kind of violence makes it particularly hard to overcome. Das Gupta and her colleagues (2003) highlight this fact in describing the troubled history of the Marriage Law in China in 1950. The legislation was originally designed to eliminate arranged marriages and child marriage; it was intended to give women the right to demand divorce and inherit property. But since it threatened established power relations within the family, it met with stiff resistance. For men and older women to lose control over their daughters and daughters-in-law was unacceptable. The authors of this troubled history note that according to some estimates, the Marriage Law in China led to some 70,000 to 80,000 suicides and murders of young women between 1950 and 1953. Intimate partner violence is not only the most common kind of brutality experienced by women at the hands of men, but the most likely to lead to "higher levels of emotional distress, suicidal thoughts and suicidal attempts."[12]

BEGINNING TO TELL

Although the statistics in China today show no great improvement from half a century ago, there are some signs of change. It is hardly surprising, however, to find that wherever they can be gathered, they turn out to be depressing.

One reason for the large number of female suicides in China today is the sex imbalance already discussed in Chapter 1. Whereas male suicides far outnumber those of women in the West, the reverse is true in countries with deficits in the female population. Valerie Hudson and Andrea den Boer, professors at Brigham Young University and the University of Kent, respectively, note that "approximately 55 percent of all female suicides in the world are Chinese women of child-bearing age."[13] It is a tragic commentary not only on the degree of violence women have to endure outside marriage but on the desperate circumstances facing them within it.

Another depressing factor in relation to violence experienced by women in China is the reaction of the government. Although there have been several attempts to talk openly about the subject, these have been severely suppressed. The detention in 2015 of a group of five women who had been planning an awareness campaign concerning sexual harassment on public transport in Beijing sent many protestors into hiding on the eve of International Women's Day. "We're so afraid and confused," said one of them. "We don't understand what we did wrong to warrant such a ferocious backlash."[14] The China director at Human Rights Watch, Sophie Richardson, commented: "Many people find it mind boggling that the government of the second largest economy and the world's largest standing army is afraid of a group of women trying to draw attention to sexual harassment."[15]

But China is not alone when it comes to violence against women. Debasish Roy Chowdhury, deputy editor of the *South China Morning Post* in Hong Kong and an award-winning journalist, notes that "a rape occurs every 30 minutes" in India.[16] Intimate femicide, the term given to the targeted killing of women by their male partners, accounts for over half of all South African women killed in 1999, which means that roughly one woman is being killed through gender-based violence every six hours.[17] In the Democratic Republic of the Congo, just one country in which gender-based violence is used as a weapon of war, it is estimated that four women are raped every five minutes. In the US, the victims in over half the mass shootings that occurred between 2009 and 2016 were either intimate partners or other family members of the male killer.[18] And in England and Wales, according to a mid-range estimate of 78,000 people, one in every five women is the victim of sexual offenses each year.[19] And while the death rate from HIV/AIDS for males is much higher than that for females at all age groups in most of the world, the reverse is true in sub-Saharan Africa. In this region, over 600,000 excess female deaths each year can be attributed to AIDS alone. In fact, the number of deaths caused by sexually transmitted diseases among women ages fifteen to twenty-nine in sub-Saharan Africa is 2.3 times higher than that of males of the same age.

Anderson and Ray (2010, p. 1292) interpret this "extraordinary discrepancy" in terms of "the multiplicity of female sexual partners among males." They also attribute it to "the existence of violent or forced sex and the relative inability of women to negotiate safer sex practices" in sub-Saharan Africa. But sexual violence is not culturally circumscribed; nor are the dangers associated with the multiplicity of sexual partners restricted to one country. In the 2014 analysis of the top five nations in the world with the highest rates of rape, Sweden showed up as second on the list, after Lesotho, with the UN reporting sixty-nine rape cases per 100,000 inhabitants in 2011.[20] The squeaky-clean profile of New Zealand also appears to have been sullied when it comes to statistics of rape, for in 2011, police recorded 3,466 rapes and related offenses, up from 3,016 in 2010.[21] Even taking the lack of reported cases into consideration, it is clear from these statistics that of all the forms of discrimination against women, sexual violence is everywhere the worst.

So if male aggression is endemic all over the world, if sexual assault is as old as time, if attacks, beatings, stabbings, and rape are inevitable, unavoidable, inescapable, and ubiquitous, are we to assume that nothing can be done? Are women doomed? Is violence against them preordained? And must all efforts to curb it, all legal instruments designed to punish it, all attempts to shield women from its nefarious consequences founder on these ancient rocks?

Although national laws still have supremacy over international standards of human rights in many countries, including the United States, major strides have been made in the creation, ratification, and implementation of legal instruments to protect women from discrimination. But how useful has such legislation proven to be when it comes to intimate partner violence? How far can international law go in implementing equality at the domestic level?

Can paper protect women from violence?

GOOD INTENTIONS

In 1993, the UN adopted the Declaration on the Elimination of Violence Against Women. This historic document, the first of its kind in human history, condemns violence against women outright, in words. It states that such violence undermines the fundamental freedoms of women and impairs their enjoyment of those rights. It recognizes the roots of gender-based violence in historically unequal power relations between the sexes and acknowledges that this inequality has led to domination over and discrimination against women by men for centuries. It further notes that violence against women has severely retarded their full advancement and that opportunities for them to achieve legal, social, political, and economic equality in society will continue to be undermined if endemic violence is allowed to prevail.

So far, so good. To put such noble principles into words is a very important step. The Declaration is justly considered a landmark for women's rights. By identifying violence against women as an international concern, it created a language and a vocabulary to speak about issues that have been suppressed and suffocated for millennia. Since its ratification, a quarter of a century ago, global efforts to eliminate all forms of violence against women have intensified, national policies supporting its aims have been gradually implemented in many countries, and research as well as growing media attention have increasingly demonstrated international determination to address this issue in recent years.[22]

Prior to the UN Declaration, other international commitments had already paved the way, of course. This story is nothing if not evolutionary. As already mentioned, the International Labour Organization's Convention of 1958 against discrimination in employment and occupation addressed one aspect of the problem affecting women in the workplace. The UN General Assembly Declaration on the Elimination of Discrimination Against Women addressed more concerns in 1967. And as Chapter 5 will show, the Convention on the Elimination of All Forms of Discrimination Against Women (CEDAW) laid the foundation for all future efforts to implement gender equality among the members of the UN. The path to gender equality is certainly paved with good intentions, and a great deal of paper in the bargain.

General Recommendation No. 19 of the CEDAW Committee, for example, clearly established violence against women to be a form of discrimination. Prior to the Convention, violence against women had not been thought of in those terms. But by insisting that countries adhering to the Convention must protect women against such violence—whether it occurs within the family, in the workplace, or in any other area of social life—this document extended a legal arm of protection over women in all walks of life. Such commitments are reiterated, moreover, in other regional treaties, such as the Inter-American Convention on the Prevention, Punishment, and

Eradication of Violence Against Women and the Protocol to the African Charter on Human and Peoples' Rights on the Rights of Women in Africa. The basis for the protection of women against all kinds of violence and in all states has been established on the foundation of international human rights law.

But the challenge posed by the implementation and enforcement of such laws is quite a different matter. Unfortunately, more than a year after the notorious New Delhi case and despite another highly publicized gang rape which also took place in India since then, not a single one of the urgent proposals of the Justice Verma Committee has as yet been implemented. According to one article, many of those recommendations had "vanished from public memory and, more tragically, from the memory of government authorities charged with providing women safer public spaces and more effective policing."[23] The 644-page report may have been difficult to read but it was entirely realistic; it had recognized that far more was needed than legislation to create a safe society for women.

"Our original mandate was to recommend changes to the law," explained Abhishek Tewari, counsel for the committee. "But . . . the solutions to problems of sexual assault and rape required a much larger, holistic approach. [We] came to realize that there had never been a serious study in India directed at understanding the psychological factors that drive rape."

Factors which hamper the implementation of laws against violence are deeply rooted in social and gender inequity. In a 2006 study originally intended to look for new ways in which women's empowerment could be conceptualized in India, women factory workers continually brought up the issue of violence against them as the dominant theme.[24] Almost 70 percent described sexual harassment as a "serious offence," and 38 percent of the interviewees had either experienced it themselves or witnessed it happening to their colleagues. But none of the women were prepared to take legal action. Although the majority said violence—or lack of it—would be "a major way in which to measure women's empowerment" over time, not a single one was able to overcome the psychological factors inhibiting her to speak of this violence.

In Brazil, too, seven years after the enactment of the Maria da Penha Law, there was a 78 percent increase in the number of police stations and courts specializing in gender and domestic violence.[25] But like the paper trail laid by international efforts to establish legal rights and protection for women, the proliferation of court activities and police administration does not necessarily address the fundamental problem. The reality is that intimate partner violence, marital rape and sexual abuse still carry too many stigmas against women themselves. The prevalence of domestic abuse is high, but according to the World Bank, only 29 percent of women who experience domestic violence are reporting it.

The enforcement of laws against hate speech is also a serious concern, even in Europe. There have been numerous cases of female journalists who have felt obliged to leave social media since receiving explicit gender-based threats. For years after Laura Boldrini was elected president of the Italian Parliament she was the target of repeated hate speech. And an investigation was opened in the United Kingdom in February 2014 against two police officers who used denigrating language against a nineteen-year-old woman who was attempting to lodge a complaint with them for domestic violence.[26] Jo Cox may have been stabbed to death for ostensibly political motives, and Diane Abbott, the first black MP in the UK, may receive a disproportionate amount of abuse for racial reasons, but a recent study in Denmark shows that female politicians are regularly subjected to digital harassment and abuse, including "direct threats of rape," simply because they are women.[27] In fact, even as women become more politically engaged, it appears that they are becoming more targeted for violence, with implications for democracy at large.[28] In an effort to prohibit sexual harassment and other forms of gender-based violence, including oral hate speech, the Istanbul

Convention was opened for signature in 2011, but the failure of many Member States of the Council of Europe to ratify the convention since then is also an indication of how long, how slow, and how arduous is the path to ensuring the protection of women against all forms of violence.

THE FACES OF VIOLENCE

Violence has many facets, many faces. It assumes different forms at different times—some physical, such as wife beating, others sexual, such as rape, and many emotional and psychological, all verbal. In order to better evaluate its protean shapes, it might be useful to summarize briefly what sort of violence is being discussed here, where it is most commonly found, and who most often commits it. We need to assess not only how badly or how often a woman is raped, or sexually assaulted, or abused, or beaten, or exposed to physical aggression, but also whether she is a target of *domestic violence*, a victim of so-called *honor killing*, or a casualty of *war crimes*.

Admittedly, it is not always easy to distinguish the cause, and often tempting to simply calculate the consequences, when gathering statistics about violence. But while motivations are difficult to assess, it is necessary to look a little more closely at the character of violence in order to measure the effectiveness of the legislation needed to control it.

DOMESTIC VIOLENCE

A study by the World Health Organization finds that one woman in three in the world will experience violence sometime during her lifetime and one in four will experience domestic abuse. She will be violated, in most cases, by someone she knows, either a former or current male partner, or a family member or colleague, and will be subjected to abuse in the course of her intimate relationships by a husband, a boyfriend, a family member, or a friend. Domestic violence can take place at home, at work, or on the street; it can be driven by private grievances or be related to public shame. The only factor of any certainty associated with such crimes is that they constitute the overwhelming majority of cases of violence against women.[29]

Domestic violence within the family home, sexual harassment in the workplace, and aggression on the streets constitute the most chronically underreported crimes and at the same time the most common forms of violence against women in the world. According to recent research, "intimate partner violence may be a predictor of other forms of violence" too.[30] It can lead out of the private and into the public sphere, from the family circle to social conflict and state insecurity. And it is statistically far more prevalent even than war crimes against women. Domestic violence does not respect economies or social status; it is not specific to any one religion or culture. It ignores all frontiers.

At Home

The vulnerability of women who are abused at home is exacerbated by the fact that they are being violated in the one place where they are supposed to feel safe. They are at high risk because they simply have nowhere else to go. Between the years 2000 and 2006, about one-third of homicides in the Canadian province of Alberta were related to domestic violence. And in the course of one year during this period, over 14,000 women and children sought places in safe shelters that were unable to take them in. According to a study conducted by WHO (2015), incidents of "intimate partner violence" experienced by women in the domestic sphere range from a low of 15 percent in Japan to a high of 71 percent in Ethiopia. Indeed, the greatest number of acts of violence reported by women take place where "home" is literally the only shelter there is, in an often-hostile environment, in provincial and often remote rural settings, in countries such as Bangladesh, Ethiopia, Peru, and the United Republic of Tanzania.

Depressingly enough, the first sexual experience for many women and girls in the world is also most frequently forced.

One of the most notorious stories of home-based domestic violence comes from Brazil. In 1982, Maria da Penha suffered two murder attempts by her husband, who first shot her in the back and then, when she returned from the hospital after his first murder attempt, tried to electrocute and drown her. Maria da Penha initiated legal proceedings against her husband, but it took two decades of sluggish progress through the court system before he was eventually sentenced in 2002. She had become paraplegic as a result of these attacks, but he served only two years in prison for his crimes. It was a case of "one too many" that led to many more. Ultimately the Inter-American Court of Human Rights held the government of Brazil responsible for failing to take action against domestic violence offenders. In response, the Brazilian government enacted a comprehensive law on domestic and family violence, which, befittingly enough, is called the Maria da Penha Law.

In Pakistan, an estimated 5,000 women are killed each year as a result of domestic violence, with thousands of others maimed or disabled. In a 2003 study conducted in the gynecology wards of three Pakistani hospitals, 97 percent of the 218 women interviewed said they had been victims of some form of assault, ranging from verbal abuse and threats, to being subjected to beatings or nonconsensual sex.[31] It is because the abuse against women in Pakistan is "endemic in all social spheres" that Shahnaz Bokhari converted her family home in Rawalpindi into her country's first shelter for battered women with children in 1999.[32] Two years later, she was arrested for "abetting an attempt to commit adultery" after sheltering a woman from an abusive husband, and it took another two years before she was cleared of the charges. Despite the fact that Bokhari and her family have received numerous threats as well as being subject to frequent police raids, her Islamabad-based Progressive Women's Association has uncovered over 5,675 stove-death victims among the 16,000 cases they documented of violence against women.[33] The term "stove-death victims" has actually been coined to describe the fiery deaths meted out to young wives in Pakistan, most between eighteen and thirty-five, many of them pregnant. In Islamabad alone, 4,000 women are believed to have been set ablaze over an eight-year period, for such reasons as the failure to give birth to a son, becoming a second wife when the husband lacks the financial means to support the first, and long-running animosity with mothers-in-law. Bokhari, who braves death threats in order to fight the practice, has wryly commented:

Either Pakistan is home to possessed stoves which burn only young housewives and are particularly fond of genitalia, or looking at the frequency with which these incidences occur, there is a grim pattern that these women are victims of deliberate murder.[34]

The Progressive Women's Association has also reported 7,800 cases of acid attacks against women between 1994 and 2008 in the Islamabad area alone. In South Asia, over 100,000 women apparently die, without complaint, in "innocent" fires every year. This astonishing number, if it does not raise a few questions, should at least raise brows.

At Work

Domestic violence has a direct impact on women at work. A US study analyzing the effects of wife beating and women battering on their employment status in 1998 found that seventy-one sample victims lost their jobs, quit their jobs, were absent from work, were late for work, were prohibited from working, or were unable to attend school as a result of violence.[35] The results of surveys in Chile and Nicaragua, too, show that domestic violence has restricted women's ability to participate in the labor market and had devastating effects on their earning power. According to Anke Hoeffler at Oxford University and

James Fearon at Stanford University, "Women who suffered [intimate partner violence] report significantly poorer health when compared to non-abused women. They have difficulty walking, struggle with daily activities, and suffer from pain, memory loss, dizziness and vaginal discharge. They also report significantly higher levels of emotional distress."[36] It is easy to imagine that in such cases working might be difficult.

Perpetrators of violence also harass women when they are trying to work. They persecute them with abusive phone calls during work hours, they appear unannounced and uninvited in the workplace, and they stalk their victims when they leave. The increased absenteeism, as well as the health and psychological problems that result, invariably affect more women than men. There is evidence that in a number of countries among employees working in call centers, women were more often sexually harassed over the phone than their male colleagues, with three out of every four of the perpetrators being men. And in 2007, a survey of 30,000 women and men across thirty-one European countries showed that 2 percent of all workers and 5 percent of those aged fifteen to nineteen years had been bullied or harassed in the workplace, with women affected more, especially those on temporary contracts.[37]

A 2016 study conducted for the United States Equal Employment Opportunity Commission (EEOC) by the Select Task Force on the Study of Harassment in the Workplace states that "workplace harassment remains a persistent problem," with "almost fully one third of the approximately 90,000 charges received by EEOC in fiscal year 2015 includ[ing] an allegation of workplace harassment." The task force also concluded that all too often workplace harassment goes unreported, that "common workplace-based responses by those who experience sex-based harassment are to avoid the harasser, deny or downplay the gravity of the situation, or attempt to ignore, forget, or endure the behavior." They further add: "Roughly *three out of four* individuals who experienced harassment never even talked to a supervisor, manager, or union representative about the harassing conduct . . . because they fear disbelief of their claim, inaction on their claim, blame, or social or professional retaliation." The authors of the study confirm as their bottom line that "there is a compelling business case for stopping and preventing harassment."

On the Streets

It is not only at home or in the workplace but also in the streets that women face violence. According to a recent report, more than 1 million women and 370,000 men are stalked annually in the United States.[38] As many as 1 in 12 women as against 1 in 45 men will be stalked in their lifetimes, with most stalkers by an overwhelming margin (87 percent) being male. A stalking inventory published in 1999 illustrates that in 141 cases of actual femicide and 65 incidents of attempted femicide over the course of a single year, there is a significant link between physical assault and stalking.[39] At least 76 percent of femicide victims and 85 percent of attempted femicide incidents were directly associated with stalking, mostly perpetuated by the victims' intimate partners. This analysis proved definitively that stalking is closely correlated to lethal and near-lethal acts of violence against women. Coupled with physical assault, it often leads to murder or attempted murder.

HONOR KILLINGS

We are fastidious about words, especially when reading and writing about violence against women. With a subject this volatile, it is easy to give and take offense, and so research papers and statistical studies generally steer clear of graphic language and employ a nonspecific vocabulary instead. For example, few findings use the word "murder" outright in speaking of extreme acts of violence toward women that lead to death. If we have come up with the term "femicide" in recent years, it may also be to sanitize as well as Latinize the act.

The word "injuries," for example, is frequently used to account for the numbers of women dying in India. Female deaths attributed to "injuries" in that country exceeded 225,000 in 2000, according to research, which is a much higher statistic than is laid at the door of maternal morbidity.[40] Although excess female deaths are more evenly distributed across age groups in India, cardiovascular disease and "injuries" are given as the most important causes. This statistic leads to the strong presumption that women are dying as a result of violence perpetrated against them.

One term that has become prevalent in modern usage is "honor killing." What this euphemism amounts to is an act of murder—burning, disfigurement, and sexual mutilation, leading to death—perpetrated in the name of morality and "virtue" against anyone who is thought to have brought shame on family or community through acts of "vice." The most pernicious aspect of this kind of violence is that it tries to exonerate itself from being a crime under the cover of righteousness. It also hides motivations of vengeance beneath codes of behavior that seek impunity on the grounds of religious authority and cultural exceptionalism. But some researchers, such as Hoeffler and Fearon, are beginning to call it by its name: "Across the world there are a number of harmful traditional practices that constitute violence against women. Examples include female infanticide and prenatal sex selection, early marriage, dowry-related violence, female genital mutilation (FGM), [and] 'honor' crime."[41] The authors of this study add the maltreatment of widows among these "harmful traditional practices," which in its extreme form can even lead to an incitement to suicide.

But honor killing, per se, is primarily a crime against young people, the average age of victims, worldwide, being twenty-three years old. It is also a crime primarily directed at women. In a study for the *Middle Eastern Quarterly* in 2010, the psychotherapist Phyllis Chesler found that over half of the victims were daughters and sisters and about a quarter were wives and girlfriends of the perpetrators. She also found that honor killings depended on family collaboration, were often carried out by multiple perpetrators, and invariably involved torture before death. This included being raped or gang raped before being killed; being strangled or bludgeoned to death; being stabbed between ten and forty times; being stoned or burned to death; being beheaded or having one's throat slashed. More than half the honor killings committed, moreover, were justified on the grounds that the victim was "too Western." This was true in the Middle East as well as in Western countries.

Honor killings have accelerated significantly worldwide in the twenty-year period between 1989 and 2009. This may mean that crimes of this kind against women are genuinely escalating, perhaps as a function of jihadist extremism and Islamic fundamentalism. Or it may be an indication that honor killings are being more accurately reported and prosecuted. The internet may also account for their wider reporting. But more studies are increasingly being undertaken as well. A 2004 analysis in Iraqi Kurdistan,[42] based on interviews of fifty-two judges, politicians, lawyers, police officers, women activists, survivors, and witnesses, reveals that few honor killings were prosecuted, all those convicted were granted considerable leniency, and the judgments of local councils were preferred. It also shows, moreover, that religious leaders view reform as motivated by Western values and conducive to immoral behavior. An analysis conducted between 2000 and 2001, based on verbal autopsies gathered about the deceased to determine the cause of deaths among young, single women of reproductive age in the West Bank and in Jordan, found quite a number of suspected honor-related deaths and honor killings. Of 625 Jordanian students questioned on the seriousness of family violence in 1998, for example, 13 percent of males and 11 percent of females reported personal exposure to an honor-related femicide.[43] According to interviews conducted in 2005 and 2006 in urban areas in Jordan, 28 percent of the 200 individuals questioned personally knew an honor-killing victim, 4 percent reported an honor killing in their extended family, and 1 percent had an honor killing in their immediate family. But at the same time 95 percent of the interviewees either disagreed or strongly disagreed with the statement that "honor killings are morally just."[44]

Many murders of this kind are closely associated with religious fundamentalism. In his March 2015 interim report regarding the human rights situation in Iran, Secretary General of the United Nations Ban Ki-moon drew particular attention to a series of acid attacks against Iranian women and the inadequate response of Iranian authorities to these incidents of violence motivated by religious zeal; he noted that they were of a magnitude that was drawing considerable attention to the problem, both domestically and internationally, "with concerns being expressed that the attacks might be linked to the approval of the plan on the protection of promoters of virtue and prevention of vice." Laws for the protection of women, as we have seen, are not easy to implement. In stark contrast, government-sponsored plans arising from religious laws that pervert and violate women's rights are applied swiftly and effectively through the zealotry of "morality police" and "promoters of virtue."

In Afghanistan, for example, shelters provided by Western governments for women who are threatened by honor killings or disfigurement have come under serious attack in recent years, not only by powerful conservative elements in the society but also from the government itself. In 2011, lawmakers came close to making these shelters illegal; in 2013, they were almost successful in annulling a law barring violence against women completely. According to reports of statements by one of the influential senior clerics in the country, Habibullah Hasham, a woman who tries to flee from a violent husband is "breaking the order of the family and it's against the Islamic laws and it's considered a disgrace. What she has done is rebelling." Manizha Naderi, who runs Women for Afghan Women, an organization that operates shelters and safe houses in thirteen provinces in the country, avers that about 15 percent of these abused women can never leave; they live in a kind of no-woman's land, because neither society nor their families will ever accept them. In many cases, it is the women in the families, the mothers themselves, who are the most virulently opposed to daughters who have attempted to escape the definitions of "virtue" set by society.[45]

One way that religious authorities "promote virtue and prevent vice" in a country is through hate speech. Misogynist language provokes domestic as well as state- and culture-sponsored violence and has been most manifest in recent years in the virulent vocabulary of religious fundamentalism in the Middle East. In October 2006, for example, during a Ramadan sermon given at the Lakembe Mosque in western Sydney, Australia's senior cleric, Sheikh Taj el-Din al-Hilali, reportedly announced that women who did not wear the hijab out of doors were like "uncovered meat."[46] Addressing five hundred worshippers, the sheikh expounded at length on the topic of adultery and the responsibility of husbands to keep their wives at home. "If you take out uncovered meat," he proclaimed, "and place it outside on the street, or in the garden, or in the park, or in the backyard without a cover, and the cats come and eat it, whose fault is it, the cats' or the uncovered meat? The uncovered meat is the problem." He concluded that if the woman had been veiled and in her home, "no problem would have occurred." It was men's responsibility to control their wives. Such verbal violence, intimidation, and abuse is ultimately the most difficult to eradicate because it is taken up from the pulpit and echoed in the streets, repeated in the market place, and finally lodged permanently in the hearths and homes of people.

When ideas of this kind, voiced by figures of so-called moral rectitude and spiritual authority, take root in people's minds, they assume an absolutism that is difficult to question or dislodge. According to Udwin, the lawyer for one of the rapists in the New Delhi murder of 2012 echoed this same obdurate stance against women, bolstered by violent language: "If my daughter or sister engaged in pre-marital activities," he stated in a televised interview, "and disgraced herself and allowed herself to lose face and character by doing such things, I would most certainly take this sort of sister or daughter to my farm-house, and in front of my entire family, I would put petrol on her and set her alight." He did not disown the comment either. "This is my stand," he said, when questioned by Udwin. "I still today stand on that reply." His position reflects the opinion of an important segment of the population in India at this time, who, even if they do not condone the murder of Jyoti, nevertheless continue to blame her for the rape.

The words of the sheikh and the Indian lawyer betray a funda-mental cause of violence against women. But misogynist language is not limited to one particular culture or religion. Women were also the prime targets of hate speech during the period of religious and political upheaval in Europe, in the sixteenth and seventeenth cen-turies. The fire and fury of misogynist language aroused both Jan-senists among the Catholics and Puritans among the Protestants. It incited many secular authorities and common folk, eager for scape-goats, to massacre between 50,000 and 200,000 so-called witches over three hundred years. In our own time it is implicit in speech patterns that demean women, on screen and in our homes, from seem-ingly anodyne mother-in-law jokes to pornographic verbal abuse that promotes vulgar political partisanship. It privileges the bimbo and beauty queen roles traditionally allocated to women by autocrats and dictators of every stripe, and has poisoned Western democratic processes with a degree of calumny unheard of since the pre-libel days of eighteenth-century England.

The stories of abducted brides and kidnapped girls, of enforced marriages and sex trafficking, whether in Nigeria, Syria, or other countries of sub-Saharan Africa, echo the same slanders against women and similarly suppress the aspirations of girls, particularly in relation to education and political empowerment. A study of the mo-tives and strategies of Boko Haram, for example, based on data gath-ered in a ground-breaking collection of testimonies, shows that this group's ultra-Salafist language and ideology deliberately target individuals on the basis of religion and gender.[47] It also shows how effective and efficient it is to focus violent attacks on women and girls, because the knock-on effects are so devastating. According to the report, since women are the key transmitters of values and beliefs, the kidnappings, imposed marriages, and forced conversions endured by the 276 women and Chibok girls who were abducted by the Boko Haram group make strategic sense. It was a religious war crime that took place over a single night, April 14–15, 2014, with women as its primary victims.

WAR CRIMES

War crimes can be motivated by ethnic hatred, incited by religious prejudice, or provoked by political partisanship. Whatever the cause, whenever women are targeted specifically for sexual abuse, most of us find ourselves tongue-tied. Journalists and political commentators call it "the hidden atrocity." Researchers and academics talk about "sexual violence in conflict" or "wartime sexual violence." The general public shies away from the horrific idea of mass rape provoked by ethnic hatred by co-opting terms like "genocide." While we had no trouble echoing the notorious phrase "weapons of mass destruction" used by governments in relation to distant wars, we are less at ease describing the more intimate threat directed at women and girls. But one thing is clear: these women and girls cannot be called mere casualties. According to Zainab Hawa Bangura, the UN Special Representative on Sexual Violence in Conflict, sexual violence in conflict needs to be named for what it is and treated as the war crime that it is, rather than gagged and muffled as so-called collateral damage.

Rape

Rape has long been used as a war tactic. Sexual violence and physical abuse directed at women and girls have been employed as conscious strategies on a large scale and throughout history during or after armed conflicts. Women as old as grandmothers and girls as young as toddlers have routinely suffered violent sexual abuse at the hands of military and rebel forces, because rape is an age-old weapon, one of the most reliable, and the least costly of missiles. It is cheap, brutal, and devastating because it can so effectively humiliate opponents, terrify ordinary citizens, and destroy entire societies in a relatively short period. It has been deployed in all wars, across all frontiers of time and place right up to today.

According to UN briefings for February 2015, approximately 1,100 rapes were being reported each month in the Democratic Republic of the Congo, with an average of thirty-six women and girls being violated every day. It is believed that over 200,000 women have so far suffered from sexual violence in that country since armed conflict began in 1996. The rape and sexual violation of women and girls is also pervasive in the conflict in the Darfur region of Sudan. Between 250,000 and 500,000 women were known to have been raped during the 1994 genocide in Rwanda, and sexual violence was a characterizing feature of the fourteen-year-long civil war in Liberia. The UN Action Against Sexual Violence in Conflict cites appalling numbers of women raped during civil wars in Africa and Europe over a period of some twenty years. More than 40,000 women were raped in Liberia (1989–2003), more than 60,000 were raped during the civil war in Sierra Leone (1991–2002), and up to 60,000 were raped in the former Yugoslavia (1992–1995). During the conflict in Bosnia alone in the early 1990s, between 20,000 and 50,000 women were assaulted in this same way.

Rape and sexual assault continue long after the immediate dangers of armed conflict is over. In camps for internally displaced persons, many thousands of women, hounded from their homes under a barrage of gunfire and mortar, take refuge from death only to find themselves victims of rape. In war-torn northern Uganda, for example, where there were about 180 camps for internally displaced persons in 2005, housing an estimated 1.4 million people fleeing the nineteen-year war between the government and the rebel Lord's Resistance Army, at least 60 percent of the women in the largest of these camps encountered some form of sexual violence. The report (Akumu, 2005), based on a nine-month study in Pabbo Camp, about 236 miles (380 kilometers) north of Uganda's capital, Kampala, was called "Suffering in Silence," proof once more that wartime violence against women beggars description, defies being named. The report revealed that six out of ten women in Pabbo Camp were being physically and sexually assaulted, threatened, and humiliated by men. According to the representative of the United Nations Children's Fund (UNICEF) in Uganda, the victims were mainly girls, some as young as four years old. Since then women and girls in Afghanistan, Kurdistan, and Syria have been suffering the same fate.

Sex Trafficking

In addition to rape and sexual assault in times of armed conflict, another weapon used against women living in war zones is to be trafficked as sex slaves. War has always afforded useful economic incentives to a society, from the sale of sausage, as Brecht brilliantly symbolized in his satiric drama *Mother Courage*, to the manufacture of arms. Many men avoided starvation and chronic unemployment in the past by becoming mercenaries and going off to fight in wars whose aims and origins they barely understood. Many run away from similar forms of desperation today, or are being seduced by the prospect of illusory glory, petty power, and the possibilities of crude extortion. But women have invariably borne the brunt of war's trafficking and have been one of its most common commodities. Of approximately 2.5 million people trafficked and enslaved each year, both across international borders and within countries, about 43 percent are kidnapped for purposes of commercial sexual exploitation, of which the International Labour Organization estimates 98 percent are women and girls.[48] Based on data from European countries, 95 percent of these women, even if they were not enslaved in war zones, experienced physical or sexual violence during transport.

But sometimes, as in the case of the Syrian stronghold of the Islamic State in Raqqa, the sexual enslavement of women ignores even the pretense of commerce. Marriage is imposed, forced—levied, almost—particularly on girls whose families are poor. Marriage contracts include no names and provide no trace of the true identity of the Islamic State fighters, and women, once married, can be "passed on and raped" by up to fifteen of these militants.[49] Several escapes have been recorded by families who have tried to save their daughters from such imposed alliances; in other cases, in which families force their daughters into marriage with a fighter, the girls themselves have rejected it, with mixed results, including suicide. Among the many acts of violence being perpetrated by this radical group are specifically sexual ones, and it is recorded that several hospitals and physicians in the region have remarked on the rising number of women patients who have been subjected to brutal and abnormal sexual practices.

There will be further discussion and a closer focus on the specifically religious nature of these crimes against women in Chapter 4, but the questions that must be raised here concern the issue of accountability. And the cost of violence against women. Recent research claims that "the total cost of female homicides is estimated at around $105 billion" on a global scale.[50] How are such conclusions reached? Why is violence proving to be so expensive? And who is paying for it?

THE VIOLENCE DEFICIT

In addition to physical, emotional, and psychological costs, violence can also have drastic economic consequences. These range from general health issues to women's reduced capacity to function in society, from permanent disability and trauma to lower economic productivity for women and increased expenses placed on public services and employers. Violence against women is not only a serious crime but is costly for society, because it is a critical factor influencing a woman's financial autonomy and agency. It lowers her productivity and has a direct impact on her ability to seek economic opportunities and stand on a par with men.[51] Beyond the human rights perspective, there is a strong social and economic rationale for ensuring that women are protected from this pervasive historical form of inequality.

But, as Lomborg and Williams affirm, the costs of domestic violence to society are not only "vast" but "poorly understood" because research has generally "underestimated the scale and effects of such abuse."[52] How do we even begin to measure the cost of violence against women? What precisely does it include, and how should its impact on economies be evaluated?

One way to approach this challenge is to examine the immediate consequences of violent behavior and the provision of services required to deal with them, and there are three main elements to consider in such an examination. The first relates to the scope of these costs, the second to their scale, and the third to the criteria being used to measure them.

Scope

To begin with, it is important to understand the scope of our estimates regarding the economic toll of violence on society. What do they include? Are they direct costs based on relatively limited expenses or indirect ones that are not as easy to calculate? The former are admittedly more measurable than the latter. They concern health care and social services needed by victims, for example, expenses incurred by police deployment and court procedures, and the costs to the state of incarceration. They might also include long-term financial burdens to the international community for the pursuance of war crimes, as well as accounting for the immediate, tangible consequences at an individual level. But indirect and more comprehensive costs must also be considered; these may be more difficult to calculate but cannot be ignored. They include time lost from paid work and volunteer labor when a woman is the victim of violence. They entail the consequences of diminished productivity on society, and reduced income on a family when a woman loses her employment. And there are still more intangibles that are even harder to evaluate, such as the impact of pain and suffering on an individual's finances, and the cost of psychological disorders caused by violence. As research evolves, we are beginning to measure the long-term economic consequences of impaired mental health and chronic illnesses that women suffer as well as the second-generation effects of violence on their children.[53] The cost of ruined lives may not be obvious, but its scope is enormous.

Scale

Secondly, the question of scale needs to be addressed. A study has to include a broad combination of statistics in order to be valid because there are a host of variables to consider. For example, even in the case of a seemingly straightforward and easily measurable expense, such as gauging police costs in the case of domestic violence against a woman, a wide range of data needs to be considered. To estimate the scale of expense, we have to know how many women call the police for help in any given period, the average time spent by the police force in addressing such disturbances, the hourly rate for both officers and administrators, and which of their services might have been used elsewhere had this violence not occurred. In other words, the equation is itself barely calculable. The cost can only be obtained by first evaluating the use of the police service, then multiplying this by the cost of that service per victim, and finally subtracting from the total the use of the service had no violence occurred. Even if the mathematics were less complex, we would still have to take geography into account. Depending on where the violence takes place, the costs would naturally differ, so the issue of scale also has implications. For instance, the feasibility of drawing inferences in national terms from costs incurred at a local or regional level would need careful consideration. We would have to know whether a few selected victims from one particular hospital were being used to illustrate national health care usage, or whether an attempt to come up with countrywide samples of victims may have ignored specifically egregious cases. Unless studies are based on broadly representative samples, they cannot be used to hypothesize the costs of violence on a national scale. At best they merely prove that calculating the cost of violence is data intensive by indicating all the variables that should be included in such estimates.

Criteria

Finally, accuracy is a vital factor. And for accuracy to be reliable, a clear criterion of measurement needs to be established. Studies that do not explicitly state the criteria used to measure violence tend to be far less reliable than those that do. They are also easier to dismiss because their accuracy can always be questioned. But the dismal fact is that however careful the criteria, however scrupulously accurate the measurements, no study has yet come close to enumerating the full costs of violence against women.[54] There are several reasons for this. Certain criteria, such as reduced life satisfaction, do not show up in estimates at all, and are a challenge to measure in economic terms. Furthermore, the criteria used to measure the costs of violence can remain opaque for cultural reasons too. Even more important, in order to avoid a backlash resulting from high figures, studies tend to present the lower end of their estimates to the public, perhaps for cultural reasons. And, finally, the sad truth is that women are the least reliable source of information about the violence inflicted on them. They often cover up the facts and frequently shy away from sharing details because of social norms and individual fears. Since they are more inclined to suppress and deny rather than to accuse and condemn intimate partners or close family members, accuracy and reliability are not easy to establish and clear criteria to measure the intangible costs of violence are not always possible to achieve.

All this implies that any estimate of this subject is usually an underestimate, and it indicates that, in spite of this fact, it may still be worth considering what we know in light of all we do not. Much may be discovered, including humility, while trying to reach conclusions about what is missing from the calculation. The real deficit lies in our imaginations.

Regardless of all these difficulties, the United Nations has used information currently available to estimate that 12 to 58 percent of girls and women worldwide will experience some kind of violence against their person at least once during their lifetime. This wide-ranging assessment is no small achievement, for it reflects both low and high levels of incidence in developed European countries as well as in Africa, Latin America, the Middle East, and Asia.[55] Another study that attempts to control the slippery data in order to arrive at a systematic assessment of domestic violence in some nine countries also shows that intimate partner violence typically costs between 1 to 2 percent of GDP.[56] This is a rough estimate, given the range of differences among the countries included, the variable methods deployed, and the year of reference, but it is significant nonetheless. For example, in 2006 the cost of domestic violence in the EU25 was €16 billion.[57] In Colombia, focusing only in Bogotá, Baranquilla, and Barancabermeja, estimates for domestic violence came to $8.8 trillion in 2003 pesos, or 3.93 percent of GDP.[58] The estimates for South Africa between 2012 and 2013 ranged from R28.4 billion (0.9 percent of GDP) to R42.4 billion (1.3 percent of GDP).[59] In sum, it seems that "intimate-partner violence costs the world about 25 times more [than terrorism]: around 5.2 percent of global GDP."[60]

Indeed, rape costs the United States more than any other crime.[61] In 2000, 36 percent of rape and sexual assault victims lost more than ten days of work, meaning that employers could pay almost $5 billion annually for violence against women as well as traditional crimes like murder. Even though this estimate unfortunately excludes the costs related to sick leave and disability insurance, it nevertheless has raised awareness of this issue and recent studies are now beginning to include a wider range of criteria when assessing the heavy price paid for violence against women. Lomborg and Williams's article, based on one such study conducted in 2010 for the Copenhagen Consensus Center, concludes that according to the most conservative of these estimates "the total cost to the United States of the almost 5 million domestic violence cases per year is about $460 billion . . . That's nearly 10 times the entire Justice department budget."[62]

In spite of the ambiguities involved in measuring the impact, assessing the extent, and evaluating the costs of violence against women, this wide range of estimates highlights two important facts: domestic violence imposes a significant economic burden on national budgets, and there is an urgent need for better data collection and a clearer consensus regarding the real costs of this violence. UN agencies are slowly developing ways to overcome the lack of harmonization and the absence of adequate country estimates in order to apply the appropriate remedies. They are bringing international pressure to bear on countries to implement population-based surveys, to integrate data into administrative and reporting systems, and to break up and separate existing data according to gender.

Although the high prevalence of violence worldwide justifies this urgent call to action, budgets have not always matched the rhetoric. Despite the universal acknowledgment of the issue, very few resources are being devoted to this issue by governments at this time. In fact, only $100 million was invested in programs related to violence prevention by 2015 by the UN Trust Fund.[63] Most studies related to violence, moreover, rely on data concerning its nature and scope rather than its economic impact. An alternate way of measuring how much society pays for violence might be to calculate the rising accountability costs involved. In other words, instead of assessing what women lose as a result of domestic violence in economic terms, it may be useful to evaluate what men might owe, in fines. If a perpetrator's aggressive act can be properly evaluated according to its cost to society, and he can be penalized financially on a generally accepted scale of evaluation, there may be some chance of calculating the consequences of these crimes more accurately.

Men have rarely had to pay for their violent behavior toward women. Only in very recent history—the last half of the twentieth century—have perpetrators of rape, sexual aggression, and abuse been called to account. Even then only rarely have they been punished or incarcerated for their acts, let alone compelled to compensate their victims or pay fines for their crimes to society. Ten years ago, a front-page article in the *International Herald Tribune* noted "spotty prosecutions, vague statistics, old-fashioned judges and unresponsive governments" when it came to confronting this endemic problem. More recently, in spite of increased exposure by the media and high-profile cases in the political domain, we are seeing evidence of covert intimidation and overt threats, of flat denials and the use of so-called hush money intended to silence women who try to draw attention to this issue. All this is glaring proof not just of the ongoing attacks against women, but how much we are all paying to pursue this ancient war. It is a grim indictment of how far we still are from real equality, despite priding ourselves on our record of human rights.

But perhaps because of the extreme cases of sexual aggression against women lately, precisely because of the verbal and physical abuse directed at them in these high-profile court cases and vulgar political scandals, the press and the public in many countries are finally directing greater attention to the issue.[64] Worldwide women's marches, nationwide calls for legitimate curbs on gratuitous aggression, and a rising generation of youth demanding the right to go to school and remain at home in safety may indicate a turning of the tide of public opinion regarding violence, particularly against women and girls.

It is surely time to address the causes and seek solutions to this appalling phenomenon.

CONCLUSION

It is as difficult to assess the price of violence with exactitude as it is to measure its motives. But when words fail, perhaps numbers might prevail. When moral imperatives prove inadequate, perhaps budget constraints could curtail violence against women.

The impact of the 2012 New Delhi rape and murder of Jyoti was dramatic from a financial point of view. Since women make up a significant percentage of employees in the outsourcing sector of India's information technology businesses, there were some negative consequences to the economy when the labor force was hit in the immediate aftermath of the rape. Due to the time difference between India and the United States, one of the primary requirements for employment in transnational call centers is the ability to work night shifts. But the fate of the young female physiotherapy student sent such shock waves through the industry that many women quit their jobs in the wake of Jyoti's death, for fear of assault on the roads.[65]

The statistics speak for themselves. According to a survey conducted by the Associated Chambers of Commerce and Industry of India, at least 2,500 women in the Delhi–National Capital Region and in other major cities were reluctant to work on night shifts following the gang rape case. In the Delhi–National Capital Region—where 250,000 women work in over 2,000 business process outsourcing companies—the efficiency of female employees in these companies decreased by as much as an estimated 40 percent. Productivity was also affected in the workforce of other cities, such as Chennai, Bangalore, Mumbai, and Hyderabad. An overall 80 percent of women said that they feared traveling on public transportation at night after the rape case, and one in three workers either quit her job or reduced her working hours after dark.[66] In fact, after December 16, almost 90 percent of the women who took part in the survey in Delhi began to leave their offices immediately after work hours, due to the atmosphere of insecurity caused by the event, and more than 80 percent said they left soon after the sun set.[67]

Violence is contagious. It is like a disease and proliferates in conditions conducive to its spread, affecting more and more people as long as it remains unchecked. Indeed, we are witnessing an epidemic of violence against women in our time and an epidemic requires that rigorous measures be put in place if it is not to cause wholesale devastation. Early detection and interruption is required; quick identification of transmission and effective treatment are needed; and the mobilization of a whole community is vital if behavioral norms are to be changed.

Women could be the key to all these measures. Since they are its first victims, they would know best how to interrupt the cycle of violence, when to block its transmission most effectively, and where to stem its spread. If they were given the chance to function freely in society without discrimination, without segregation, and without commodification by the market, they would ensure that incidences of violence would decrease, and general levels of security could subsequently improve. Everyone loses when women are abused. Everyone, including the abusers, suffers the consequences and bears the costs of violence against women. The insecurity that results in society as a whole ultimately undermines the safety of men as well as women if violence against women is exonerated, justified, and ignored. As Hannah Arendt, the great Jewish writer of the Holocaust, pointed out, when we oppress people, any people, including half the human race, we do damage to our inner selves, and we deny the very essence of who we are.[68] Violence against women is violence against us all.

The rape of the twenty-year-old Ozgecan Aslan, the Turkish psychology student, is a case in point. She was also gang raped, like

Jyoti, on a bus on the outskirts of Istanbul in February 2015, and the consequences of this action are increasingly evident. On one hand, the contagion of authoritarianism has spread in Turkey, affecting its political stability and alliances; on the other, Ozgecan's death has shone an arc light on the stark gender gap in Turkey, which was ranked 131 out of 144 countries in terms of equality in 2017.[69] It has highlighted the fact that only 33.6 percent of the country's women are participating in the workforce and just 14.6 percent of the country's legislators, senior officials, and managers are female. It has also drawn attention to the 1.7 million bus drivers currently employed in Turkey, 1.1 million of whom have no training, have passed no formal tests, and have been conducting part-time businesses with no proper qualifications. Although the public outrage caused by this rape and murder forced the government to issue hurried promises that it would address this glaring problem, there have been other, less measurable costs borne by civil society, where political opposition and freedom of speech are being curtailed. As history has demonstrated time and again, any attempt to ensure "security" by clamping down on basic freedoms is bound to prove expensive in the end.

Moreover, women themselves are becoming aware of the expense. They are beginning to measure their worth in economic terms and use it to insist on change in society. In spite of the odds stacked against them, they have begun to find ways to circumvent the prevalence of violence through legislation and have been able to achieve political "value" to government through their economic independence. And the results have been immediately beneficial to society as a whole. In the United States, enactment of the Violence Against Women Act of 1994, which mandated $1.6 billion for prevention programs over a five-year period, is estimated to have led to an overall savings totaling $14.8 billion.[70] In South Africa, too, economic literature on violence against women predicts that as her income rises and her access to shelters and job training improves, a woman's threat-of-leaving power increases and she becomes more independent of her abuser.[71] Consequently, empirical evidence clearly demonstrates that increased economic independence is a major factor in reducing violence against women, and economic exclusion—when women have no bank account, no formal savings or chance of credit—leads to a higher incidence of violence against them.[72]

Women's economic independence is critical to equality.

3

WOMEN AND WORK

*Empowering women and girls with more choices and
more freedoms is crucial to achieving a better future for all . . .
Women's agency and freedom are among the crucial means for
enhancing development . . . The way in which economic progress
is judged in the contemporary world tends to give a much larger
role to men's needs and demands despite all the progress that has
been achieved in enhancing the voices of women in the last half-
century . . . Countries that have expanded opportunities for
women and girls in education and work in recent decades have
largely achieved greater prosperity and moderated population
growth while limiting child mortality and achieving social progress for all . . . These greater opportunities and freedoms have
had truly astonishing results . . . There is an overwhelming need to
pay attention to the needs of girls and women.*
—AMARTYA SEN, 2012

DIVISION OF LABOR

The naked truth is that, regardless of background, culture, and race,
a higher percentage of men work outside the home in comparison to
women. This has been the case and still is true almost everywhere in
the world, across all frontiers of time and place. The preponderance

of men in comparison to women in the labor force has been a reality that is common in every age. Women have always assumed responsibility for household chores and child rearing; they have always been considered better suited for domestic work than men. According to age-old traditions, men have hunted, women have gathered; men have gone to war, and women have cared for the young. And this division of labor has been passed down from generation to generation.

Patriarchy has maintained this split between male and female roles for over six millennia.[1] Although, as Austrian-born American historian and poet Gerda Lerner eloquently testifies, women have always shared the world and its work equally with men, although they have been central to the making of society and the building of civilization—preserving memory, shaping culture, and forging links between generations—it is men who have recorded this shared history and men who have, until very recently, defined women's work. Their views of women have shaped the relationships between the sexes down to the present.[2]

One of the results of this gender-defined division of labor is that men and woman have invariably been described as essentially different creatures, almost as different species, associated with different worlds.[3] And these differences have become embedded not only in social customs and traditions of societies but in the very language used to distinguish between the sexes. Men have been considered "naturally" superior and more rational, and women have been seen as "naturally" inferior in intellect and weaker in body. Since they have also been perceived as more unstable both emotionally and spiritually, it has been "natural" to keep them at home. These rigid definitions emerged millennia ago, but they are still prevalent today.

Indeed, such notions about sex-specific roles in society have proven so obdurate that we have ended up believing that the division of labor is simply in the "natural order of things." Although the very word "labor" has associations that are intimately related to the birth process and female physiology, until relatively recently women have had restricted access to the actual labor force. It is still more difficult for women to find jobs than it is for men, even in the twenty-first century. Still more women work at home, or stay at home and do not get paid for the work they do there, and more men get paid more to work outside it. The variation in percentages can be very small or quite large; the reasons for the differences can be multiple and ambiguous; but the pattern persists nevertheless.

THE EXTREMES

The labor force imbalance is evident even in countries where gender equality is highly advanced. In Denmark and Germany, for example, 66 percent of the adult men held jobs outside the home in 2016, as compared to 58 percent of the women in Denmark and 54 percent in Germany. The gap between the sexes in the labor force may be narrow in these countries, but it still exists—all 8 to 12 percentage points of it.

At the other extreme, in Saudi Arabia, the difference between men and women in the workforce is as wide as 59 points. Here 79 percent of adult men work outside the home, as compared with only 20 percent of Saudi women—over seven times more than in Denmark.[4] In Iran, the gap between the sexes is similarly large, showing a difference of a full 57 percentage points, with 73 percent of the men in the labor force as against a 16 percent participation rate for women. In India, the second most populous country in the world, the gap is also a significant 49 percentage points (79 percent male and 30 percent female).

Figure 3.1 shows male and female labor force participation rates for the world in 1980 and 2016. It also indicates various regions and particular income groups, providing a fairly detailed summary of the problem. The gap between working men and women is evident everywhere. The difference lies in the range of 13 to 17 percentage points in sub-Saharan Africa and East Asia and the Pacific and

Figure 3.1

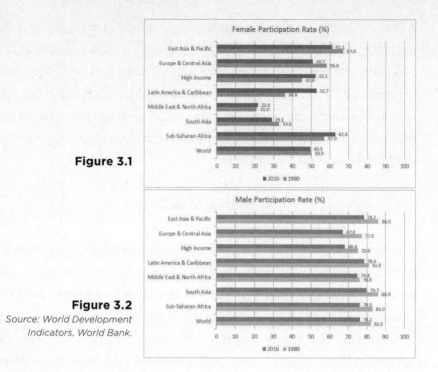

Figure 3.2

Source: World Development Indicators, World Bank.

widens to 51 to 53 percentage points in South Asia and the Middle East and North Africa. It is worth noting that these figures mask the different types of jobs held by men and women. This issue is addressed in detail later in this chapter, but in light of the extremes under discussion, the gender difference in labor force participation should be viewed as an underestimate. The true extent of gender disparity that exists in these economies is grim given that women are typically concentrated in low-paying sectors of the economy.

The sobering news conveyed by these statistics is that over the past thirty-six years, between 1980 and 2016, the global female labor force participation rate has remained virtually unchanged; it has stagnated at about 50 percent. Similar evidence can be found in the United States, where even though the married women labor force participation rate went up from 2 percent in 1880 to 70 percent in 2000, it has stayed relatively constant since 1990.[5] Although the difference between male and female participation has narrowed slightly over this period, it is only because the rate for working men has fallen somewhat, from 82 percent to 76.7 percent, and even so, the gap between the sexes still remained large in 2013, at close to 27 percentage points.

In those regions of the world where female labor force participation has increased over this period (sub-Saharan Africa, Latin America), the rise has been linked to improved levels of education among women, declining fertility rates (themselves linked to rising levels of education), and other trends in the global economy. For instance, globalization—in particular the opening up of many countries to international trade—has contributed to the growth of export-oriented industries, many of which (garments, light manufacturing) have attracted large numbers of women. The process of economic development itself, with improvements in various infrastructures (electricity, water, transport), has helped remove or lighten the impact of various constraints on women's mobility and has made it possible for more women to join the labor force. Increases in the age of marriage are also thought to have had a favorable impact on participation rates by allowing women access to paid work before they embark on the unpaid labor of family life and children.

Nevertheless, these factors are also influenced by social norms, and as a result, their effects have been varied and fairly uneven across different regions of the world. For example, significant improvements in education in the Middle East and North Africa have had much less of an impact on female labor force participation than in Latin America. And in East Asia and the Pacific, female participation rates have actually fallen since 1980, as rapid economic growth has allowed many women to opt out of the labor market.

Not surprisingly, various restrictions embedded in the law—often imposing limitations on women's access to work—have also had an adverse impact on female participation rates. In this area too, the statistics reveal the extremes. In Iran, for example—a country with a large and rapidly growing population of increasingly well-educated and cyber-savvy youth—women lack even basic freedoms, let alone equality in the workforce. Their right to travel, to work, to choose where to live, to be paid equal remuneration for work of equal value are all severely restricted. Their powers within the family are limited, exposing them to the possibility of domestic violence in as well as outside of marriage, providing them with no protection from sexual harassment in the home or from unequal remuneration and exploitation at work. Instead, the laws of the land expose them to discrimination at every level of society and have a direct bearing on their economic empowerment and personal liberty of choice.

By contrast, in most Nordic countries, gender equality is widespread, and this has naturally had an impact on women's participation in the labor market. In Sweden, for example, maternity benefits are well established. Both parents have access to the mandatory minimum length of paid parental leave. The retirement age for both men and women is the same, and since laws have been put in place for nondiscriminatory hiring, men and women can both work in the same kinds of jobs, for broadly similar pay, at night as well as during the day.

Having considered the extremes in these statistics, it is important to state, from the outset, that parity in female labor force participation is not what will guarantee gender equality. Nor is it remotely in the interests of equality or desirable for its implementation in the world that such statistics should exclusively govern a country's economic policies. The relevant question is whether noninvolvement in the labor force has been imposed on women, explicitly or implicitly, by the laws and regulations of a country. The important issue is whether the work environment is conducive to women's participation, promotion, and proper remuneration if and when they need or choose to join the labor force.

Earlier chapters have explored how the gender gap in the labor force may have been kept artificially large as a result of demographic factors and the rise of violence against women. Later chapters will show how it could be narrowed through a stronger adherence to the norms of human rights and a change in discriminatory legislation, through the questioning of cultural assumptions and priority given to the education of girls. The aim of this chapter is to look specifically at the equality of opportunity that exists between men and women in the workforce, and the forms of gender discrimination that impede women's participation in the job market.

PARTICIPATION AS EQUALITY OF OPPORTUNITY

The variables involved in measuring job market participation, however, are laced with ambiguities, some of which actually arise from the need to protect women's rights. There is no reason why a woman should join the workforce if she does not want to. There is no reason why working outside the home should necessarily be an optimal decision for everyone. Since a woman may or may not join the labor market for a whole range of reasons, it must be her autonomy of choice that serves as the gold standard for gender equality and not the degree of her participation. Since causes are much more difficult to gauge than consequences, however, we have to use the outcome as a proxy for calculating equality of opportunity.

And the outcome clearly demonstrates that gender discrimination in the workforce is inefficient in the long run. When it leads to the exclusion of women from the labor market, it reduces the gross domestic product per capita. When it manifests itself via the exclusion of women from managerial positions, it distorts the allocation of talent and depresses economic growth.[6] But when such discrimination can be overcome, the economy invariably improves. Amartya Sen (1999, p. 191) argues that decreasing work-related gender inequalities can make "a positive contribution in adding force to women's voice and agency," thereby empowering women within both the public and private spheres.

We cannot gauge the boundaries of personal motivation or the multiple influences that bear on a woman's decision to participate in the workforce, but we can measure the results. And there are at least three dimensions to these results, all of which require their own qualifiers.

One concerns the actual numbers of women engaged in paid employment, as shown in Figure 3.1. It has to be borne in mind that shifting social norms can produce fairly uneven results across different regions of the world. Significant improvements in education in the Middle East and North Africa, for example, have produced far fewer results in terms of female labor force participation than in Latin America. And in East Asia and the Pacific, as noted earlier, these rates have actually fallen since 1980, as rapid economic growth has allowed many women to opt out of the labor market. Conversely, in Eastern Europe, the numbers show that women over fifty-five years of age experienced a dramatic *increase* in labor participation, but this was only because of changes in social supports and the withdrawal of retirement benefits. Global labor participation rates sometimes can mask the reasons for these disparities.

A second dimension that needs to be borne in mind concerns the unequally shared family responsibilities linked to looking after children and the care of the elderly. Many women forgo or curtail their employment opportunities for these reasons and because of these responsibilities, which could account for the 27-percentage-point disparity mentioned earlier. According to the UN's *World's Women 2015* report, women's participation in the labor force is lower at all stages of life, with the narrowest gap between men and women's participation occurring in the years before childbearing, between the ages of fifteen and twenty-four, and, as one might expect, the highest when many women are occupied with the care of children, between twenty-five and fifty-four years of age.

The third dimension of the female labor force, which may be the most difficult to measure, relates to the unpaid domestic activities or community service done by women. Marilyn Waring (2004) in her book *Counting for Nothing: What Men Value and What Women Are Worth*, claims that the actual daily hours of work performed by women outstrip those of men by a wide margin, but the statistics on labor participation invariably exclude the women who stay at home, who do unpaid domestic work, and who remain unsalaried. We have still not learned how to measure this kind of work. Nor have we found ways to evaluate the loss to women themselves, to their families, and to society as a whole when they have less independence and economic autonomy. We are still inclined to fall back on the traditional idea of the home as the woman's "natural" place.

THE PLOUGH THEORY

A recent concept that is closely linked, both literally and metaphorically, to the issue of female labor force participation may cast a new light on this old tradition. The so-called plough theory[7] redefines our ideas about what we call "natural" and evaluates patriarchal practices in slightly more down-to-earth terms. It does this by exploring the theory that agricultural technology rather than either biology or theology has influenced the historical gender division of labor.

The Australian feminist Pat Brewer notes in the article "On the Origins of Women's Oppression" that with the invention of the plough, a significant change took place in early agrarian societies, "from collective tilling controlled by women . . . to the individual activity controlled by men."[8] Ploughing, she claims, is an isolated task whereas tilling is communal; ploughing requires greater physical strength whereas tilling, which depends on handheld tools and is very labor intensive, can be conducted by women. According to this theory, which has also been tested by Alberto Alesina, Paola Giuliano, and Nathan Nunn (2013), the differences in agricultural methods practiced in the preindustrial period account for the classic differences in gender roles. "Since plough cultivation required significant upper body strength and bursts of power, which were needed to either pull the plough or control the animal that pulls it, men in these societies had an advantage in farming relative to women" (p. 470). As a result, the classic division of labor, which leads men to work outside on the land while women specialize in activities within the home, produced the characteristics of societies associated with patriarchy to this day.

The authors find a "strong and robust" relationship between "historical plough use and unequal gender roles today," which cuts across all stereotypical assumptions about which countries are or are not developed. In light of this hypothesis, it is not surprising to find that Switzerland, for example, which was one of the last countries in Europe to give women the vote, was a solidly plough cultivation society in the preindustrial period. As the authors attest, "Traditional plough-use is positively correlated with attitudes reflecting gender inequality and negatively correlated with female labor force participation, female firm ownership, and female participation in politics." In other words, long after we leave the land, its patterns of thought and behavior stay rooted in us.

Alesina et al.'s analysis attempts to go beyond the links between plough use and female labor force participation, however. It also seeks to explore causality and to explain the mechanisms behind these relationships. Using data from the UN's Food and Agriculture Organization, the authors identify the geoclimatic suitability of specific locations for growing "plough-positive crops" (wheat, barley, and rye) and "plough-negative crops" (maize, sorghum, and millet), which are grown in soil whose characteristics make use of the plough difficult. Apart from plough use, these two sets of cereals are otherwise very similar in terms of where they have been cultivated and by whom. Both kinds have been grown in the Eastern Hemisphere since Neolithic times; both require similar preparation for consumption; both are used for making flour, porridge, bread, and beverages; and both "produce similar yields and therefore are able to support similar population densities." But the difference between them is rooted in the use of the plough.

Consistent with studies made by Pryor (1985), Alesina et al. argue that location characteristics—such as whether the soil is shallow, sloped, or rocky—predicts cultivation of plough-positive or plough-negative crops. And they have also found that wherever the plough was adopted, it predicted the gender norms of today. That is to say, the status of women in any particular country today can be gauged according to its traditional use of the plough in the past. In exploring the data, the authors even cross geographical and historical boundaries to test their hypothesis. They find, for example, that the plough hypothesis also accounts for why immigrants originating from different places but now living in the same host country still follow the gender norms of their original lands. They claim that individuals from cultures that have historically used the plough invariably maintain their traditional gender norms as immigrants, and women from those same cultures are less likely to participate in the workforce even when living abroad. In other words, when people pass through airport immigration, they often bring their invisible ploughs with them. Although these may not be seen among the suitcases, the patriarchal habits they support are easy enough to distinguish.[9]

When such metaphors are sanctioned by religion, as previously noted, they became all the more absolute. The earth as a female deity exists in many forms of religious worship, from the days of the Greeks to the establishment of Buddhism, when "[t]he earth deity in the form of a beautiful woman rose up from underneath the throne, and affirmed the Bodhisattva's right to occupy the vajrisana."[10] The relationship between the sexes from early biblical times was also interpreted according to farming metaphors; a man's duty to cultivate the earth was the same as a husband's duty to be fruitful with his wives. According to Genesis 2:5, before the creation of Adam, "there was not a man to till the ground,"[11] and the Quran 2:223 also advises men that "[w]omen are your fields: go, then, into your fields whence you please." It is easy to understand, given such terminology, why a division of labor that gives man the right to "plough his furrow" in every sense of the word is associated in the traditional mind-set not only with the "natural" but even with the "divine order of things."

But these metaphors and mythic archetypes have had a very deleterious effect on the role of women in our own day. "Plough cultures" have specialized production along fixed gender lines, which, as Alesina and colleagues attest, has "generated norms about the appropriate role of women in society" even when such roles are convincingly contradicted by the reality on the ground. According to the Food and Agriculture Organization (2017):

> *On average, women make up 40 percent of the agricultural labor force in developing countries, ranging from 20 percent in Latin America to 50 percent or more in parts of Africa and Asia. They generally work as subsistence farmers, paid or unpaid workers on family farms or as entrepreneurs running on- or off-farm enterprises. In addition, women provide the bulk of unpaid care and domestic work in rural areas, thereby supporting current and future generations of rural workers within their households and communities. Despite their significant contribution to the agriculture sector, rural women typically find themselves in disadvantaged positions. Compared to their male counterparts, they tend to face more restricted access to productive resources and assets, financial services and social protection. Gender-biased social norms, laws and practices also limit women's involvement in gainful work and their participation in workers' and producers' organizations, especially in organized labor institutions such as trade unions.[12]*

So it is women who are sowing the fields and reaping the harvest; it is women who are now, in no small measure, holding the plough and feeding the world. And yet, in spite of this, gender-based attitudes about the division of labor have endured. They have persisted even when the main focus of the economy has changed from agriculture to industry and services, from rural to urban employment. And such attitudes still affect the participation of women in activities no longer connected to the soil, such as market entrepreneurship or politics. Men have moved from farms to firms without losing their grip on the handle of the plough.

Patriarchy has used myths to sanction its legitimacy that have solidified over time into dead clichés, hardening our attitudes and narrowing our perceptions with regard to women's roles.[13] While there are many reasons for the bias against women and the prejudices toward them, the myths embedded in "plough culture" have kept women in the home by emphasizing the biological differences between the sexes. And in the process these myths have shoved women into the ground, lowering their potential, undermining their abilities, and diminishing their prospects of prosperity. The plough has effectively buried women alive for thousands of years.

Perhaps the "plough theory" will help us demystify the origins of gender norms. Perhaps the time has come to call a spade a spade and debunk the old taboos.

EVALUATING VALUES

Traditional values have created far more obstacles for women than for men when it comes to finding jobs. The World Values Survey, which provides a wealth of data on different standards and moral principles across the world, offers particularly useful information regarding attitudes toward women in general and perceptions about women in the labor force in particular which illustrate some of these prejudices.

The next figures, drawn from World Development Indicators (2011) and World Values Survey (2010–2014), provide quick visual summaries of the high percentages of people across a broad spectrum of countries who hold on to traditional attitudes with regard to women working outside the home, women working for pay, and whether women do a good or bad job when they join the workforce.

Working Outside the Home

Out of a sample of sixty countries where data were collected over the course of four years, from 2010 to 2014, an average of 39.4 percent of people interviewed agreed that "when jobs are scarce, men should have more right to a job than women" (Figure 3.3). This average covers similar extremes as noted in the comparisons between Sweden and Saudi Arabia. In other words, the positive response to the question regarding men's greater right to a job than women varied from 83.4 percent in Egypt to only 2 percent in Sweden and 5.7 percent in the United States. Not surprisingly, these numbers correlate well with female labor force participation in these countries. In other words, wherever men are perceived to have more right to a job than women, fewer women are found working outside the house. The bottom line is that the social norms and the expectations imposed on women still favor work within the home as opposed to paid work outside it.

Working for Pay

According to the *mores* of certain cultures, not only should men be the ones with a right to a job, but women, if they work at all, should not be paid. In other words, some people think there is a moral stigma associated with a woman who works for pay. Money is perceived as corrupting, and since women are thought to be easily corrupted, a

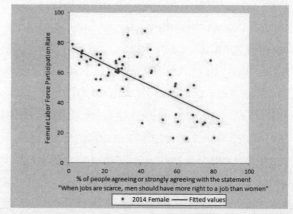

Figure 3.3: Should men have more right to a job than women?

woman who works for money is exposing her vulnerabilities to corrupting influences. The prohibition against work, whether implicit
or explicit, is defined in terms of protection, of preservation, particularly of chastity. In certain cultures, to leave the house and step
into the workplace, therefore, is tantamount to selling your body if
you are a woman. In fact several dictionaries still define a "working
girl" in colloquial English slang as a prostitute.

It is bad enough that a woman has difficulty finding a decent job
in certain societies, or earning a reasonable living wage when she
does, but if she is expected to work for nothing, it is even worse. And
if she persists and maintains the job in spite of all the odds, she is
often damned for it. Her decision is seen as damaging not only her
own reputation and that of her family but her children's too. In twenty-
four out of the fifty-nine countries covered in the World Values Survey, the majority of individuals said that they thought it was bad for
children and detrimental to their happiness and well-being if their
mothers go out to work (Figure 3.4).[14]

DOING A BAD JOB

In addition to being blamed for sacrificing the future of her children if
she works for pay, a woman who seeks employment in certain cultures
is frequently condemned as less capable than a man of doing a proper

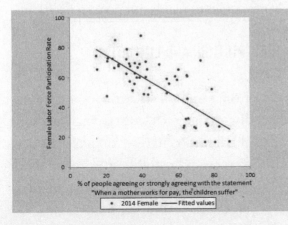

Figure 3.4: Do
children suffer if
women work?

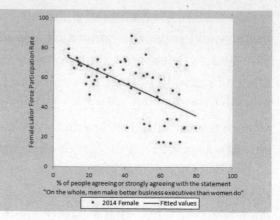

Figure 3.5: Are men better workers than women?

job anyway. So even if she manages, against all odds, to find a job, she is more than likely judged as doing it incompetently. The common prejudice among those who participated in the World Values Survey is that women are not only less entitled to jobs and are bad mothers if they work outside the house, but are failures in the bargain.

In Figure 3.5, it is clear from the data gathered that the majority of people in twenty-five of the sixty countries believe that men make better business executives than women. This is a very damning attitude and profoundly unjust as well as untrue. Although the lack of physical and human capital can sometimes put women at a disadvantage when accessing the workforce, this is very different from being considered less capable of holding a high position, less able to wield responsibility, or less adept than men when it comes to making important decisions.

EXCLUSION, RESTRICTION, AND LIMITATION

The negative consequences of such traditional attitudes and values are all too familiar. At worst, discrimination against women leads inexorably to their poverty and ghettoization in the workplace. At best it imposes constraints on their upward mobility and keeps them trapped under the proverbial glass ceiling. Whether women fail to find adequate jobs or try to succeed, they all suffer some form of exclusion, restriction, and limitation. In the following pages, the three factors that check women's full participation in the labor force will be analyzed more closely.

Poverty and Exclusion

As Virginia Woolf pointed out when she raised the question about the relationship between women and poverty in 1928, there can be no clear, irrefutable, and authentic "this or that" reason why women are, generally speaking, poorer than men.[15] The data related to gender and poverty, like those used to assess the gender pay gap, are fraught with technical complexities. Poverty, according to Thibos, must be evaluated with more than an economic yardstick:

> *The feminization of poverty, as a lived reality, represents something larger than the lack of income or a state of financial need for women. While the very definition of poverty implies the inability to meet basic needs such as food, clothing, or shelter, being poor also implies the absence of choice, the denial of opportunity, the inability to meet life goals, and ultimately, the loss of hope. Thus, a feminized poverty extends beyond the economic domains of income and material needs to the core of individual and family life.[16]*

Evaluations of poverty are usually based on household income or expenditure surveys. The numbers of the poor are estimated in relation to a particular poverty line according to how many people live in poor households. But this measure provides a very inadequate picture of the reality. We know that an important dimension of the "missing girls" problem, discussed in Chapter 1, is that, when it comes to food and health care, parents invariably give preference to sons. So although both women and men are considered to be equally poor in any given household, men invariably consume more than the women in terms of food, medicine, and fuel. This suggests that the incidence of poverty is probably much higher among women than among men, even when they are living under the same roof. In other words, there are more poor women in the world than men, whichever poverty line is used to estimate their number.

However, a mere disaggregation of the poverty data in terms of how resources are used according to the sex of household members may not accurately reflect gender inequality either. Even if one were to assume, unrealistically, that consumption levels for women and men living in the same household were the same, sex differences in poverty rates are likely to emerge simply because women's labor force participation is lower virtually everywhere. As noted, even when women do work, they earn less than men for comparable work. The United Nations' excellent study *The World's Women 2010* points out, moreover, that since the ratio of women to men increases with age, extended family households tend to include more women than men. And since women work and earn less in their lifetimes, more of these households are likely to be below the poverty line, contributing to sex differences in poverty rates.

But unfortunately, poverty is not magically eradicated by finding work. Even when women are employed, the real question is what kinds of jobs they have access to and whether these jobs are well paid. So another dimension of this problem concerns the quality of work that is open to women in the labor market. The legal environment as well as cultural habits can also restrict women to certain kinds of jobs. The "ghettoization of labor" or "horizontal occupational segregation," which is another term used for the restrictions on female participation in the workforce, is a phenomenon that crosses all cultural boundaries and affects women of all races.

Occupational Segregation and Restriction

One of the reasons for the gap between men and women's earnings is that women frequently find themselves working in traditionally "female jobs." Even if they are allowed by law to work in the same industries as men, they still tend to concentrate in employment fields or work in professions classically associated with women, such as nursing, teaching, routine office work, and care of the elderly and disabled. Since these jobs constitute what many consider to be the service functions of society, they are most frequently perceived as "women's work." As a result, they are given little value and even less prestige, and are consequently among the lowest-paid jobs in the labor force. They offer limited or no opportunity for advancement. They are accompanied by little recognition and no social status. And even though these services are crucially important to those who need them, no outward validation is given to those who undertake them.

In principle, there is nothing wrong with some sectors being male dominated and others being female dominated as long as the outcome is equally to everyone's advantage. But when occupational segregation or ghettoization is the result of gender discrimination, it can lead to loss of personal autonomy as well as lower growth for the economy as a whole. By legally restricting women's access to better-paid jobs and undervaluing the worth of the jobs they are obliged to assume, women are effectively cribbed, cabined, and confined within a narrow sector of underpaid employment.

There are two main types of ghettoization of female labor. The first is by sector, due perhaps to educational bias or governed by preference or choice, as, for instance, if a woman prefers to be a supermarket cashier rather than a truck driver, a teacher rather than a banker. Although this appears to be a form of occupational segregation, it need not be discriminatory as long as both women and men are given equal opportunity to enter the profession. The second kind of ghettoization is based on hierarchic limitations and is not governed by choice. For instance, although the percentage of women in the textile sector may be high, women tend to be assigned lower-level positions while managerial positions are reserved for men.

Such ghettoization may vary according to the size of a company. For example, using data across eighty-seven developing countries,

Mohammad Amin and Asif Islam (2014) found that the percentage of female managers is much higher in the service sector than in manufacturing firms. Furthermore, they found that the higher percentage of female managers in the retail sector vis-à-vis manufacturing is not uniform: It is much larger for the relatively smaller firms and those that are located in relatively smaller cities.

Such segregation of the female labor force is not only caused by obstructive attitudes in the workplace; it also is due to legal restrictions that have proven difficult to address or remove in many countries. Hampered by legislation, women have been penalized economically for their reproductive and childcare responsibilities. They have been forced into "false choices," between career or family, as the philosopher Mary Midgley (1983) discusses in her book *Women's Choices* about the alternatives faced by working women in contemporary society. Women have also found themselves "protected" by family law from making such choices, which leaves them effectively dependent on their husbands. And furthermore, some of these husbands have the right by law to curtail their wife's freedom to engage in high-paying jobs that are considered "dangerous to their health." As a result, one of the consequences of occupational segregation is the gender gap in wages. Although this gap has been closing, according to the International Labour Organization's latest data, women still earned only 75 percent as much as men in the United Kingdom, 62 percent in Japan, and 58 percent in Korea, to take a few examples.

But Preston (1999) has shown that gender differences in qualifications are not sufficient to explain such differences. They are more likely to be linked to gender inequality in the workplace. As is made abundantly clear by the Women, Business and the Law data, traditional attitudes as well as legal restrictions can actively prevent women from becoming entrepreneurs, from accessing capital and credit, and from stepping beyond the confines of occupational segregation into well-paid, high-profile positions of authority.[17]

Limitations to Upward Mobility

Even if women manage to break out of the ghetto, how far can they actually go? Even if they have avoided being pushed to the bottom of the economic heap, what about their prospects at the top? Are women fairly represented in positions of authority in the labor force, on decision-making boards and in executive positions?

One of the most damning proofs of continued gender inequality in the world is the glaring absence of women in the higher echelons of the private corporate sector. What makes these data especially discouraging is that they may fly in the face of economic common sense. Linking the relationship between gender diversity and performance is no easy task, given the multitude of factors at hand. It is thus no surprise that *The Economist*, citing a handful of studies, has questioned the link between women in the boardroom and firm performance.[18] However, there is ample evidence suggesting consistent patterns of positive outcomes connected to the presence of women in important decision-making positions. Quoting a broad range of studies, the World Bank (2012, p. 204) argues that low gender diversity on corporate boards "is seen by many as undermining a company's potential value and growth. Higher diversity is often thought to improve the board's functioning by increasing its monitoring capacity, broadening its access to information on its potential customer base, and enhancing its creativity by multiplying viewpoints. Greater diversity implies that board directors can be selected from a broader talent pool." Indeed, there is persuasive evidence that companies benefit greatly from fostering an increase in the number of women board directors. A study by Lois Joy, Nancy Carter, Harvey Wagner, and Sriram Narayanan (2007) comparing the top and bottom quartiles of women board directors at Fortune 500 companies found that wherever there were higher numbers of women on the board, the companies thrived. Analyzing financial measures such as return on equity, return on sales, and return on invested capital, this study established that companies with more women board directors were able to outperform those with fewer such directors by an astonishing 42 to 66 percent.

This pattern has been found to be consistent across a variety of different industries. In a 2011 study, Catalyst, a US nonprofit organization, found that the Fortune 500 companies in the top quartile in terms of female board representation—with women making up between 19 and 44 percent of their boards—had a return on sales (i.e., net income as a percentage of revenue) that was 16 percent higher than that of companies with no women on their boards. The chief executive of Catalyst put it succinctly: "Diverse business leadership and governance are correlated with stronger business performance, employee engagement, and innovation. Shareholders beware: a company with no women at the top is missing one of the biggest opportunities in the marketplace today." According to research from the index provider MSCI, which looked at 6,500 boards globally, companies with "strong female leadership" (primarily measured by women on boards) were correlated with higher return on equity than companies without such leadership (10.1 percent versus 7.4 percent) as well as a superior price-to-book ratio (1.76 versus 1.56).[19]

A study by Hagen Lindstädt, Kerstin Fehre, and Michael Wolff (2011), moreover, found that when more women were on their boards, German companies were far better at retaining talent. They also had a far lower employee turnover, which in turn suggests greater employee satisfaction. A 2014 study of 3,000 companies from around the globe by the Credit Suisse Research Institute also found a marked correlation between high performance and the number of women on company boards.[20] In this study, companies with at least one female director had generated a compound excess return per annum of 3.5 percent for investors over the previous decade. Companies where women made up at least 15 percent of senior managers had more than 50 percent higher profitability than those where female representation was less than 10 percent. There is evidence as well that companies with greater participation of women on boards have stronger ethical foundations. According to the 2015 MSCI study: "[P]ublic companies with more women on their boards are less likely to be hit by governance scandals such as bribery, fraud or shareholder battles."[21]

The facts are staring us in the face; the evidence is palpable. It is better for business if women rise to executive positions. And yet this reality continues to be ignored. According to Deloitte (2017), in the United States, 20.2 percent of board directors at Fortune 500 companies were women in 2016. And data from the European Women on Boards organization indicate that the situation in the European Union is only marginally better; by 2015 boards of STOXX 600 companies had an average of 25 percent female board members, partly reflecting the existence of quotas in Norway, Iceland, Spain, France, and, most recently, Germany.[22] In Norway, legislation was approved in 2002 requiring state-owned companies to have at least 40 percent representation of each sex. But Norway (close to 43 percent by 2016) is an outlier: Among the 35 countries in Europe, only Iceland (44.6 percent), France (41.2 percent), and Sweden (36.9 percent) come anywhere close. At the other extreme, the Republic of South Korea, an otherwise highly industrialized and "modern" nation, had only 2.3 percent women on its various boards of directors in 2016, the lowest among all countries for which data are available.[23] Only twenty-one of the Fortune 500 companies in 2016 had a woman chief executive, about 4.2 percent of the total. The equivalent ratio in Europe (for the 350 largest companies listed in the S&P index, and where Europe is defined as the EU plus six other countries) was also a mere 4 percent. These are abysmally low statistics for the so-called developed democracies in the world.

SIGNS OF CHANGE

As grim as these statistics seem, however, there are signs of change. The first of course was the Convention Concerning Discrimination in Respect of Employment and Occupation launched by the International

Labour Organization in 1958. It began slowly, and women's participation in the workforce was very limited before the latter half of the twentieth century. As Jens Peter Jacobsen writes, "It was only in 1963 that the US passed the Equal Pay Act, making it illegal to pay women and men different wages for equal work; it took a while for other countries to follow suit (e.g., Ireland in 1976; Japan in 1987)."[24] But since the mid-twentieth century, policies have been put into effect all over the world that promise to introduce new patterns of behavior in relation to women at work. Although some governments continue to impose legal restrictions on a woman's agency and limit the scope of her actions, many others are finally introducing new policies that promise to reverse the age-old negative patterns. A range of incentives is emerging that will certainly make it easier for women to take part in vital roles and enter into higher positions in the labor force in many countries. These incentives include quotas for women in decision-making positions, in both the private and the public sectors, that could ensure their participation in parliaments, in local administrations, and on corporate boards. There are also new laws in certain countries mandating equal pay for equal work, penalizing employers for firing pregnant women, and instituting parental leave and maternity benefits in order to provide women with the choice and opportunity of work outside the home.

These signs of change, though far from sufficient to address the glaring inequalities facing women in the labor force, are nevertheless encouraging. They are a necessary first step to recognizing the detrimental consequences of inequality on the well-being of society. And the trend can be irreversible as well as irresistible, although Turkey and Iran, among others, have shown regressive tendencies in this regard. Some of these incentives will be explored in greater detail in the following pages so as to gauge their scope, assess their limitations, and evaluate their impact on women's participation in the labor force.

A RANGE OF INCENTIVES

The *Women, Business and the Law 2014* report examines a total of twelve incentives that make it easier for women to work. According to the data related to these cases, the countries with the highest number of restrictions against women embedded in the law also offer the fewest incentives for them to work. Oman, Saudi Arabia, Iran, the United Arab Emirates, and Yemen, for example, have twenty or more restrictions each, which limit women in some form or other and offer them very few incentives, if any, to work. By contrast, Hungary, Spain, and the Slovak Republic have created six or more additional incentives for women to work, with the result that there are zero discriminations against women (relative to men) embedded in the law of these countries, and it is far easier for women to enter the paid labor force. Furthermore, the data suggest that gender-specific laws may influence women's decisions to participate in the labor market. For instance, the presence of a nondiscrimination clause in hiring along gender lines has been shown to be associated with greater female employment relative to men.[25]

The issue of incentives turns out to have a bearing on the all-important question of income inequality. The data show that countries which offer a relatively larger number of incentives making it easier for women to work outside the home are also countries that have better income distribution: Their Gini coefficients tend to be lower, other things being equal, and this is very encouraging.[26] These results make sense. The more disadvantaged half of the population is empowered by incentives that make it easier to access the labor market in varying ways. This, in turn, promotes a more even sharing of the fruits of economic growth and prosperity. When women can work outside the home, they are more likely to decide on the allocation of assets and the use of cash inside it, and this will have important implications for family welfare. Alternatively, diminished opportunities and restrictions on resources will have adverse consequences for economic outcomes. According to the World Bank (2012, p. 18), "[I]n Ghana the mean value of men's landholdings is three times that of women's landholdings. Similarly large gaps are observed in use of fertilizers and improved seed varieties in agriculture, and in access to and use of credit among entrepreneurs." As a result, women were less likely to plant the more profitable crops that men were growing, and this was at considerable cost to the family in terms of total output produced. Of course, similar patterns exist in much of the developing world, with Ghana being not the exception but rather the rule.[27]

Those of us who have been perturbed by the implications of rapid economic growth on income distribution trends during the post–World War II period may find it hopeful to identify an area where governments could implement policies that lessen the widening gap between the rich and the poor. It is encouraging to see that simply by providing women with greater incentives to work and ensuring the means for them to reap higher benefits for the work they do, the fruits of economic development can be distributed in a manner that leads to improved social stability.

But progress can sometimes hide regressive factors that impede gender equality. In professions such as the law, medicine, and engineering, for example, where women are better represented in developed countries, institutional implementation often lags behind theoretical principle. Although "family-friendly" and "female-friendly" practices identified in a survey carried out by Yale Law Women (2014) are on the increase, enabling more women to become partners in firms, the principal obstacle to professional development has to do with the reluctance of countries to implement adequately paid maternity leave. Despite the fact that the majority of the world's countries offer it—some even offering a guaranteed wage of 50 to 100 percent of salary—most seem to grant only twelve to fourteen weeks of leave or less. At the generous end of the scale are Norway and Sweden, which offer a year or more to women who have given birth; not surprisingly, female labor force participation rates in these countries are among the highest in the world. But the United States offers women only twelve weeks, without pay, putting it in league with Lesotho, Swaziland, and Papua New Guinea. And at the low end, we find Oman, Nepal, Sudan, the United Arab Emirates, Thailand, and Tunisia, which offer no more than between forty-five and sixty days of maternity leave, sometimes paid and sometimes not, depending on the country.[28] There is clearly a long way left to go.

THE CHALLENGE OF QUOTAS

One way might be quotas. The evolution of thinking on this subject is worth examining. An interesting story is associated with quotas at the corporate level and in parliaments. On the corporate front, Norway has played a pathbreaking role. Back in 2002, senior politicians in Oslo noticed that women's representation in corporate boards was only 6 percent, a surprisingly low level given the remarkable progress that had been made in the country in reducing the gender gap in a number of areas. So the government decided to introduce voluntary quotas for publicly listed companies that year, with a 40 percent target for women's participation in corporate boards by 2005. However, by 2005, the target was not achieved, and what had begun as a well-intentioned exercise in good corporate citizenship was soon transformed into amendments to the Public Companies Act, making quotas mandatory and setting a new deadline of 2008. Companies unable to meet the target by 2008 would initially be subject to fines, followed by deregistration from the Oslo Stock Exchange and, in the case of outright noncompliance, dissolution.

These measures naturally generated interesting and, at times, contentious debate. Opponents of the legislation put forward two lines of argument. The first addressed the need for diversity. Since there was a perception, in 2002 in Norway, that very few women were both qualified and able as well as ready to serve on company boards, it was felt that a relatively small number of them were being asked to serve on a relatively large number of boards. This stirred considerable criticism as the quota critics considered such an imbalance a highly undesirable outcome. A second line of argument was more philosophical in nature. It concerned the right of governments to tell corporate boards how to run companies which were ultimately responsible to shareholders. Such perceived interference in the democratic process was also considered inappropriate.

An alternative view might be that neither of these arguments is particularly persuasive. The initial lack of large enough numbers of women ready to serve on boards could be a transitional issue, soon addressed by the emergence of training institutes and other educational initiatives aimed at teaching otherwise highly educated women how, for instance, to read a company's balance sheet and income statement. On the issue of whether governments should dictate or not dictate the composition of corporate boards, the fact of the matter is that governments impose a broad range of regulatory practices on companies all the time, including a whole battery of fiscal and tax obligations pertaining to their operations, all of which are generally motivated by some aspect of the public interest. Over the past decade, for instance, a growing number of governments have been imposing constraints on companies based on issues relating to environmental protection. If there is well-substantiated evidence that companies with more women directors are actually better run, one could indeed argue that government would have an *obligation* to demand that companies boost gender diversity at the board level.

A related argument that has sometimes emerged in this debate has to do with the benefits of meritocracy, the idea that jobs should go to the best-qualified people, even if, in this particular instance, that should mean corporate boards overwhelmingly made up of men. It is, of course, difficult to argue against the virtues of meritocracy. However, it is glaringly obvious that the world has *not*, by and large, been run according to meritocratic principles. Although there are, of course, many exceptions, the fact is that chief executives, prime ministers, and presidents often appoint their loyal buddies and cronies—otherwise known as campaign contributors on occasion—to serve on their boards or in their cabinets. Former Spanish prime minister José Luis Rodríguez Zapatero came under significant criticism in 2004 when he decided to impose a 50 percent quota of women serving in his cabinet of sixteen ministers. Critics never saw the need to confront an otherwise obvious fact: namely, that in a country with over 46 million inhabitants, it should be theoretically possible, without having to sacrifice meritocratic principles, to find eight qualified women—irrespective of whether they are personally known or part of one's "inner circle"—to serve in the cabinet. An equally interesting question in this context would be how long it might have taken Norway to achieve a 40 percent target for women directors in the absence of binding legislation. It could have been at least a hundred years, and this assumes a substantial acceleration with respect to the previous half century. Male Norwegian chief executives prior to 2002 were, no doubt, very much committed to the principle of gender equality, but not when it came to the composition of their own company's boards.

Similar arguments can be made regarding quotas for elected legislative bodies. Although it is an improvement over the 1995 average of 10 percent, the Inter-Parliamentary Union reports a world average of only 23.3 percent women in combined houses of national parliaments as of May 2017. The statistics by region offer few surprises, ranging from 18 percent in the Arab states, 19.4 percent in Asia, and 28.1 percent in the Americas, to 41.7 percent in the Nordic states. Interestingly, Rwanda outstrips the Nordic states with 55.7 percent, using its gender quotas as a fast track to gender balance.

Although women are poorly represented in the lower levels of government, they are rarer still in the upper echelons of decision-making. According to Geiger and Kent (2017), as of March 2017, "there were 15 female world leaders [then] in office, eight of whom were their country's first woman in power." Since some of these women served as both head of state and head of government, this translates to only 9 out of 152 elected heads of state in the world and only 8 out of 194 heads of governments.[29]

The use of quotas as a mechanism for the political empowerment of women has not been free of controversy, as illustrated by the story about Norway. Some, repeating the meritocracy argument, insist that quotas violate the principles of liberal democracy, which should allow voters to make the ultimate decision on who gets elected. Others argue that quotas, far from introducing a discriminatory practice, are actually a sensible way to compensate for long-standing barriers that have prevented women from being adequately represented. In a historically male-dominated political system, women's qualifications and suitability for office have been consistently downgraded. As a result, the world has not been able to benefit from the insights and experiences that women could have brought to political decision-making. A less charitable way to express this is to say that humanity has actually suffered immeasurably as a result of decision-making biases that are the direct result of a male-dominated political landscape. According to certain thinkers, we need only glance back at the blood-soaked twentieth century and gauge the impact of its violent and grizzly excesses to confirm this fact. Indeed, if we look more critically at current habits and practices in our highly vaunted democracies, we see that political parties rather than voters control the nominations in most countries. In other words, contrary to received opinion, quotas in no way violate voters' rights and are therefore quite in keeping with "democratic" principles.

More and more countries are making use of electoral quotas. In some cases, such as in Uganda, the Philippines, Nepal, and Burkina Faso, constitutions are being amended to this end. There are other examples, in much of Latin America, Belgium, France, and Slovenia, for instance, where changes are being introduced to electoral laws. Such adjustments in the law can produce healthy results, and their demonstrated effectiveness can lead to rapid emulation. Argentina, for instance, was the first country in Latin America to introduce candidate quotas, in 1991, with party electoral lists required to have a minimum of 30 percent women among candidates for all national elections. Other countries in the region followed suit in the ensuing years. Progress is taking place even in countries where women were traditionally proscribed from any role in elected bodies. In early 2011, for instance, Saudi Arabia issued a royal order amending the composition of the previously all-male, 150-member Consultative Council by allocating 20 percent of its seats for women members. According to UN Women (2017a), as of June 2016, out of the 46 countries that had single or lower houses composed of more than 30 percent women, "40 had applied some form of quotas—either legislative candidate quotas or reserved seats—opening space for women's political participation."[30]

Such progress is encouraging, but there are also examples of inertia that impede development. As of May 2017, India, for instance, had quotas at the subnational level but not for its national parliament, where the share of women members was only 11.6 percent, some 12 percentage points below the global average. A constitutional amendment to establish a 33 percent quota for women in parliament has been debated many times since it was first introduced in 1996 but has faced stiff opposition from some parties on the grounds that upper-caste women will displace lower-caste men. In addition, women's organizations have opposed the introduction of a system of subquotas within an overall quota for women, with some shares being allocated to lower-caste women, Muslim women, and other groups. So, the politics of gender quotas have fallen victim to the nastier politics of caste. Clearly, even among the emerging economic giants of the world, much work remains to be done, which might account for the previously mentioned disparities in the allocation of resources in India. There are also many countries where there is a substantial gap between the quota set by the law and the actual results on the ground. In some cases, despite every effort to ensure parity, women are being placed at the bottom of party electoral lists.

Quotas are clearly not an end in themselves. They are meant to be an instrument to achieve a better outcome for women, a tool to boost the sharing of prosperity in countries. It is hoped that they will not be needed in the future as people understand the value of having women in decision-making positions and social norms change. But although quotas remain controversial, the discussion about them reflects a shift in the broader debate about equality. There is an increased tendency to move away from an emphasis on the desirability of equality of *opportunity*—meaning, in this particular context, the removal of barriers that prevent women from voting—toward the need to ensure equality of *outcomes*, or results. If women are still grossly underrepresented in political decision-making bodies half a century after the removal of restrictions on voting rights, then other means have to be used to ensure a speedier removal of the thousand and one hidden barriers that have impeded and curtailed their political empowerment. Radical decisions have to be taken and more effective means for their implementation have to be found in order to ensure that women can more rapidly and actively contribute to improving social welfare.

In respect to this wider debate, the evidence in a number of different studies is really quite encouraging. For instance, some countries with quotas for women in parliament show higher female labor force participation rates. Quotas also appear to have an impact on government spending priorities. These studies reveal that there is greater spending on social services and welfare in those countries where quotas are implemented.[31] In other words, quotas have begun to ensure that the quality of political decisions will differ. A 1993 study carried out in India looking at data for 265 village councils found that once a quota established a one-third share for female membership, there was considerably more investment in infrastructure relevant to the needs of women and children. Also in India, a 2004 study on *panchayats* (local councils) discovered that the number of drinking-water projects in areas with female-led councils was 62 percent higher than in those with male-led councils.[32]

Quotas may also have far-reaching and meaningful results for gender equality in the Indian state of West Bengal.[33] Since 1998, one-third of village council leader positions in this area were reserved for women on an ad hoc basis. The study explored the effects of this policy for two electoral cycles, or ten years. The findings are fascinating. Initially, public opinion toward female leaders was negative, and villagers rated female leaders as less effective than men despite similar performance. However, exposure to female councilors over a ten-year span altered perceptions of gender roles both in society and in the home. The negative bias male villagers held toward the effectiveness of female local leaders was gradually reduced. After ten years, women were more likely to run and win local-level political races in villages that had instituted the quotas for positions unaffected by them. So while quotas may not be an end in and of themselves, they clearly can achieve positive ends.

PARENTAL LEAVE AND CHILDCARE POLICIES

Traditionally one of the main deterrents to female labor force participation is the fact that women rather than men are expected to be the primary caretakers of children. This may be a preferred choice, but where it is not, it can serve as a deterrent to family prosperity as well as gender equality. Although such attitudes may be changing in certain parts of the world, the usual pattern in most countries is that the woman gives up her job outside the home in order to take care of children. And if she does not, absent childcare, she is faced with the painful choice of having a successful career or a family. This is particularly true for women at the top end of the labor force, women who have overcome all odds, risen above implicit as well as explicit impediments and reached managerial positions in their professions. A study in the United States found 49 percent of high-achieving women to be childless, as compared with only 19 percent of their male colleagues.[34]

Parental leave and childcare policies can therefore provide incentives to keep women in the labor force and allow them alternatives to these stark choices. By enabling women to maintain their jobs after having children, these policies can give them greater motivation to look for work outside the home and can encourage them to strive for long-term careers and high-paying positions that demand greater investment of time.

Most of the research on the impact of such policies at this time concerns maternity leave benefits. But the results of this research are not without ambiguity. In general, there appears to be a positive link between maternity leave and women's participation in the labor force, showing that a higher percentage of women work outside the home in those countries offering access to such benefits. However, there is no consensus on the right duration of this leave, and, in the absence of parallel measures of support, there is also some uncertainty regarding its consequences. If maternity leave is too short, it may discourage women from entering the labor force in the first place. But if it is too long, it may discourage employers from hiring women altogether.

In several developed countries, policies regarding paternity leave provide an alternative or complement to maternity benefits. Since the primary aim of these policies is to counteract low and decreasing birth rates and provide higher incentives for working women to have children, they do not necessarily focus on increasing women's participation in the labor force. But Jochen Kluve and Marcus Tamm (2009) have found that parental leave does bear directly on women's decisions to return to work. The 2007 Elterngeld Reform in Germany that Kluve and Tamm analyzed aims to readjust the decline in household earnings after the birth of children and tries to make childbearing more attractive for working women by offering incentives for fathers as well as mothers to participate in childcare. But when the authors compared households before and after the law went into effect in early 2007, they also found a significant increase in women who go back to work after parental benefits expire.

The research on childcare policies also produces mixed results. Florence Jaumotte (2003) identifies a positive impact of these policies on female labor supply in countries that are members of the Organisation for Economic Co-operation and Development (OECD). She shows that tax incentives, childcare subsidies, and paid parental leave increase female labor participation, particularly in relation to full-time employment and the availability of part-time work in the field of childcare. Susan Averett, Elizabeth Peters, and Donald Waldman (1997) reached a similar conclusion in their earlier studies related to the childcare tax credit system in the United States. When childcare expenses can be deducted from the tax bill, there is a substantial impact on female labor, and more women take advantage of the tax credit to go back to work. But although Baker, Gruber, and Milligan (2008) show that the subsidized "$5 per day childcare" program in Quebec was widely used in the late 1990s with a resulting rise of women in the labor force, they also discovered that children in such programs suffered from behavioral and health problems in the long term. On one hand, therefore, it is clear that affordable or subsidized childcare can have a positive impact on women's labor force participation. On the other, there is evidence that such childcare can have a negative impact on children's behavior and health. The fact that these results confirm age-old attitudes about children suffering from their mother's decision to work only adds to the burden faced by women who need to find employment for their family's material well-being.[35]

CONCLUSION

Although women are still less likely to work outside the home than men, there has been a positive trend in this regard in recent years, except in certain Middle Eastern countries, where women's participation in the workforce has increased very timidly or not at all. In spite of all the cultural impediments facing women, in spite of the legal restrictions they encounter and the policies and customs of exclusion they have to overcome, there has been a dramatic rise in the numbers of working women across the globe over the past three decades.

This evolution, while significant, is not linear, however. According to Goldin (1995), the participation rate of married women in the labor force first declines and then rises as countries develop. The initial decline is due to rising economic stability in the household. When families become wealthier, it is more likely that women feel less obliged to work outside the home; this is because the family can afford to "carry" certain of its members who do domestic unpaid work. However, as women become more educated and a country more developed, they discover it is more to their financial benefit to work outside rather than in the home. The social stigma of paid employment also decreases when women can access white-collar jobs.

When women seek and find employment outside the home, it is not only due to changing laws and growing opportunities and incentives. They also enter the labor force because of other important factors. Seema Jayachandran (2014), a professor at Northwestern University, has identified three: growth of the service sector, changes in technology, and relatively recent scientific and medical innovations—all of which, for varying reasons, contributed to expand job opportunities for women.

There has been an increased demand for employment in the service sector in recent years. Since this is a domain in which women often have some advantage over men due to greater experience, it has provided more jobs for them than they might find elsewhere. Significant changes in demographics, a sharp increase in numbers of school-age children and the elderly, the expansion of institutional as well as commercial food industries—all these and other opportunities in the service sector have enabled women to find work that is less physically demanding but more mentally as well as psychologically intensive. The problem is that jobs in the service sector are invariably less well paid, precisely because a service is not considered to be a product.

Women also have a greater incentive to look for jobs outside the home because of recent improvements in technology. With more time on their hands, thanks to the availability of home appliances, electricity, sanitation, and running water,[36] they can join the labor force and earn more than they would doing "women's work" at home. Traditionally responsible for domestic unpaid work, such as cooking, cleaning, laundry, and childcare, they are liberated by labor-saving devices that cook, clean, do laundry, and entertain children. In fact, according to Ramey (2009), the time spent on home production among prime-age women in the United States decreased from forty-seven hours per week in 1900 to twenty-nine hours in 2005, principally because of the sales boom in dishwashers, washing machines, vacuum cleaners, and similar appliances.

But health and reproductive care have had the greatest impact on the lives of women. Recent discoveries in science and medicine have given women control over when and how many children they have. This relative control has not only influenced their participation in the labor force but has also broadened their career choices and resulted in smaller gender gaps in education. According to Goldin and Katz (2002), lower fertility rates are directly linked to higher levels of education for women in the United States. The ability to choose when they bear children has also allowed more women to embark on better-paid careers, such as law and medicine, which require considerable early investment in time, training, and experience before yielding financial rewards.

It is ironic to consider that an increase in the participation of women in the labor force over the last fifty years may, to some extent, be an unintended consequence of factors entirely unrelated to changing legislation or economic policy. Although many incentives aimed at increasing female participation in the labor force have been consciously adopted and painstakingly implemented in various countries, it would seem that the rising number of women at work could also be attributed to good plumbing as much as to new laws, to the contraceptive pill as well as to maternity benefits, and to the rising numbers of the elderly who need to be cared for as well as the need for increasingly better childcare services.

As we see in the next chapter, it does not matter, in the end, how many technological or even logistical changes improve the quality of life of women; it does not make a difference how much more time they have on their hands to enter the workforce, once they are freed from domestic obstacles and obligations. The bottom line is that there are other barriers far more entrenched than blocked drains or the lack of vacuum cleaners, other factors that curb and check a woman's aspirations and narrow the range of jobs that she could look for or might find. Ultimately, it is not just the lack of schools or job incentives that will impede her access to education and employment. It is culture that brings the strongest influence to bear on whether a woman will go out to work.

Culture controls the roles and often conflicts with the rights of women. And when culture also hijacks religious belief to sanctify interpretations regarding these roles and rights, the first to lose economic independence in society and personal freedom in the home are women. The next chapter explores the high costs not only to women but to society as a whole when the status quo of male superiority is privileged by a patriarchal culture.

4

THE CULTURE QUESTION

*It is time to effect a revolution in female manners—time
to restore to them their lost dignity. It is time to separate
unchangeable morals from local manners.*
—MARY WOLLSTONECRAFT, 1792

*Behind us lies the patriarchal system; the private house,
with its nullity, its immorality, its hypocrisy, its servility. Before
us lies the public world, the professional system, with its
possessiveness, its jealousy, its pugnacity, its greed.*
—VIRGINIA WOOLF, 1938

WHAT IS IT?

The culture question has worried specialists in many fields, from
labor law to demographics, from violence to human rights. What exactly constitutes this thorny question has been and continues to be
particularly difficult for economists to address, especially in relation
to gender. In the abstract, no one can deny that a specific work ethic
and a system of personal values affect the economy; no one disagrees
that culture has a role in guiding a population toward or away from
prosperity. Indeed, how could it be otherwise? For it is impossible to
make sense of certain phenomena—such as Japan's emergence in the

twentieth century as a global economic power—without appealing to the role of culture. Prosperity clearly depends on the relationship between culture and economics, and we cannot properly tackle the problems raised by the latter without recognizing their links with the former. But what those links are exactly and how to measure their impact have been less obvious.

Economists and policy makers have therefore tended to avoid the subject and have generally focused on concrete criteria rather than less tangible phenomena to gauge the pace and quality of development. They have looked for measurable factors that can influence prosperity in practical ways. In fact, much of the past century, as well as this book, has been dedicated to these very ends. It seems an obvious method to follow: Look for the problem, define its nature, and then fix it. Along the way, however, we have learned that successful economic development is not so easy to fix nor so tangible a phenomenon to define. It is a complex concept. Its determinants are many in number, multifaceted in scope, and intricately connected. They are also ambiguous, especially when it comes to the links between women and culture.

Indeed, the mere conjunction of these two factors can sometimes confound rational argument. To discuss the impact of culture on women in the Middle East—for example, to assess its relationship to the extremely low female labor participation rates and poor innovation capacity in this region—can disturb as much as it determines.[1] Any suggestion that cultural criteria might have had something to do with the stagnation of the Chinese economy between the fifteenth and the nineteenth centuries or the rise of capitalist industrialization in Britain over the same period can raise the very hackles it has attempted to redress. As a result, experts have watered the question down to broad generalizations, redefined it to the point of pabulum, or taken refuge in bland and uncritical expressions of political correctness in order to avoid giving offense.

SHIFTING DEFINITIONS

Although generalizations may be valid in principle, they are difficult to use in practice. The more all-encompassing a definition, the less helpful it tends to be. To say that "culture matters," as Harvard professor David Landes (2000) does, for example, or to claim that "culture makes almost all the difference" to social and economic outcomes is to state an important but fairly superfluous fact. If our definition of culture includes a whole panoply of values, beliefs, attitudes, practices, symbols, and human relationships, if we feel that it is "expressed through religion, language, institutions, and history"[2] as well as art, collective memory, psychological hang-ups, and childhood nightmares, then the notion becomes too broad to be pertinent and too vague to be useful. As with the rule of law in relation to gender, there are "thick" and "thin" formulations of culture too: A definition that contains everything may finally explain nothing at all.

Culture has not always been so protean in its implications. There was a time, in the heyday of anthropology, when it was a useful term of theoretical analysis. But having escaped the confines of abstraction that it occupied a century ago, its definitions have proliferated in recent years. Sherry Beth Ortner, a distinguished American cultural anthropologist, in her review of anthropological literature (1984, pp. 129–130), argues that culture can no longer be defined as "something locked inside people's heads"; it is not "some abstractly ordered system" but rather something that communicates the views and values "of acting social beings trying to make sense of the world in which they find themselves." It has to be understood in relation to shifting social issues now, to evolving civic codes and symbols, to personal interpretations that fluctuate with technological, political, and economic change. Culture has become an evolutionary process rather than a fixed state.

Over the past century, our understanding of culture has been forced to adapt to all kinds of new data that have also contributed to its shifting definition. We must now acknowledge the impact of natural resource endowments, of geography and climate, of demographics, and of technology on culture, and even of a country's ability to project military power abroad. We must reassess, redefine, and reshape its meaning in relation to globalization, to expanding international trade, and to migratory flows, whether voluntary or coerced; we must rethink its relationship to government policies affecting education and the distribution of benefits and power in society.[3] We can no longer assess single cultures in isolation either, because of the borrowings among them.[4] The synergies between all these different factors, moreover, are as important as are the competing paradigms for how to achieve economic prosperity.

How in the world can we analyze the economic consequences of a word that we cannot explain, especially when it bears on a subject like gender equality, which is already difficult to define? Perhaps words are at the root of our problem.

LACK OF LANGUAGE

Our first challenge may be to overcome the paucity of language. If we are at cross-purposes on the subject of culture, it may be because our terms of reference, in and of themselves, have become confounded. Words like "religion," "culture," "tradition," and even "belief," for example, overlap and contain contradictory interpretations across geographic and temporal divides as well as across disciplines. When we say "culture" nowadays, we are unclear whether we mean "religion" or "tradition." Or both. When we use the term "tradition," we do not know whether we are speaking of abstract beliefs or are referring to literal, concrete behavior. Or both. We have invented new terms like "faith traditions," "faith communities," and "belief systems" just to cover the widening gaps and fault lines between these terms.

Indeed, to even refer to all these issues as "questions" of culture, when many consider their beliefs to be the "answer" to the world's problems, indicates the contradictions inherent in language.

According to Karen Armstrong, the well-known feminist theologian and authority on religious history, it is English itself that is at fault:

> The words in other languages that we translate as "religion" invariably refer to something vaguer, larger and more inclusive. The Arabic word din signifies an entire way of life, and the Sanskrit dharma covers law, politics, and social institutions as well as piety. The Hebrew Bible has no abstract concept of "religion"; and the Talmudic rabbis would have found it impossible to define faith in a single word or formula, because the Talmud was expressly designed to bring the whole of human life into the ambit of the sacred. The Oxford Classical Dictionary firmly states: "No word in either Greek or Latin corresponds to the English 'religion' or 'religious.'" In fact, the only tradition that satisfies the modern Western criterion of religion as a purely private pursuit is Protestant Christianity, which was also a creation of the early modern period.[5]

But a proliferation of signifiers does not necessarily clarify what they signify. Words must cross vast contextual distances to arrive at meanings common to all. Is there really no distinction between a "traditional" carpet design and the "custom" of subjecting little girls to genital mutilation?[6] Is "faith" in an unknowable Source of creation the same as "belief" that a woman should cover her face in public? And are spiritual concepts that define our metaphysical place in the universe the same as customs that give us a sense of "social identity"? Are we demonstrating obedience to the laws of God or the imperatives of a market culture when we argue about what we do or do not wear, what we eat or do not eat, and above all what we think, question, believe, doubt, say, insist, or deny to be women's role in society?

The only thing such questions have in common is that they all make us nervous.

FEAR

It is hardly surprising that economists and policy makers have found themselves held hostage by the culture question. The ambiguities inherent in it have provoked anxieties and engendered fears, especially where change is concerned. Indeed, there have been occasions in the past when not only individuals but entire societies have been made nervous by the culture question. Some countries have even become paralyzed by it, with far-reaching consequences to their economic development. But what some consider a threat, others can interpret as a challenge, and certain nations have overcome their anxieties with equally dramatic results for their prosperity. Since China and Britain have already been mentioned in this regard, it might be useful to look more closely at these countries to contrast opposite reactions to the challenge of cultural change.

China

What happened in China between 1405 and 1430 that transformed it from the preeminent naval power in the world to a society threatened by change? What caused this great civilization of the East to withdraw into isolation for the next four centuries, even as European nations crossed the Atlantic and staked claims on the Americas? Before this period, Admiral Zheng He was already leading armadas around the Indian Ocean and beyond; he was commanding up to sixty-two ships, some of them five times larger than the typical Portuguese caravel, which would later round the Cape of Good Hope. But in 1433, fifty years before the West achieved this feat, the Ming emperor suddenly banned foreign travel. The state archives were purged; all records pertaining to the construction of Chinese seafaring vessels were systematically destroyed, and so were the ships themselves. Even the transport of supplies along the Chinese coast from south to north was proscribed.[7] Why?

Although many answers to this question have been suggested, the cultural one prevails. The sinologist Étienne Balazs blames China's stillborn technological prowess on the excessive authoritarianism of its religion, and he identifies Confucian orthodoxy as responsible for this early manifestation of stultifying totalitarian control:

> The word "totalitarian" has a modern ring to it, but it serves
> well to describe the scholar-officials' state if it is understood
> to mean that the state has complete control over all activities,
> absolute domination at all levels . . . Nothing escaped official
> regimentation. Trade, mining, building, ritual, music,
> schools, in fact the whole of public life and a great deal of
> private life as well, were subjected to it . . . A final
> totalitarian characteristic was the state's tendency to clamp
> down immediately on any form of private enterprise (and
> this in the long run kills not only initiative but even the
> slightest attempts at innovation), or, if it did not succeed in
> putting a stop to it in time, to take over and nationalize
> it . . . Most probably the main inhibiting cause was the
> intellectual climate of Confucianist orthodoxy, not at all
> favorable for any form of trial or experiment, for
> innovations of any kind, or for the free play of the mind. The
> bureaucracy was perfectly satisfied with traditional
> techniques. Since these satisfied its practical needs, there
> was nothing to stimulate any attempt to go beyond the
> concrete and the immediate.[8]

But culture can be Janus-faced. When one examines China's development over the last two-and-a-half millennia—a period under the presumed spiritual and moral guidance of Confucius—one sees remarkable creativity and progress as well as economic stagnation. During this time, despite periods of backwardness, decay, and mass killing, the Chinese also invented printing, paper, the compass, gunpowder, porcelain, and silk, all of which have contributed in various ways to the advancement of civilization. There may even be a Confucian-based ethic at the root of China's recent rapid growth, as Lee Kuan Yew, Singapore's first and long-serving prime minister, claims there is in East Asian prosperity today (Zakaria, 1994), since values of "thrift, hard work, filial piety and loyalty to the extended family, and, most of all, the respect for scholarship and learning" could provide the cultural soil that gives rise to new levels of prosperity.

At the end, however, causes of economic performance based on cultural and religious values alone might obscure rather than clarify the issues, for China's recent rapid growth perhaps is less linked to Confucianism than to the forces unleashed through its integration with the global economy, its efforts to introduce more secure property rights, and its active encouragement of internal migration from the countryside to the cities. A macroeconomist might even point to a weak exchange rate as the primary engine of Chinese economic growth over the past two decades. When analyzing economic progress or regress, there are clearly problems with using cultural explanations in isolation.

At least one other author has suggested an additional factor as being responsible for China's past economic and technological stagnation, apart from Confucian orthodoxy and the state's tendency to clamp down on private enterprise. And it is a significant one. American sociologist Jack Goldstone (1996) believes that the centuries-long inertia in the Chinese economy also stemmed from the confinement of women to the home. The severe restriction on the employment of women outside the household in China seriously curtailed the supply of female workers to labor-intensive industries, such as textiles, and the economy of the state was fatally affected.[9] This pattern was maintained right up to the mid-nineteenth century, by which time such employment was becoming the norm in the West. The country's aborted technological development and economic growth could well be linked to the restricted mobility of half its population.

Goldstone also thinks restrictions on time were as significant as place; not only *where* but *when* women had freedom of movement was also important. According to him:

> *In northwest Europe, with its pattern of late marriages and nuclear families, there existed a stage in the life course of most women—between puberty in their early teens and marriage in their mid-twenties—when they were available for labor and routinely performed work for wages outside their natal households.* No such stage existed in the life course of Chinese women, at least from the Ming through the end of the Imperial era (to 1911). *This would have posed a great obstacle to the creation of textile factories along the lines of their development in Europe and North America at any time in China's late Imperial history.* (p. 3)

Curiously enough, a country that insisted on keeping half its population behind locked doors and effectively shackled its women by footbinding practices may ultimately have constrained its own progress and straitened its prosperity for centuries. By keeping its women imprisoned, China limited its own freedom.

There seems to be a chicken-and-egg dilemma at the heart of the culture question; our second example may illustrate the reverse of this conundrum.

Britain

What was the reason for Britain's economic success during the Industrial Revolution? What was responsible for this famous case of culturally determined development? The alleged superiority of a

Protestant ethic has often been touted as its cause, but we should exercise some caution in attributing more than a peripheral role to Protestantism alone.[10] Industrial capitalism did not occur until almost 300 years after the rise of Calvin and Luther, and it is not at all clear, as economic historian J. Bradford De Long (1988, p. 1146) points out, that Protestantism initially favored a capitalist spirit: "Strong Protestantism—Calvin's Geneva and Cromwell's Republic of the Saints—saw theology and economy closely linked in a manner not unlike the Ayatollah's Iran. And religious fanaticism is not often thought of as a source of economic growth." Indeed, it was not until the development of the slave trade in the eighteenth century that profit seeking and wealth accumulation became morally acceptable in England. So while religious fanaticism may have been more quickly allied to political and economic pragmatism in Ayatollah's Iran, MIT professor Peter Temin suggests that the Protestant culture in Europe can be seen as only partially responsible for the rise of industrial capitalism. It would appear that its success was less dependent on ideological factors than on a particular set of technologies and a specific system of social organization.[11]

More significantly, perhaps, than the role of the Protestant ethic was a belief in individual accomplishment and the legitimacy of man's mastery over nature. This cultural characteristic, which was the key to enhanced productivity, contributed significantly to the economic success of the Industrial Revolution. Epitomized in Adam Smith's analysis of the division of labor in *The Wealth of Nations* (1776), the prevailing idea underlying the British model consisted of the separation and specialization of the individual in the workplace in a narrow set of tasks. Such an idea of mastery enhanced people's social capabilities; it led to a rapid assimilation of the latest technologies and legitimized the pursuit of science and knowledge for their own sake. Above all, it challenged the age-old, quasi-feudal norms of English culture implicit in traditional agrarian societies and spread its influence far beyond English shores. Thus it was that Britain, a small, insular, but highly disciplined nation—the leading scientific innovator of the time and an industrial giant actively seeking to project power abroad—ultimately became the model for the economic development of nineteenth-century Meiji Japan, under the leadership of finance minister and noted statesman Okubo Toshimichi.

But apart from the changes envisaged by Adam Smith and implemented in industrial Britain and elsewhere, there was another dynamic in the workplace that broke with old traditions even more radically, even more shockingly. This important change led to a new definition of "mastery"; it introduced a new dimension of "individual accomplishment" that was to have long-lasting consequences across the world. More significant than the division of labor, more consequential even than the Protestant work ethic, was the recruitment of women and children into British factories in the nineteenth century.[12] This is what fundamentally changed the country's economy and set it on a new path. And this change was to prove far more challenging and would take much longer for other countries, including Japan, to emulate.

This secondary, gender revolution within the industrial one not only reduced costs and prices by swelling the labor force with hundreds of thousands of female workers but contributed to demand by giving women more money to spend. Most important, it deepened the reach of transformation from the workplace into the home itself. The status of women changed most quickly in those societies where the impact of the Industrial Revolution took root most rapidly at the domestic as well as national levels. The sense of individualism and empowerment which became widespread in Britain in the nineteenth century was stimulated by financial and social incentives, and these, in turn, influenced family life as well as the economy at large, promoting innovation and self-improvement that even cut across the class system. As a result, questions were finally raised and principles articulated about universal suffrage and human rights, both of which emerged as defining issues of the time.

THE BACKLASH

The issue of incentives and human rights will be discussed more closely in the following pages, but the "success" and "failure" stories in relation to cultural change cannot be complete without reference to the backlash that has paralleled them. The positive and negative examples of proactive and preemptive response to cultural change in Britain and China need to be set against the growing fear of women's freedom clearly evident in Syria, Iraq, Egypt, Libya, Iran, Pakistan, Afghanistan, and parts of sub-Saharan Africa. The rise in the status of women has been violently rejected by the conservative faction in some of these countries, leading to abductions, rape, and increased violence against women and girls; their recruitment into the workforce and their economic autonomy have been blamed for all kinds of social ills, from the rise in divorce rates to the collapse of civil society. Although their participation in the workforce has been critical to economic growth, women and girls have been the first casualties, and gender equality has been the immediate target of this backlash in our times.

The nefarious influence of Western culture is frequently seen, by fundamentalist elements in many countries, as the cause of rampant materialism and rapid urbanization, of irresponsible industrialization and even postcolonial corruption. But Western culture is also the victim of its own brand of fundamentalism, which is protean and can take many forms. It can be a political ideology as well as a form of religious extremism; it can be rooted in scientific materialism or offer us the illusion of liberation and financial agency. While converting us to the sacred faith of human rights, the Western brand of fundamentalism has bound us hand and foot to the ideology of the bottom line; it has brainwashed us into becoming disciples of the unrevealed religion of the modern age: materialism. As a result, while appearing to champion their rights, Western culture has paradoxically provoked the backlash against women in some cases. Our Western preoccupation with physical appearance, commodification, and a dogmatic belief in personal gratification has muffled the female sex in a veil of tanned and exposed flesh that has greatly contributed to the onslaught of fanaticism against women and girls.

Indeed, the link between political commercialism and religious fundamentalism lies precisely in how they both treat women. The preponderant emphasis on the female body, for example, whether stripped of clothing or covered from top to toe in obscuring cloth, dominates the discourse of both. The obsession with sexuality, the definition of gender as identity, and the promotion of ideologies profoundly materialistic in their interpretation of reality also characterize both. Interestingly, both are built on the politics of paranoia, too, governing people through intimidation and the desire to be "saved," one way or another. Religious as well as materialistic dogmas, both governed by fear, are intrinsically antithetical to gender equality.

Of course, one should be careful in reading the facts and interpreting the evidence. But it does look as if the changed status of women, which has triggered debates about their rights, has simultaneously given rise to fundamentalist wrongs against them. The historical contrast between China and Britain as well as the more recent cultural backlash against gender equality in other countries proves that however complex and ambiguous it might be, women's relation to culture cannot be ignored. If women's rights are threatened by cultural traditions and religious beliefs, the prosperity of that society is invariably undermined, to the detriment of all. And if women are given greater opportunities of economic independence, that society as well as its cultural prosperity is also enhanced, to the benefit of all. Failed states and failed economies lead to the failure of culture in its broadest sense, with women as the primary casualties.

And that collapse *is* worth fearing.

INCENTIVES

It has been generally accepted by contemporary economists that failed states and failed economies are associated with the failure of incentives. In the Soviet Union, for example, the prevailing economic paradigm during the twentieth century was central planning, an ideologically driven system in which government bureaucrats made all the decisions about production, distribution, and prices of goods and services. The Communist Party suppressed positive incentives to growth; in their stead it attempted to establish a new cultural model, defined by a set of abstract values, habits, beliefs, and attitudes that were underpinned by a fairly complex institutional infrastructure. But this model, which was imposed through terror and repression in the early years, gradually proved to be a mirage as the decades passed. Instead of being willingly held and therefore culturally authentic, people's so-called values under communism were, for the most part, rational accommodations to the prevailing orthodoxy, moral compromises made in an effort to feed a family and to survive.

In other words, it did not greatly matter, in the Soviet Union, whether people believed in the system or not: What mattered was that the system affected their behavior. Central planning offered no scope for private property, no possibility for entrepreneurial initiative, and no price system. Wage differentials were extremely narrow, promotion was not linked to performance, and lifetime employment was more or less guaranteed. As a result people had no idea about the scarcity value of things and therefore no incentives to economize resources; people regulated the temperature in their apartments in the winter by opening their windows, for example, as there were no thermostats. By the time the Soviet Union collapsed it was an environmental wasteland. This inevitably produced a culture of passivity and paralysis, but the absence of a work ethic in the Soviet Union was not a reflection of laziness or lack of discipline: it was a natural and indeed logical response to an environment in which cultural incentives were radically eroded.

It is worth repeating that people will respond to incentives, whether these are positive or negative, intelligent or perverse. Give them cheap gasoline and they will drive their cars instead of walking, and pollute the air. Give them lifetime job security and no stimulus for advancement, and they will slack off and pretend to be working when they are not. And the same is true for the role and participation of women in the economy. Curtail the opportunities for women to educate themselves, and they will soon look like and increasingly be perceived as pieces of furniture. Limit their access to the job market and to knowledge, and they will begin to sound intellectually inferior and be treated as such. Clearly, incentives that have had a role in shaping people's attitudes toward the other sex may go a long way toward explaining discriminatory behaviors.

Another example of the cultural role played by incentives that can highlight their importance for gender equality is to be found in Indian history. According to David Landes (1994), India was the world's leading producer of cotton goods in the seventeenth and eighteenth centuries with a major presence in the Asian markets. These goods were also popular in Europe, but the high demand from abroad did not lead to technological improvements in production on the subcontinent. At least one plausible, if partial, explanation for this puzzle was that, unlike Britain, where there were powerful economic incentives to find mechanical substitutes for human skills and manpower, India had an inexhaustible supply of cheap labor, frequently female, which was readily available to use existing technologies. Indians were not necessarily less inventive than the British; they just operated in an environment in which the economic incentives for invention and innovation were different from those prevailing in Britain.

Just as negative incentives influenced behavior, effort, and priorities in India, with direct consequences on the economy and gender equality, so too positive incentives in the United States and the United Kingdom encouraged improvements in the lot of women in the nineteenth century, with long-term prosperity for the economy at large. Thomas Franck (2001), a former international law professor at New York University, provides examples to buttress this claim by showing how the emergence of a middle class in the aftermath of the Industrial Revolution in the United Kingdom increased the demand for high-quality children's education. This opened up the teaching profession to women and gave them an incentive not only to enter the workforce but also to raise the level of literacy throughout the land, because new supply had to meet the rising demand. The demographic consequences of the Civil War in the United States also created new openings for women, just as it expanded opportunities for all African Americans to improve their lot, and this in turn provided many with further incentives to seek higher qualifications in medicine and in the law. The ripple effects of these cultural shifts in society led to a whole range of improvements in the Western world. Progress in transport and communications increased people's mobility, and the associated demonstration effects proved powerful catalysts to precipitate further change.[13] All of these changes, in turn, influenced people's willingness to participate in and form opinions about the management of society, enhancing the level of informed and politically active citizens, including women. So the widespread economic impact of gender equality in Western countries was clearly linked to improved incentives.

A final example of the role of incentives in a culture can be found in Ghana. Many economists in the early 1960s thought that Ghana, with its rich environmental resources, would develop faster over the longer term than South Korea, which had poor natural endowments and complicated geopolitics at the end of the Korean War. How much of Ghana's stunted development since then has been due to culture? How much of its potential at the time of its independence has been wasted because of bad economic policies that have undermined all incentives for progress? As in the case of other countries where gender equality has been undercut by negative incentives, the policies have been so poor in Ghana during the last several decades that they spawned corruption, induced political instability, and beset the country with numerous ills. Political instability in developing countries like Ghana has led to an inability to look beyond the next year and an unwillingness on the part of investors to plan for the long term because of the associated risks. And these conditions are invariably linked to negative incentives for the enhancement of gender equality.

In a nutshell: What may appear to be a cultural trait may, in fact, be an economic incentive and thus may be amenable to change if and when the underlying conditions in a country are altered. From this perspective, poverty and underdevelopment are due less to culture than to economic malfunction. And by extension, the lack of gender equality, the oppression of women in society, and discrimination against them in the family, in the workplace, and in government are not necessarily culturally determined either but could be linked to a lack of positive incentives and the proliferation of negative ones that block their progress. A good example of this is provided by the relative success of various diasporas all over the world, ethnic or national communities that often are highly successful once they establish themselves abroad. In many of these communities, women play a preponderant role as soon as they find themselves with the incentives for improvement. This fact seems to suggest that so-called backwardness at home may have had more to do with the underlying policy framework and the incentives in an economy than with any particular cultural attributes. We need to be cautious, therefore, against undue pessimism about countries or continents allegedly under the influence of the "wrong" kind of culture.

In fact, there is considerable evidence that the notion of culture per se might be a mirage and in some ways "wrong," in and of itself. The anthropologist George Peter Murdock (1965) cites sixty-four elements that are common to the cultures of Korea and Ghana, from community organization to dream interpretation, from etiquette to inheritance rules.[14] He argues that although behaviors, such as eating rice with chopsticks or not, will differ across cultures, "all . . . are constructed according to a single fundamental plan—the 'universal cultural pattern,'" a concept he believes is based on the "psychic unity of mankind." Murdock claims

> *that all peoples now living or of whom we possess substantial historical records, irrespective of differences in geography and physique, are essentially alike in their basic psychological equipment and mechanism, and that the cultural differences between them reflect only the differential responses of essentially similar organisms to unlike stimuli or conditions. (p. 91)*

Or, *unlike incentives*, he might have convincingly added.

CULTURAL EXCEPTIONALISM

In the culture of materialism that currently prevails, it is not very fashionable to speak about a "universal cultural pattern." Where is the individual branding in that? Where is the possibility for identity politics if we are going to admit to the "psychic unity of mankind"? Even as we become more and more interdependent for global trade, for shared resources, for environmental protection, for food security and safety, for communications and technology, we are being pulled apart by various kinds of tribalism, by obsolete forms of nationalism based on racial distinctions, and by the suspect logic of cultural exceptionalism. What is even worse, we are seduced into believing that these "isms" are associated with our inviolable human rights.

Over the past quarter century, even as "feminism" and the demand for women's rights has gained ground, there has been a parallel debate about the relationship between human rights and culture. It is at these crossroads, after all, where the greatest strain occurs at times of social transition.[15] It is here that global and national issues intersect with family and domestic life and the old fault lines between the sexes yawn wide. It is here that we experience the increasing tension, already discussed, between tradition and change, between the demand for women to stay at home and the pressure for them to go out to work. If hackles are raised when economic failure is traced to the issue of gender, it may be because the conjunction is so domestically combustible.

As soon as human rights are linked to women, the goalposts shift, the frame of reference slips, and the definitions slide from the protection of rights to the preservation of culture, from the question of culture to the importance of customs, from custom to traditions, from tradition to religion, and from religious law to articles of absolute faith. At the end, the debate invariably leads to the intractable question of whether such rights should be considered as universal or merely a reflection of Western values. And the discussion founders on the rocks of cultural exceptionalism.

This argument, sometimes disguised as pluralism and often concealing despotism, is rooted in the idea that human rights bear little relevance beyond the shores of Europe and North America. An example of such logic can be seen in recent steps taken to prevent discrimination against women in Afghanistan. As already mentioned, the Convention on the Elimination of All Forms of Discrimination Against Women (CEDAW) prohibits practices discriminatory toward women that are prevalent in many parts of the world. Indeed, the unanimous resolution of the UN Security Council passed in October 1999 censured the Taliban for its treatment of Afghani women on these very grounds.[16] But this resolution still did not prevent radical fundamentalists of all stripes from arguing against it. Claims of cultural relativism and exceptionalism, accusations of neoimperialism and racism immediately came to the fore. Since these arguments were defending the nation's so-called right to determine its own standards of what was "discriminatory," without any obligation to abide by so-called outside interference, it looked as if women were being sacrificed to national sovereignty.

Whenever human rights are set in opposition to national sovereignty, the received wisdom of our time, as noted by Franck (2001, p. 192), holds that "states have a sovereign right to be let alone and not to be judged by international human rights standards." But in the human rights versus culture debate, we find that these states often insist on being "let alone" in relation to gender issues. When it comes to matters of military or economic aid, for example, there has been little or no such demand for independence. The flaw in such logic cannot be ignored. Since the proponents of cultural exceptionalism always follow the same line of defense and deploy the same allegations to promote their positions, it may be useful to look at the three arguments they invariably use in rejecting gender equality. These are national sovereignty and rights of legitimate spokesmanship; cultural imperialism and the accusations of racism and neocolonialism; and religious absolutism and the authority of doctrinal beliefs.

National Sovereignty and Legitimate Spokesmanship

Behind the argument that independent states should be let alone and not judged by international human rights standards, one finds the primacy of national sovereignty. This is the first line of defense against the universality of human rights, and it is always deployed to reject norms established by the international community. Although initially it may be couched in cultural terms, in pleas for tolerance, and in calls for diversity rather than conformity, this argument has a defiantly political purpose. It uses national sovereignty to reject any ideas that are politically inimical to a country's leadership.

According to this logic, State leaders alone are the ultimate deciders; they have the final say in how to govern their people. No neighboring nation, no external coalition of nations, and certainly no international institution supported by the majority of nations in the world can impose its values or guidelines, its models or principles on that sovereign State. No external power, whether political or economic or cultural, has the right to influence its policies. And to attempt to do this, to suggest the need to do it, to claim the authority to do it on the grounds of "human rights" is tantamount to an assault, an act of war. It is perceived as undermining the sovereignty, as threatening the security, and as violating the independence of that nation.

This implicit and sometimes explicit accusation immediately politicizes the definition of culture. It opens up a minefield. It turns the word into a weapon and hurls verbal missiles and language bombs into the debate. But on closer scrutiny, the logical weaknesses of this argument are evident. Even when not using democratic criteria based on corrupted or distorted statistics to bolster its legitimacy, leadership needs some evidence of its validity. If this is asserted on the basis of force rather than freely granted popular support, then it is most likely to be tyrannical. The great English historian Edward Gibbon long ago noted that claims of legitimacy are most vociferous when references to the abuse of rule are most absent. As he famously stated in his analysis of the decline and fall of the Roman Empire, "It is sufficiently known that the odious appellation of *Tyrant* was often employed by the ancients to express the illegal seizure of supreme power, without any reference to the abuse of it."[17] The claims of those who deny such abuse, moreover, are rarely disinterested and hardly objective. When leaders hold on to power at the cost of the rights and freedoms of others, their legitimacy is most likely to be self-serving and least likely to be freely granted. And when half the population they claim to represent has been forcibly silenced, the motives of a particular elite must be considered patently suspect. In such cases, a government rarely represents all the people of its country, for it almost never speaks on behalf of its women.

Under the Taliban, for example, women neither chose their government nor were asked about who they wanted as their spokesmen.

They were never consulted about whether they could join the labor force, or if their daughters might go to school. These choices were appropriated by the men, controlled by men, and dictated by those men who claimed to speak on behalf of Afghan society. And it was these same male leaders who, in the name of national sovereignty, forced women to bear the brunt of their insecurities; who, under the guise of protecting their culture and traditions, denied women their rights to vote, to be educated, to earn money, to own property, or to travel freely. In other words, the majority of those who thought that such evident and universal rights would shake the stability and undermine the national sovereignty of the country were men. It would seem, therefore, by a curious twist of irony, that the solemn and sacred subject of national identity has in some countries become inextricably entangled with women's clothing and women's jobs.

But one need not refer to extreme cases to see evidence of such violations of legitimate spokesmanship at work. Franck (2001) tells the fascinating case of Sandra Lovelace, a Canadian Maliseet native who lost her right to live on ancestral lands because she married out of the tribe. In 1979, she took her case to the Human Rights Committee of the International Covenant on Civil and Political Rights, arguing that no similar penalty applied to men. The committee upheld her claim. This in turn forced the Canadian government, eager to abide by its international human rights obligations, to repeal what was clearly a discriminatory tribal law in 1985. Upon closer examination, however, anthropologists noted that a rule that appeared on the surface to have been a manifestation of some tribal customs, adopted in ancient times, perhaps to facilitate group survival, was, in fact, copied relatively recently from male-dominated Victorian society and imposed by male elders on the women of these First Nation peoples.

Moreover, paraphrasing Radhika Coomarswami, the UN special rapporteur on violence against women, Franck (2001) claims that practices such as female genital mutilation, flogging, stoning, and amputation, as well as laws restricting women's rights to marriage, divorce, maintenance, and custody, are inauthentic perversions of religious dogmas rather than cultural norms. Accordingly, the criterion of free choice is all that can resolve the conflict between human rights and issues of cultural pluralism. "Cultural diversity should be celebrated only if those enjoying their cultural attributes are doing so voluntarily," Coomarswami states. "By protecting choice, voluntariness and the integrity of female decision-making, we may be able to reconcile the dilemma between cultural diversity and the need for the protection of women's human rights."[18]

If the claims of legitimate spokesmanship are not voluntarily supported by the majority on the basis of free choice, then this argument against the universality of human rights is clearly flawed. Which leads to the second line of defense.

Cultural Imperialism, Racism, and Neocolonialism

Behind the argument for exceptionalism or pluralism based on claims of "cultural hegemony," one frequently finds a very plausible desire for retaliation against the long and bloodstained history of racism in the world. This second line of defense against the universality of human rights is based on the idea that their imposition is a new form of imperialism, the new face of neocolonialism. It insists that criticism against any country's so-called cultural practices is just racism.

As already indicated, at the root of this accusation is the theory that the human rights system and all its supporting institutions are manifestations of Western domination and supremacy. According to this argument, De Long's (1988) references to the absence of the Protestant ethic in Japan and China and the significance of this absence in relation to the economic development of these countries proves the cultural myopia of Western ideas. The importance of individualism and empowerment in industrialized Britain, and the long-term impact of these developments on questions of universal suffrage, also bolsters this line of argument. These examples, according to critics, confirm that notions such as universal human rights are not universal at all. The values of respect for diversity, belief in tolerance, support for gender equality, and even democratic methods of election and representational government may characterize Western civilization but are irrelevant to other societies in the world. They are intrinsically alien to races and cultures that have a different history, different traditions, and a different set of political, religious, and geographic circumstances. And to assume otherwise is a sign of racial paternalism, neocolonialism, and cultural imperialism.

Such accusations take full advantage of Western guilt over its colonial and racist past. Europe and America have, finally, begun to develop a salutary sense of shame in this connection after five centuries of brutality toward others and themselves. There is a changing of attitudes in the West that, even if only skin deep so far, is remarkable, considering the blood spilled in the name of racial superiority and ethnic cleansing, even in the recent past. And the impact of this change has been relatively fast, given the rooted prejudice of centuries that preceded it. Being racist is, generally speaking, considered a stigma now, and although some deploy it as a form of provocation, few would dare advertise their intolerance toward those of a different culture and color. These principles have a long way to go before taking root in our consciences and in our actions, but except in extreme cases, which ironically prove the rule by attempting to break it, they have already made a dent in our social laws and public behavior.

Sadly, this invaluable awareness actually undercuts the argument in support of human rights. If, according to David Landes (2000), a culture that is allowing for and enabling positive economic development is judged as doing the *right* thing, then it is all too easy to give the impression that the culture which does not do so is somehow *wrong*. And when negative outcomes detrimental to development are attributed to the *wrong* sort of culture, it is all too easy to cause offense, to undermine self-esteem, and to give the impression of a blinkered judgment rooted in racism. "Coming from outsiders, such animadversions, however tactful and indirect, stink of condescension" is how Landes succinctly puts it (p. 2). Accordingly, despite the validity of opinions such as Murdock's in support of a "universal cultural pattern" and the "psychic unity of mankind," the debate is immediately sabotaged, without need of any bombs.

But the flaw in this argument is that it is based on false premises. To argue that tolerance is a Western value is to ignore the facts. The West has been permeated with prejudice and zealotry for millennia; the civilizations of Europe have produced the most brutal and bloody examples of intolerance and fanaticism in the world. Judeo-Christian beliefs, which are foundational to Western culture, have instigated some of the greatest violations against human rights in history, more often than not in the name of one of the sustaining pillars of any culture: religion. According to the Old Testament, "Anyone who blasphemes the name of the Lord is to be put to death. The entire assembly must stone them. Whether foreigner or native-born, when they blaspheme the Name they are to be put to death" (Leviticus 24:16). According to St. Thomas Aquinas, heretics "deserve not only to be separated from the Church by excommunication, but also to be severed from the world by death" (quoted in Franck, 2001). In keeping with such statements, millions in England, in Holland, in France, in Spain, and in most other countries of Europe were subjected to inhuman torture and punishment in the centuries leading up to the Reformation. The magnificent tract titled "The Grand Inquisitor" in Dostoyevsky's *Brothers Karamazov* is a sobering reminder of the extent to which fundamentalist attitudes are very much part of the DNA of Western civilization.[19]

Furthermore, the behavior of Western leadership toward its own people as well as others over the past four hundred to five hundred years is more like a saga of intransigence than an inspiration for the

Universal Declaration of Human Rights. The admission of crimes against humanity certainly did not come naturally to the white race. Centuries passed before the Catholic Church admitted to the brutal religious intolerance it exported to Latin America. A civil war and another century of assassinations had to ravage North America before racism, though still practiced, finally became an ugly word. And as for granting rights to women, as we have seen in the preceding chapters, that has taken the longest time of all. The statistics for domestic violence in many countries today are proof that the defense of human rights is definitely not intrinsic to Western culture. The fact that women were not given the right to vote in most countries until well into the twentieth century, and that Harvard Law School did not even admit women until the 1950s, can be taken as symbolic of the many restrictions to women's empowerment in the West for the past 2,000 years. The vast majority of countries today still treat women as second-class citizens.[20]

It is significant to note, moreover, that the principal international institutions established to defend human rights only emerged in the last half century. They were not the product of the Western imagination at all but the result of two world wars and responses to major crises and challenges sweeping across the planet. The driving force of the Universal Declaration of Human Rights and the animating principles governing its infrastructure and its supporting institutions have less to do with Western norms than with innumerable other factors, such as the spread of universal education, the process of urbanization, the progress in science and technology, and the revolution that has transformed information and communications industries, even in the most remote places. All these factors, to a greater or lesser degree, have had an impact on societies everywhere; they have transcended innumerable barriers—geographic, religious, and ethnic—and have had a profound impact on our ways of thinking.

Interestingly enough, the first group of people to be affected, the first whose lives have been revolutionized by these sweeping changes, have been women. Since the origins of dominance and subservience are so intimate and so very hard to overcome, this counter-argument in defense of the universality of human rights invariably leads to the third argument used by the proponents of cultural exceptionalism.

Religious Absolutism and Doctrinal Beliefs

Behind the definition of culture in religious terms, one finds the inviolability of belief. This third argument against the universality of human rights is the hardest to confront, because it is often based on a rejection of reason. The need for logic is dismissed with this line of thinking because gender equality, in addition to rational thought, is invariably sacrificed to doctrinal absolutism. Although, paradoxically, the more absolute a doctrine, the less reliable it proves to be, cultural exceptionalism, in this case, rests squarely on and takes refuge in the unquestionable authority of blind faith.

There is no point in entering the bloodstained arena of theology to prove the point. The grounds of this argument are splattered with far more than the ink spilled by many besides priests and clerics, scribes and self-appointed interpreters. Some have been sincere and some venal, some sadly misguided and some well-meaning, but what is common to their interpretations, their justifications, their qualifications, their commentaries, their translations, and possibly even their distortions of varying sacred texts over the past four millennia is that all insist on the divinely ordained inferiority of women. By claiming the right to "mediate between humans and God,"[21] male clerics of all cloths have not only controlled the sexuality and reproductive functions of women but wreaked violence upon them by divine command.[22] They have kept women in an inferior status, legally as well as socially, in the home as well as in society at large, and appropriated God's name to this end. Since male clerics have been the primary interpreters of the Word of God, they have also been the exponents of the Will of God. But the old patterns and traditional habits they have established in society, partly for purposes of stability and partly, no doubt, to maintain their own powers, have not always been godly. They have been marked by the enduring power of patriarchy.

"Even when there was an initial attempt to introduce greater sexual equality," affirms Karen Armstrong (2004), writing about the distortions of religious truth in history, "men hijacked the faith and dragged it back to the old patriarchy."[23] Whenever the status quo was threatened by cultural change, it was all too easy for old habits to be given divine authority. As the Jewish Women's Archive *Encyclopedia* confirms, "With the entrenchment and spread of the Babylonian Talmud and its further interpretations, social inferiority was hardened into law."[24] And yet these laws were invariably man-made. The discriminatory statements in the New Testament—that women should veil their heads and keep silent in the assembly, for example, that wives should submit to their husbands and should not teach or speak in church, in fact all references illustrating women's inferiority—were not the words of Christ himself but were compiled, according to Armstrong, "when Christianity was beginning to retreat from its early radicalism" and "the conventional requirement[s]" of patriarchy were once again being reasserted.[25] And the same pattern also occurred in Islam. Women were at the forefront of its early development. The Prophet permitted the presence of women at prayer in his lifetime, but they were kept out of the public mosques after his death.[26] And as time passed they were excluded from much else too. As Raqiya Abdalla (1982, p. 102) writes in her book about female genital mutilation, "[R]eligious teachings [of Islam] have been manipulated to demonstrate that men have a sacred as well as a secular right to dominate," and that to argue against them was to risk apostasy.

The flaw in the argument of doctrinal absolutism rests not only on the fact that it has been constructed, by and large, by men rather than God but also on its application. Religious texts, such as the Bible and the Quran, the Bhagavad Gita and the Sutras, are often relative, not absolute, arising from a particular context as well as expressing eternal truths. They are filled with seeming contradictions and differences of interpretation that have spawned a proliferation of sects and factions over the millennia. How can doctrinal absolutism, based on one particular creed, be used as proof of cultural exceptionalism? It all comes down to who is interpreting what, and why or when one interpretation dominates all others in a culture. There is no logic inherent to this subject. As the feminist academic Anita Weiss (2014) states in relation to the thorny issue of "ijtihad," or interpretation of the Quran, "there is no consensus" as far as the interpretation of religious laws are concerned, particularly as they pertain to women in Pakistan. "Instead, different voices have called for conflicting actions all 'based on Islam.'"

Such problematic logic is reflected in the contradictions that exist between civil and religious courts even in the same country. In Israel, for example, where Judaism is the state religion, the rabbinical marriage ceremony is naturally imposed by law, and no marriage with a Jew can take place without the authority of the rabbinate. As a result, thousands of people who do not meet the religious definition of any faith, or who cannot prove their religious heritage, or who are considered "questionable Jews" or in some way religiously "taboo" may not marry in Israel at all. They are obliged to live in violation of religious standards, with so-called Domestic Union Cards[27] as a stopgap measure, or else travel to another country for a civil marriage ceremony, which they cannot have in Israel. The ultimate irony is that such civil marriages, forbidden by the rabbinate, are not considered a circumvention of its authority and are recognized in Israel, once they have taken place elsewhere. And a further twist in logic is that a Jewish couple who has married abroad will still have to divorce in the rabbinate, because religious authorities alone can divorce couples. The rabbinate therefore has to arrange the divorce of couples it has pronounced ineligible to marry.

Furthermore, if doctrine is to serve as grounds for law, as the sharia is, for example, it has to be consistently applied. To insist on applying one set of religious laws while ignoring others surely undermines their overall authority.[28] But there can be such wide discrepancy of interpretation in religious matters, even in countries holding to the same belief system, that there may be no single way to implement the laws regarding women. A comparison may serve to illustrate this point. The Islamic Republic of Iran and Saudi Arabia have the highest number of restrictions against women: twenty-three in the case of Iran and twenty-nine in the case of Saudi Arabia. However, Tunisia and Algeria only have about ten restrictions of this kind, and Turkey has just four at the present time. The growing divergence of opinion in the Muslim world provoked by the rise of politicized and radicalized Islam has thrown differences of religious interpretation, especially regarding women, into sharp relief. The ways in which gender discrimination is expressed ranges across a wide spectrum and appears to be as *non*universal as women's rights. Clearly, countries that share the same religious tradition deal with the issue of equality in radically different ways.[29] The rejection of human rights on such grounds, therefore, rests on circular logic, because if religious doctrine is subject to cultural relativism, it can hardly be absolute.

It may be futile to note the inconsistency of this line of logic, given that consistency has in any case been rejected by cultural exceptionalism, but it is hard to ignore one kind of consistency that is being unwittingly promoted by such contradictions. Even the most cursory glance at ways in which women have been treated and are still perceived within the Christian, Buddhist, Hindu, and Zoroastrian faith communities illustrates a baleful similarity. Perhaps it is time, after more than four millennia, to draw aside the veil of censure and constraint on women in the name of God. Perhaps it is time to demand accountability for cultural crimes.

CONCLUSION

On March 19, 2015, a terrible crime took place outside the main mosque in Kabul. A young woman was kicked, beaten, run over, dragged through the streets behind a truck, and finally burned before being thrown in a polluted river. She had been accused by the mullah in the mosque of committing blasphemy. Several young men who heard the cleric raise his voice against her then dragged her out of the mosque, incited into a frenzy of revenge. The crowd that gathered was told that she was an apostate who had burned the Quran and deserved to die. Several policemen standing by did nothing to defend her. Many took videos of the attack. Highly placed officials, including a female political figure, claimed that such retaliation was justified. The woman's family vouched that she was mentally unstable, but by then she was dead. The internet was flooded with her blood-reddened face as she begged to know what her sin had been.

After the furor died down, journalists, women's activists, and international human rights organizations began asking the same question, and it gradually emerged that the woman, Farkhunda, who was twenty-seven years old, had committed no sin at all. In fact, she was a devout Muslim. A religious scholar herself who had just qualified as a teacher and knew the Quran by heart, she had been remonstrating with the mullah in the mosque about his monopoly on selling talismans and "holy" amulets to the women. In other words, her real "crime" had been to break with tradition. Her only "blasphemy" had been to argue with a cleric. Her so-called act of apostasy had been to make a distinction between the injunctions in the Quran and the superstitions being sold to a bunch of uneducated women whose children would go hungry if they wasted their money on such rubbish. The mullah's fury against her, for undermining his reputation and his means of livelihood, led to false accusations and the incitement of the crowd. Even her family, it was later said, had been intimidated into saying that she was mentally unbalanced, because they feared for their reputation. This kind of behavior should not be dignified by being called "religious." It was a glaring example of a cultural crime.

When the remains of the woman were gathered up and prepared for burial, the women of Kabul took the unique step of breaking with tradition: They refused to allow the prayer leader of the mosque to preside over her funeral and turned him away. Furthermore, they violated the custom that women should remain at the back of the crowd during a funeral and strode in front of the mourners, wearing masks of the woman's blood-drenched face. They carried her coffin to the graveyard themselves. It was unprecedented.

What was even more significant was that a large circle of men surrounded and protected them as they challenged the customs of their country. This remarkable action, which echoed the events that had taken place a month before in the wake of the attack on the psychology student in the southern Turkish province of Mersin, showed a growing awareness by many people in Kabul, men and women alike, of the distinction between a cultural tradition and divine injunction, between custom and religious faith. Only when social laws are differentiated from spiritual principles can gender equality finally be recognized.

Despite great scientific strides over the centuries, our religious thinking may still be "remarkably undeveloped, even primitive" in this regard.[30] We are inclined to be literal-minded. We translate moral exhortations into material injunctions; we confuse spiritual principles with social laws. It is easy to confound these two aspects of religion and deify culture in the process.[31] But perhaps the time has come to distinguish between the universal principles implicit in all faiths and the cultural mirages we elevate to the level of religious doctrine. Perhaps it is time to question those assumptions that crush half the human race in the name of culture.

There was a time when, and there are still areas of the world today where, acts of brutality could take place in zones of combat with very little consequence to the perpetrators. Atrocities could be inflicted on innocent citizens with impunity; slaughter and butchery and carnage and cold-blooded murder could take place without recourse to justice; acts of ruthless cruelty and crimes of unspeakable violence could be committed and no one was held to account for these so-called casualties of war. But this sort of justification is no longer acceptable today. It is no longer possible to claim that the end justifies the means and that those who condone the massacre and plunder of a whole community bear no responsibility for it. We have defined the meaning of "genocide" now to expose rather than hide murder. We have begun to identify "war crimes." We are able to speak about "crimes against humanity" at last. And humanity finally includes women.

There was a time, too, when, and there are still many areas of the world today where, rape and sexual assault could occur with very little consequence to the offender, as indicated in previous pages. The default reaction in many cultures has been to blame the woman for "asking for" rape, to absolve and to exonerate the rapist, and to avoid all institutional responsibility for applying proper justice on grounds of noninterference in domestic matters. In Victorian England, a man could face transportation to "the colonies" for stealing a loaf of bread; he might, however, receive no more than a reprimand and ten days in jail for beating his wife, smashing her face into the floor, ripping open her stomach, and leaving her for dead.[32] It is only now that a new vocabulary has emerged giving us words like "femicide" to define gender crimes. Although it is still rare for a rapist to be called to account, the Universal Declaration of Human Rights and its accessory conventions have established grounds to protect women against such abuse.

We are facing a similar paradigm shift in relation to cultural crimes in the name of religion. There was a time when, and there are still many areas of the world today where, wrongs committed on the basis of belief were either justified "by" God or else blamed "on" Him. They were either sanctified as proof of Divine will or condemned as evidence of its nonexistence. In either case, we rarely raised the question of human accountability when confronted by the blood spilled and the victims sacrificed to religious prejudice and persecution. We have been quick to blame abstractions and ideology and slow to identify the actual perpetrators of these acts. And we have tended to blame the victims of religious fervor for their gullibility rather than those who took advantage of them. It has even been customary, until very recently, to exonerate the more private and perverse crimes committed in the name of religion. The ranks of orthodoxy tend to close when it comes to accountability.

But although this tendency has persisted and even hardened with the rise of extremism in recent decades, although we have heard much talk about the "violence of Islam," the "latter-day Crusades," and the "clash of civilizations"—all terms that blur the boundaries of human responsibility—perhaps times are changing. It has recently become fashionable for religious leaders to apologize. We are even beginning to speak about the criminality of "incitement," the consequences of "hate speech." Perhaps it will one day be possible to call to account those who commit cultural crimes in the name of God in courts that promote human rights.

The next chapter traces the history and explores the range of those rights in order to show the vital importance of including women within their pale. It also looks for new interpretations of those rights, as distinct from the wrongs committed when women are excluded from them.

5

RIGHTS AND WRONGS

*Men suppose that all is now as it should be in regard to the
marriage contract; and we are continually told that civilization
and Christianity have restored to the woman her just rights.
Meanwhile the wife is the actual bondservant of her husband:
no less so, as far as legal obligation goes, than slaves commonly
so called. She vows a lifelong obedience to him at the altar, and is
held to it all through her life by law. Casuists may say that the
obligation of obedience stops short of participation in crime,
but it certainly extends to everything else. She can do no act
whatever but by his permission, at least tacit. She can acquire no
property but for him: the instant it becomes hers, even if by
inheritance, it becomes ipso facto his. In this respect the wife's
position under the common law of England is worse than
that of slaves in the laws of many countries.*
—JOHN STUART MILL, *THE SUBJECTION OF WOMEN* (1869)

*Sixty years have passed since the founders of the United Nations
inscribed, on the first page of our Charter, the equal rights of men
and women. Since then, study after study has taught us that there
is no tool for development more effective than the empowerment
of women. No other policy is as likely to raise economic
productivity, or to reduce infant and maternal mortality. No other
policy is as sure to improve nutrition and promote health—
including the prevention of HIV/AIDS. No other policy is as*

*powerful in increasing the chances of education for the next
generation. And I would also venture that no policy is more
important in preventing conflict, or in achieving reconciliation
after a conflict has ended. But whatever the very real benefits
of investing in women, the most important fact remains:
Women themselves have the right to live in dignity, in freedom
from want and from fear.*
—KOFI ANNAN, 2005

EMPOWERING WOMEN

We invent new words all the time and new definitions of the old ones.
This preoccupation will surely continue for as long as the human
brain has a future and language remains our means of communicat-
ing. But since each age creates its own vocabulary, our new words
today have a distinctive tone and flavor that reflect the fundamental
concerns of the twenty-first century. Our words will bear witness to
the preoccupations of this age for generations to come.

The vocabulary of our times has been influenced, in part, by the
dramatic strides in technology and the expansion of internet communication. It has also arisen out of the ubiquity of finance speak,
media jargon, and the globalization of pop culture in contemporary
society. It has probably been spawned by the spread of fundamentalism and terror as well and is marked by the monstrous mutations
of warfare and fanaticism emerging in the world.

But there are also new terms, which have taken root in World English over the last decades, that are distinguished for their sense of
universal morality. They arise from the soil of our concern with
human rights. None of these terms, if they existed before, was ever
used in quite the same way in the early decades of the twentieth
century. All of them are marked by the specific challenges embed-

ded in the Universal Declaration of Human Rights established in the aftermath of World War II.

Sometimes, precisely because these words tread such sensitive ground, the new language of human rights is distinguished by a kind of linguistic anxiety. Whenever it is deployed by corporations and institutions, for example, it adopts a tone of bland noncommitment, the color of political correctness, in deference to diplomacy. But at other times, the vocabulary of human rights acquires a more dynamic, more virile tone, perhaps. One example of a new word associated with this vocabulary is the term "empowerment." It glows with a sense of urgency, of budding responsibility and the new energy released in civil society. But what does this word mean? What associations does it carry? How does it promote gender equality, and will the empowering of women necessarily lead to the establishment of equal rights for everyone?

The verb "to empower" is defined not only as the act of conferring power upon or making a person powerful; it also connotes the art of enabling, of self-actualization. It carries the implications of increased independence, of evolving self-esteem, of gaining access to civil rights and liberties through personal effort. Above all, it means giving individuals the confidence and awareness to gain that access, and to influence the society around them. In other words, empowering women means making it possible for them to improve social policy and legal standards for the betterment of their own lives and those of others in their communities.

No one can deny that women have been kept powerless in many societies and have been prevented from exercising control over their lives in widely divergent cultures. For centuries and in different countries and cultures, women have had no right to their own children or to control their own bodies. They have been denied an equal voice both within the home and in the community at large. They have been deprived of health care, employment, property ownership, of the right to marry or divorce at will, of the right to leave their homes or travel, or even engage in commerce. Why did this happen? What has caused women's "disempowerment"? And how has it led to their loss of autonomy in virtually every sphere of life?

The answer seems simple enough, in retrospect: It all came down to the right to vote. In other words, as long as women were not able to choose who governed them, they have not been able to change the laws that control them. And this has doubtless been a fundamental cause of their disempowerment the world over. The systematic disenfranchisement of women has effectively curtailed all their other rights. It is a fact of history, an almost universal phenomenon.

THE VOTE

The dramatic story of women's suffrage in Europe and America has often been told. The battle for gender equality since the nineteenth century has been tragic at times, replete with heroes and martyrs, and has just as often been denigrated as a farce by its critics and detractors. But achieving this right has been crucial in ensuring the confidence and encouraging the empowerment of women everywhere and in giving them the chance to participate in civic society and decision-making processes. The following brief account highlights only a few of the salient moments in this epic endeavor, illustrating the universality of this drive for political empowerment and its ultimate inevitability.

Although it has been rarely acknowledged, women in many communities, such as high-born abbesses in the Catholic Church in Europe, had full voting and decision-making rights in their councils long before the so-called modern period. During the seventeenth and eighteenth centuries, when democratic forms of government began, tentatively, to free themselves from autocratic rule in Europe, certain aristocratic women wielded considerable political influence through their literary salons. And spurred on by the growing liberalism of the nineteenth century and the incisive writings of such authors as Mary Wollstonecraft and John Stuart Mill, numerous attempts were made—some of which were rescinded later—to grant women the right to participate in local elections in countries as far-flung as New Zealand, Sweden, Corsica, and various American states and Canadian provinces. But these were isolated efforts.

For example, in the summer of 1848, several hundred people gathered in a small rural town in upstate New York to discuss, among other issues, the right of women to vote. The so-called Seneca Falls convention was the first ever collective demand for universal suffrage. By a strange coincidence, during that same summer of 1848, a lone woman entered a public gathering on the outskirts of a small rural village in northern Persia with her head unveiled, proclaiming an end to sharia law. A few years later, before she was put to death, this icon of female courage is reported to have said, "You may kill me, but you cannot stop the emancipation of women."[1] Since then, hundreds of women, in both the East and the West, have been at the heart of the so-called emancipation movement. Although the right to vote was denied to many well into the twentieth century, the demand for it has led to social, political, and religious upheavals all over the world, since the mid-nineteenth century.

In 1863, the Australian state of Victoria astonished its entire population by making the mistake of granting women the right to vote by accident, in the parliamentary elections that were due to take place next. As reported by the Parliament of Victoria, the legislators soon discovered the error and proceeded to rectify it the following year. After that, women in Victoria were again barred from voting, and another forty-five years had to go by before they were able to address the real error and regain their so-called mistaken right to vote, at last, in federal elections.

New Zealand, in 1893, become the first country to grant universal suffrage to women in reality rather than by mistake. Although various states allowed women to vote prior to 1920, it was not until after World War I that the nineteenth amendment to the US federal Constitution was passed, granting both sexes this right.

Suffrage for women was achieved in the Grand Duchy of Finland by 1906. The following year, Finland's voters elected nineteen women as the first female members of a representative parliament. But it took until 1920 for women to gain universal suffrage in the United States, almost seventy-five years after the Seneca Falls convention in 1848.

Certain countries in Western Europe took even longer to accept that women had the right to vote. Switzerland did not grant them this right at the federal level until 1971. Even then, women in the canton of Appenzell had to wait until 1991—another two decades—before being able to vote locally. Indeed, an impressive 95 percent of the voters in this canton voted *against* the extension of the franchise in a referendum in 1959, and when women were finally granted the right of suffrage, it was achieved only by order of the Swiss supreme court. In other words, the federal government finally forced the cantonal authorities to abide by what was already recognized, at that point, to be a universal human right, whether it conformed to cultural traditions or not.

Much has taken place, both in attitudes as well as in law, since women's suffrage was first debated on one side of the world and sharia law challenged on the other. In the course of the century and a half since the government of Victoria blundered into its enlightened historical error, all but five countries in the world have now granted the vote to women. Two of the most recent are Kuwait, which granted women's suffrage in 2005, and Saudi Arabia, which finally allowed women to vote in municipal elections in 2015.

The vote for women has been a critical step toward empowering them.

LEGAL RIGHTS IN THE TWENTIETH CENTURY

The vote, in and of itself, is no magic wand, however. It does not guarantee gender equality automatically, much less across the board. But it does create an environment more conducive to change. Although women's legal rights have evolved painfully slowly, once women are granted the vote, it becomes apparent that a wide range of other rights can be affirmed and enshrined in law. Once the right to vote is in place, women's priorities can be protected and their civic and economic participation in society ensured, which is why their legal status is so crucial to equality. Only as women have been gradually perceived as a significant portion of the electorate have their concerns finally been brought to the table to influence public discourse and resulting legislation.

With women wielding the vote, patterns of public expenditure in areas such as child welfare and public health began to change noticeably in country after country in the last century. For example, a study examining voting rights for women in the United States found that when states granted women the right to vote, legislators began reflecting the preferences of their expanded electorate, leading to an increase in public health spending of approximately 35 percent within a year. This in turn allowed for greater emphasis on public health campaigns at the local level. As a result of this new emphasis, better hygiene ensured a decrease of 8 to 15 percent[2] in infectious childhood diseases in the United States in the twentieth century and a marked decline in childhood mortality. The impact of the vote is slow, but it can also be deep, and widespread; it can influence the general level of health care in society as well as basic demographics.

Women's participation within government has also had a significant effect on spending patterns in society and consequently on living standards in any given country. In other words, the vote also influences where the money is going. One cross-country study from 2010, analyzing more than thirty-five years of government spending between 1970 and 2006, found that countries with quotas requiring a certain number of female legislators, as discussed previously, spent more on social services and on welfare than those that lacked such quotas.[3] A study from India, where one-third of village council head positions have now been reserved for women, found that wherever women became the head of the council, policy decisions better reflected their priorities and choices. For example, greater investments were made for the improvement of drinking water in those villages where women, who were generally the first to complain about such matters, had become council heads.[4] The vote controlled the budget.

But the greatest impact as well as challenge of women's suffrage has been felt within the family unit. Critics argued vociferously against giving women the vote throughout the nineteenth and twentieth centuries on the grounds that it would be "unnatural" and detrimental to the well-being of the family to do so. Despite wide divergences in class and culture, race and religion, these critics, generally men but sometimes women, too, have all shared a common fear of universal suffrage, a common desire to maintain the status quo. Over and over again, the concern has been that family values would be undermined if women were given more legal rights.

For example, a 1959 referendum in Switzerland to grant women the vote was soundly defeated (67 percent of the voters opposed), in no small measure through the strenuous efforts of many prominent women who founded the Federation of Swiss Women Against Women's Right to Vote that same year. Arguing that women's role in society should largely revolve around "Kinder, Kirche und Kuche" (children, church, and kitchen), Gertrud Haldimann, president of the federation, was passionate in her desire to protect Swiss women from the dangers of universal suffrage. She argued:

> *Look what female suffrage has done in other countries.*
> *Everywhere the so-called equality of women has resulted in*

*women losing their natural privileges and suffering through
having to compete with men on their own ground. A
women's place is in the home, not in the political arena. To
make political decisions, you must read newspapers, and a
woman who does her housework and looks after her
children has no time to read newspapers.*[5]

Over and over again, critics of the franchise, whether male or female, have used the old "plough" logic, maintaining that the woman's
place is at home because the outside world is full of corruption. If
women are kept out of the public sphere, they insist, it is to protect
their physical vulnerability, to shield their moral weakness, and to preserve them from the nefarious influence of materialism. If they are
denied or dissuaded from taking employment, it is for the sake of
their reputation and their health. And whenever, in response to such
attitudes over the last 150 years, women have sought redress for their
rights, these same critics, falling back on patriarchal values, have all
accused them of usurping their husbands' authority, taking away their
jobs, and undermining family unity. In the minds of many, women's
marital and maternal obligations are far more important than their
legal rights.

However, the irony is that women's presence in the public sphere
ensures their safety at home. Whenever a woman's employment
possibilities are unequal, whenever she is confined within the walls
of her home or constrained to certain hours of work in limited sectors, it is not only the woman who suffers. The consequences of
such inequalities are often accompanied by patterns of marital disaffection and authoritarianism between couples; they lead to a
higher prevalence of violence against dependent women, which spills
over from the domestic sphere to the community at large. A growing awareness of a woman's right to empowerment and the protection of her rights in society, therefore, actually ensure her rights in
the family unit.

THE LAWS

If arguments against the vote have been most shrill in the domestic sphere, it may be because legal jurisdictions, in both the East and the West, have, until relatively recently, vested authority squarely in the husband's hands.

In the East, differing legal systems have imposed similar constraints on women, whether they derive from the Confucian tradition, from sharia law as practiced in certain Islamic countries, or to a lesser degree stemming from Hindu jurisprudence. In the West, too, the Code Napoléon as well as the influence of English common law were based on similar marital power restrictions that kept women's rights strictly within their husbands' sphere of control. In other words, women's rights in relation to inheritance and marital dues, control over property and assets, or with regard to their children and their autonomy in the labor force have been limited everywhere for centuries. There has traditionally been little difference, in practice, between male authority over women's legal rights under sharia law, Asian cultural laws, or the doctrine of coverture, a legal doctrine originating in English common law according to which a woman's legal rights and obligations upon marriage were subsumed by those of her husband. Coverture arises from the legal fiction that a husband and wife are one person.

The system of coverture persisted throughout continental Europe, in Latin America, and in West Africa until the latter half of the twentieth century. In Cameroon, Haiti, Republic of the Congo, and other countries, women still do not have the same rights as men when it comes to property ownership or use of land. And in Niger and the Democratic Republic of the Congo, a married woman does not yet have the right to open a bank account without her husband's permission. When it comes to sharia law, a husband has no legal control over his wife's inheritance, and she is technically free to spend it as she wishes; but female inheritance shares are smaller than those of males. Furthermore, sharia law gives a man power over his wife's mobility; he controls her freedom to work, her right to divorce, and her parental rights. Although sharia was replaced by civil and common law practices in Egypt, Jordan, and Palestine in the early decades of the twentieth century, it has been reinstated since then in Iran, in parts of Iraq, and in sub-Saharan Africa, and it has been retained in Saudi Arabia and Afghanistan.

All vestiges of the marital power doctrine as well as sharia and traditional Asian law ensure that husbands and fathers hold more decision-making authority and that wives and children have less legal autonomy. In countries where the civil law followed the Code Napoléon, a wife had no autonomy at all over her employment; her husband could prohibit her from working. He could even prevent her from having a bank account. As a result, he could deny her the benefits of savings, or the acquisition of credit, or make other financial decisions affecting her. She was dependent on him for everything. Under English common law, a similar legal system held sway until the middle of the nineteenth century, where the doctrine of coverture had previously dominated. The same is true in nations where sharia is imposed today; as under the civil and common law systems in the past, the husband's marital authority restricts his wife's legal rights; a wife has limited authority to make decisions; her testimony in court carries only half the weight of a man's; she is required to have the consent of her husband for divorce and may be subjected to the humiliations of polygamy and domestic violence without recourse to legal protection.

By contrast, unmarried women or widows in the United Kingdom, Australia, and the United States, as well as those under the Code Napoléon, retained an individual legal identity. This was due to their status as femes soles under the doctrine of coverture, which allowed those who were unmarried to make legal decisions for themselves. This anomaly, however, was gradually rectified in the late nineteenth and early twentieth centuries. As family dynamics shifted, married women in these countries began to be given the same legal status as single ones. By the beginning of the twentieth century, a series of Married Women's Property Acts were passed that gradually rendered the old restrictions obsolete and paved the way for greater equality.

These acts, applicable across common law jurisdictions, meant that by the early 1900s, many women in the West were finally making decisions on their own, with rights that corresponded to their responsibilities. In most American states, for example, by the turn of the twentieth century, legislation had already been reformed allowing married women to own and administer property as well as conduct legal transactions. Furthermore, state census data from 1850 to 1920 show that legal reforms which increased women's economic rights resulted in more girls attending school, thereby expanding human capital.[6] Half a century later in 1961 in Singapore, where common law was still in place, old imbalances were redressed when Article 51 of the Women's Charter gave married women rights as well as responsibilities in areas where only single women had enjoyed them before.[7]

In many civil law jurisdictions in Europe and Latin America, however, women would be granted similar legal decision-making powers only in the latter half of the twentieth century. In the countries of the Far East as well, the struggle to ensure women's equal access to work took many decades and is still ongoing. And as Taj Hashmi of Simon Fraser University (2005) writes, in certain countries in the Middle East and North Africa governed by sharia law, women's fundamental rights to inheritance, to marital autonomy, to education, and even to mobility are still denied at the time of writing.

There are, however, some exceptions to the rule. A married women does retain financial autonomy under sharia, leaving her husband with all legal responsibility to support the family. Although this autonomy is not always implemented, a woman is also legally free to do what she wishes with any income she earns or any property she has. This right too, however, is often abused, since the acquisition of such property and income depend on her husband's permission. Many freethinking Muslims, such as Hashmi (2005), deplore the imposition of this "absurd, outdated un-Islamic code" but confirm that "abysmal ignorance about religion, history and culture of the people concerned are as counter-productive as the close-minded mullahs in this regard." Sharia law, like coverture, demands internal change.

Despite the differences in laws and the differing pace of change, one pattern is common in both East and West as far as women are concerned. Wherever legal restrictions have been lifted and new laws have abolished gender discrimination, women's earning potential has grown, their entrepreneurship has increased,[8] and their employment ratios show positive results relative to those of men. In other words, the granting of legal rights to women has greatly enhanced their equality.

RESTRICTIVE LEGISLATION

In hardly any country in the world today, however, do women have complete legal protection. At the time of writing, restrictions still abound and at least one legal constraint on women can be found in 90 percent of all economies covered by the Women, Business and the Law dataset, differentiating their rights from those that men enjoy. And whatever that restrictive legislation might be, it is negatively correlated to female labor force participation. In other words, wherever there are more gender differentiations in the law, women are less likely to work outside the home.

Some of these legal differences are more directly linked to women's employment than others. For instance, husbands can object to their wives getting jobs in fifteen countries of the world, and have the legal right to prevent them from accepting paid employment in these countries. In other countries, although a woman may be able to work without her husband's consent, she is prohibited by law from working in certain industries. Such restrictive legislation exists in up to seventy-nine economies, according to the WBL dataset, many of which can be found in the Middle East and North Africa, in sub-Saharan Africa, and in Eastern Europe and Central Asia. In all these countries, the participation of women in the labor force is severely curtailed.

Other types of differences exist where the link to women's participation in the workforce may be less obvious. For instance, legal differences in obtaining a national identity card may at first seem unrelated to a woman's ability to get a job. But without a national identity card, it can be close to impossible in some countries to work in the formal sector. In other examples, such as owning property, or inheritance laws, or even a woman's right to open a bank account without her husband's permission, legal differences can play a significant role in creating and perpetuating inequality in the labor force. Such differences invariably contribute to lower access to assets by women vis-à-vis men; they put women at a disadvantage once again when it comes to entering the labor market.

Although global data comparing the ownership of physical capital by men and women are sparse at this time, studies do show gaps at the local and regional levels,[9] revealing asset restrictions. In general, women own smaller shares of physical capital than men and are less likely to own or inherit estate property. Furthermore, in certain cultures, women or girls may even start off with negative assets. In India, for example, where girls are supposed to bring a dowry to their marriage, women not only have more limited access to assets but actually start off life as a liability to their parents, compared to their brothers.

Interestingly enough, this pattern can be reversed in countries where sharia law is in place and the opposite definitions of a dowry exist. In these circumstances, it is the groom who has to provide the bride with a certain amount of money, in the form of goods or property, at the time of marriage. There is no stipulated limit on this sum, called *mahr*, and its payment, which is written into the marriage contract under sharia law, can be disbursed fully or deferred in part. But in all cases, it remains the separate property of the woman, for her personal use alone; it cannot be appropriated by her family or any third party and, as such, it permits her, in theory at least, to enter married life with positive rather than negative assets. Originally intended as a deterrent to divorce, it can, however, like all laws, be abused. If her husband will agree to a divorce only on condition that some or all of the *mahr* is repaid, a woman's choices can be seriously limited. When set beside other restrictions on a wife's self-sufficiency under sharia law, her autonomy of capital based on the principle of *mahr* might be described as something of a fiction in actual practice.

CHANGING THE LAWS

So where does all this take us? What hope is there for change? Is it feasible to imagine that women can finally be empowered through the lifting of restrictive legislation?

Although the legislative picture that emerges from the WBL dataset is by and large disturbing, and shows how far the law is still being used to impose rather than lift restrictions on women's participation in the labor force, the 2014 report nevertheless contained encouraging news. Using seventeen indicators covering areas such as women's access to institutions and property, the World Bank was able to compare changes in the law in a total of some 100 countries over the past half century, between 1960 and 2010. And these changes proved to be revealing.

Although sub-Saharan Africa had the most restrictions in 1960, it had implemented the highest number of reforms by 2010. In 1960, for instance, gender inequality was glaring in Benin: Sons and daughters had unequal inheritance rights, with those of females inferior to those of males; husbands were the unchallenged heads of households, and a woman needed her husband's permission to get a job, open a bank account, sign a contract, and initiate any kind of legal proceeding. The constitution, moreover, contained no nondiscrimination clause with gender as a protected category. By

2010, most of these restrictions had been eliminated, an encouraging sign.

In Ethiopia, too, Hallward-Driemeier and Hasan (2012) found that after a reform in family law which established more equal property rights between spouses, an increase in female labor force participation actually took place in more productive sectors of the economy. This is linked in part to women's increased ability to use property as collateral to access the financial system to obtain credit. Although because of the cross-country nature of the data, a causal link is difficult to establish, there does appear to be a link between legal differentiations of gender and female labor force participation, especially in relation to property rights.

The 2014 *WBL* report also reveals significant reforms in Latin America, including evolution in the law in Argentina, Bolivia, Brazil, Colombia, Peru, and Paraguay. In Brazil, for instance, the husband used to be considered the legal head of the household with the sole right to represent the family, choose their domicile, and administer marital assets, including any separate effects owned by his wife. This exclusivity of control remained in force until the constitutional reforms of 1988, and cross-country studies demonstrated that these restrictions radically lowered participation rates of women in the workforce. A recent International Monetary Fund study, moreover, shows that in many cases, the gender gaps caused by such restrictions can be significant enough to negatively impact gross domestic product. The same study found that within five years of women being granted legal equality, female participation in the labor force increased by 5 percentage points in 50 percent of countries.[10]

Interestingly, the Central and Eastern European and Central Asian region had very few legal restrictions on women's control of their assets in 1960, and most of these had largely been eliminated by 2010. The high-income OECD countries had more restrictions, but they were also removed, at least from the books, during this fifty-year period. Sometimes, as in Brazil, the changes were implemented surprisingly late, as also occurred in certain European countries.[11] Farther east, in Indonesia, the Dutch Civil Code of 1874 was not replaced until 1974, when the Law on Marriage finally permitted a married woman to open a bank account without the authorization of her husband. It had taken an entire century to achieve, but this change was a landmark.

The regions of the world with the least progress over the last fifty years are to be found in the Middle East and North Africa, where many countries have had setbacks during this period. These setbacks are directly linked to the enforcement of sharia law. For instance, in Iran in 1975, the Family Protection Law established equal rights to work for both spouses, but in 1979, under the Islamic regime, this law was reversed, giving husbands the right to prohibit their wives from joining the workforce. An amendment to the constitution in Egypt in 2007 included for the first time a clause guaranteeing gender equality. This was promptly eliminated from the constitution in 2012, an early casualty of the backlash following the aftermath of the Arab Spring. However, in the 2014 constitution, the clause on gender equality was restored.

It looks as if we are fated to move one step forward in some cases, only to take two steps back. But despite the evidence of setbacks and the ricocheting back-and-forth of laws affecting women over the decades, progress has been made in certain countries in lifting the legislation impeding their economic freedom. More than half of the restrictions on women's legal capacity and property rights have actually been removed during the past fifty years. This is a very encouraging trend, suggesting that change is not only possible but not restricted to certain parts of the planet either. Change with regard to gender equality is both inevitable and universal.

CHANGES IN EUROPE

It is often assumed that the "West" is far ahead of the rest of the world when it comes to national laws that reflect international standards of human rights. The current status of women in countries under sharia law is frequently contrasted to that of those in the West. It is referred to in a consistently minor key and cast in a negative light with implications of cultural judgmentalism. But, as has been shown in the previous pages, the West has nothing to be proud of; both civil and common law practice in Europe and many of its colonies, including the Americas, curtailed women's legal rights for centuries. In an attempt to set the record straight, the following summary highlights how long it has taken and how hard it has been, over the past fifty years, to achieve even a modicum of equality in the West and how relatively recent the legal instruments are that have been put in place to abolish gender discrimination in certain European countries.

In Germany, the Equal Rights Act became law for the first time in 1957, enacting a reform that had a direct bearing on women's empowerment.[12] The new law no longer included the head-of-household designation. It not only affected women's chances of employment, but also removed a husband's right to manage his wife's separate income and property. Although a married woman in Germany was able to enter into employment without her husband's consent prior to 1957, the Equal Rights Act confirmed that he had to first give her notice, before insisting on the termination of his wife's work contract, if he believed it interfered with her household and maternal duties. A wife's matrimonial and familial obligations were still placed above her economic and professional interests, stipulating that the latter were permissible only if compatible with the former, but the difference now was that the wife had the right to terminate her contract herself.

Male marital authority and power were finally abolished in Belgium in 1958, when a wife was at last granted the right to work without her husband's permission. Even after this date, however, the effects of male marital power lingered regarding parental rights and property. It was not until 1965 that fathers were no longer automatic heads of the household, and the law stipulated that parents would exercise parental authority together. In 1976, a provision stating that a wife had to obey her husband was finally repealed, and from that date on in Belgium, married women were allowed to open bank accounts for the first time without permission.[13]

In 1965, French husbands finally had to relinquish their administrative authority in the family. According to the detailed report of the Assemblée Nationale, prior to this, married women could have an independent profession only if their husbands did not oppose it. They could open bank accounts without their spouse's notification only if they had separate assets and access to independently earned money. But by 1970, French law finally abolished the designation of the husband as *chef de famille*. Spouses were allowed to jointly determine the moral and material direction of the family from that time on. Even so, it was not until 1985 that equality in property administration between spouses was finally achieved in France.[14]

In Austria, it took until 1975 for the vestiges of marital power to be finally shaken. Prior to this time, the husband was the head of the household and could determine where the family lived. The civil code was even interpreted to mean that fathers could determine their children's professions. But the reforms of the 1970s finally placed spouses on an equal footing. With responsibilities defined in gender-neutral terms, husbands could no longer prohibit their wives from working, and the family residence and name could be jointly held and decided on the basis of mutual consent.[15]

Before 1984, under the Swiss civil code, married women were also denied the right to be heads of household or determine the place of marital residence. Women required the express or tacit consent of their husbands in order to pursue a profession or occupation. In the event that the husband refused consent, a Swiss judge could intervene only if the wife proved that her occupation contributed to the family union.[16] The same civil code stated that the husband also controlled jointly held marital property, and the wife retained ownership only if she had brought the property into the marriage. Even then, the administration of her property still remained in her husband's hands. The civil code reform of 1984 removed these anomalies in marital and family relations, allowing for equality in property rights and granting spouses mutual rights and responsibilities to manage family affairs.

As can be seen from these examples, progress in granting women their legal rights has been slow, even in Europe. Although universal suffrage was perceived in revolutionary terms in the early decades of the twentieth century, legal changes affecting household dynamics are an evolutionary process. They are organic in nature, and, in spite of changes on paper, vestiges of marital power remain firmly in place even now. It has taken at least half a century for the laws in many European countries to reflect the implications of universal suffrage. The interesting thing is that tensions within the family unit may indeed be heightened by the vote, but ironically enough, these tensions can be resolved only when the external legal environment begins to influence and protect women's rights in the family. As in the case of the Swiss canton of Appenzell, changes at the national and local level can occur only when there is a growing awareness of the universal nature of human rights.

It is this growing awareness that will be addressed next, in a brief overview of one of the most important charters of our times: the Universal Declaration of Human Rights.

HUMAN RIGHTS: EQUALITY AND NONDISCRIMINATION

The Universal Declaration of Human Rights, adopted in 1948 by the General Assembly of the United Nations, was the first global statement about the fundamental rights and freedoms of all human beings, regardless of race, culture, age, or gender. Forged in the fires of World War II and welded within the grim furnace of its terrible aftermath, the Declaration is a unique document, listing these rights and freedoms for the first time in human history.[17] Its thirty Articles and the accompanying covenants articulate the international scope of the bill[18] and emphasize the central role of equality and nondiscrimination at every level of human society.

The Declaration proclaims that the bedrock of freedom, justice, and peace in the world is the "recognition of the inherent dignity and of the equal and inalienable rights of all members of the human family." Article 1 of the document proceeds to state that all human beings are "born free and equal in dignity and rights." Articles 2 and 7 take this even further by articulating the specific legal protections on nondiscrimination and equality and establishing these as the underlying bedrock and foundation of international human rights throughout the world.

Subsequent legal instruments related to global issues have since elaborated on the rights and detailed the freedoms listed in the Declaration. All ensuing major human rights treaties promulgated by the international community now rest on its fundamental commitments and follow its model. Indeed, as the UN Human Rights Committee has emphasized, the ideal of "non-discrimination, together with equality before the law and equal protection of the law without any discrimination, constitute a basic and general principle relating to the protection of human rights."[19] The language of the Declaration has become embedded in contemporary thought, and its terminology has become common parlance among many peoples.

The European Convention on Human Rights (drafted in 1950 by the then newly formed Council of Europe and entering into force in 1953) is one of the regional treaties that extended the range and application of the Declaration of Human Rights across forty-seven member states. Another example is the American Convention on Human Rights, also known as the Pact of San José. This Convention, which by 2013 had been adopted by some thirty-five Member States, represents yet another international human rights instrument protecting women. It was adopted in 1969 and came into force in 1978. Both of these Conventions contain nondiscrimination clauses.[20]

Article 3 of the African Charter also expressly states that "every individual shall be equal before the law" and "shall be entitled to equal protection of the law."[21] Under Article 18(3) of this same charter, States parties also undertook to ensure "the elimination of every discrimination against women." It is interesting to note that Article 3(c) of the Arab Charter of Human Rights also engages each State party to take all the requisite measures to guarantee equal opportunities and effective equality between men and women in the enjoyment of all the rights set out in the Charter. The International Labour Organization has also sponsored a number of conventions dealing with nondiscrimination and equality in the workplace, all of which uphold the core human rights articulated by the UN Charter.[22] In addition, other Articles of the Charter also make it clear that human rights protection is a fundamental part of the UN's mission, that is, to "promote and encourage respect for human rights and fundamental freedoms for all without distinction as to race, sex, language or religion." Indeed, since its adoption in 1948, the Universal Declaration of Human Rights has spawned many similar initiatives, such as conventions and other supporting instruments, designed to broaden the scope of our understanding of equality and nondiscrimination in all domains and on a global scale.

Beyond such overall commitments to equality and nondiscrimination, which cut across a wide range of legal instruments, the international community has specifically emphasized its support for gender equality. The most significant of these commitments to nondiscrimination for women is the Convention on the Elimination of All Forms of Discrimination Against Women (CEDAW), an international treaty adopted in 1979 by the United Nations General Assembly and now ratified by 189 states, except the United States, Palau, the Holy See, Iran, Somalia, Sudan, and Tonga.

CEDAW: THE INTERNATIONAL BILL OF RIGHTS FOR WOMEN

Entrenched attitudes toward women have not altered for thousands of years, and yet, in the past century, we have seen radical changes taking place regarding their rights and role in society. In fact, any objective appraisal of the impact of the Universal Declaration surely points to the relative speed with which it has been instrumental in raising the collective consciousness regarding the plight of women. And one of the ways in which this change has been implemented has been through what has been called an international bill of rights for women. Even though it took more than thirty years after the adoption of the Universal Declaration of Human Rights for CEDAW to come into being, and even though it may take many decades more before its implications can be fully realized, the wheels were set in motion, and the legal basis for the establishment of women's rights had been put in place by the mid-twentieth century, after literally millennia of gender oppression.

The UN General Assembly adopted CEDAW in 1979, and it went into effect in 1981, entering into force in just two years, after being ratified by twenty countries. Few major human rights treaties have taken so little time to become law. The widespread support of CEDAW demonstrates that there is finally a global consensus on equality and the existence of near-universal acceptance of it as an international norm. This Convention now serves as the most comprehensive instrument protecting women's rights the world over.

CEDAW defines the right of women to be free from discrimination and prohibits all forms of gender-based constraints that limit their full equality. It sets out the principles to protect this right and establishes a process for action to end direct and indirect gender-based discrimination that hinders equality between men and women. The protection provided by CEDAW against discrimination, moreover, is specifically limited to and tailored for the legal requirements of women's rights. Article 1(1) refers to only one ground for discrimination, namely sex discrimination, but also explicitly prohibits discrimination on the grounds of marital status. This prohibition is freestanding and therefore applies to rights and freedoms "in any other field," covering both direct and indirect discrimination against women.[23]

According to the Convention, equality and nondiscrimination are "cross-cutting" human rights. That is, rather than aiming to fulfill one single set of specific human rights, these are intended to ensure that women can enjoy *all* substantive rights on an equal basis with men. The Convention does this by ensuring equal opportunities for women in both the public and the private sphere and by setting out particular obligations for states parties with regard to education, health, marriage, and family life. It also seeks to eliminate all traditional practices which discriminate against women nationally, regionally, and even rurally, and it aims to preserve and enhance the political, economic, and cultural life of women everywhere. In other words, it is intended to protect women at every level of social interaction, both private and public.

Since coming into force in 1981, CEDAW has been signed to date by 189 states. But despite the remarkable international acceptance of the Convention, there are still a number of significant stumbling blocks to its full acceptance. All legal instruments are worth less than the paper they are written on if they are not implemented, and many obstacles relating to the thorny issue of gender equality still hinder the application of CEDAW. In the following pages, we analyze some of these impediments more closely and address several issues that have dogged the implementation of the Convention during the thirty years since it was first adopted. We also examine some of the checks and balances put into place to enforce its powers and consider how stumbling blocks might gradually turn into stepping-stones.

STUMBLING BLOCKS

As mentioned earlier, despite the international respect in which CEDAW is held, several countries have still not ratified, and therefore have not implemented, the Convention. These include Iran, Sudan, South Sudan, Somalia, Palau, Tonga, and, surprisingly, the United States. Although the United States and Palau signed the treaty in 1980 and 2011, respectively, neither country has as yet put the terms of the Convention into effect. Meanwhile other nations from all over the world have done so, including some as wide-ranging in their human rights records as North Korea, Canada, and South Africa. But despite a general recognition of the intrinsic importance of gender equality, which the Convention symbolizes, certain specific terms in it are still subject to a variety of "reservations." These include religious as well as political ideologies and legal standards as well as issues perceived as being related to "national security" or "cultural autonomy." All such objections and reservations constitute multiple stumbling blocks to the ratification and implementation of CEDAW.

Even after a state signs or ratifies an international convention, it can, under the UN Charter of Human Rights, limit its obligations under the terms of the treaty on the grounds of such reservations. In the case of CEDAW, however, such reservations, according to Article 28, cannot be incompatible with the object and purpose of the Convention itself. Even so, from the time that it was established, over fifty countries of the 189 that signed CEDAW have entered into the agreement with specific reservations concerning some of its applications. Of these, thirteen countries have since removed their reservations entirely and a further thirty have revised them in part. But others still limit their obligations, thereby preventing the application of CEDAW internationally.

These reservations vary greatly and have, moreover, changed over time. Thus, certain countries may have ratified CEDAW *internationally* while excluding the *domestic* applicability of specific articles. Jordan, which signed CEDAW in 1980 and ratified it in 1992, still maintains reservations regarding the conveyance of nationality to women, as well as marital custody, maintenance, and marital status. Despite these sticking points, Jordan recently withdrew one reservation, in 2009, which related to women's freedom of movement and residence.[24]

The Tunisian reservations initially concerned treaty requirements providing equality to women in family matters. These included women's right of guardianship over their children and their ability to confer their nationality to them. They also concerned women's personal rights with regard to family name and occupation as well as rights and responsibilities in marriage, divorce, and the ownership of property, to all of which CEDAW provides for full equality. In September 2011, however, Tunisia became one of the first countries in the Middle East and North Africa region to lift each of these key reservations to the Convention.[25]

Other countries have entered less specific reservations to the treaty. For example, UN Women reports that the reservation by Saudi Arabia insists that "in case of contradiction between any term of the Convention and the norms of Islamic law, the Kingdom is not under obligation to observe the contradictory terms of the Convention." This type of reservation, of course, highlights areas of potential intransigence that no amount of international negotiation can resolve. Given these limitations, as well as the number of nations still withholding full commitment to CEDAW on the basis of various cultural, religious, and political reservations, including sharia law, the challenge for the UN has been to find ways to at least facilitate the implementation of laws where the Convention has already been fully accepted and ratified.

STEPPING-STONES

Given all these challenges, it became necessary for the UN General Assembly to take steps to address the slow response and encourage a more rapid implementation of CEDAW. As a result, in 1999, it adopted an optional protocol to CEDAW and called on all states parties to the Convention to become party to the new instrument as soon as possible. By ratifying the optional protocol, a state recognizes that the Committee on the Elimination of Discrimination Against Women—the body that monitors states parties' compliance with the Convention—has the competence to receive and consider complaints from individuals or groups within its jurisdiction. Thus, the optional protocol is at least a step in the direction of implementation. It can monitor whether terms of the Convention are actually reflected in and applied by the internal code of laws in signatory countries. It can set forth a limited enforcement of international laws in those countries. It can examine a particular state's actual compliance with CEDAW and also undertake an inquiry into systematic violations, wherever women's rights have been guaranteed by a signatory country. In other words, the CEDAW Committee has been granted a measure of international oversight to ensure interim measures to safeguard the rights of women.

As one might expect, however, to date, not many cases by either individuals or groups have been brought forward for the Committee's consideration, an indication of the continuing international resistance to the fundamental principles of gender equality. Not only is the protocol optional, but it is restricted in its actions as an enforcement instrument. Moreover, it depends for its effectiveness on individuals and groups knowing their rights and engaging in a laborious bureaucratic process, which first includes exhausting all other remedies before submitting any complaints. The optional protocol entered into force in 2000, after ratification by ten countries. By the end of 2017, eighty States had become its signatories. But while this looks like a good number, there are formidable challenges ahead. UN Women (2017b) reports that of the eleven cases submitted to the Committee so far, six have been dismissed because the complainant was deemed not to have exhausted all domestic remedies beforehand. As a result, the Committee has only ruled on five cases in more than fifteen years.

In spite of these limitations and impediments to implementation, CEDAW has become a useful educational tool. It has raised social awareness in general and delivered vital information to women in particular regarding their rights. It has also ensured that the debate regarding gender equality and nondiscrimination does not take place behind the closed doors of international institutions but is heard at every level of civil society wherever the Convention has been ratified. And it has not only drawn worldwide attention to CEDAW but has also highlighted the responsibilities of governments in States that are its signatories. Even its failures of implementation have been useful.

Article 18 of CEDAW is an example of the incremental steps by which progress is made. This Article requires all states parties to file periodic reports proving compliance with the Convention. The review process has been standardized in recent years, and the reports, submitted to and examined by the Committee on the Elimination of Discrimination Against Women,[26] have provided civil society organizations at both national and international levels with vital statistics regarding women's rights and have become the means for holding their governments to account. They also provide organizations with material for their own parallel reports. As a result, an increase in civil society involvement has drawn attention to the inconsistencies between the provisions of the treaty and domestic legislation in specific countries.[27] Global events, such as the Nairobi Third World Conference on Women in 1985 and the Beijing Fourth World Conference on Women a decade later, have also drawn international attention to CEDAW. This increasing awareness has led, in turn, to the ratification of the treaty by more States.

Indeed, just as in the Swiss case mentioned earlier, it is as if a global gold standard for human rights needs to be established before women's rights can be respected at the local level.

FROM GLOBAL TO LOCAL

A 2013 study by Hallward-Driemeier, Hasan, and Rusu has demonstrated the dramatic impact that an international treaty can have at the national and local levels. The authors show how the rate of legal reform, in areas such as women's property rights and legal capacity, can almost double in the first five years after CEDAW is ratified by any given country. When this is compared to the slow rate of change during the fifteen years prior to ratification, we can perhaps be more optimistic about how international human rights instruments can influence national legislation that subsequently changes attitudes and practice in civil society. Despite the fact that the Middle East and North Africa as well as South Asia have produced the fewest reforms over this period, we can begin to see direct, reciprocal interrelationships between the global and local levels of transformation in society.

Examples of this fascinating phenomenon, drawn from several countries in Africa, Asia, and the Far East, will illustrate the long-term implications of CEDAW in the pages that follow. They show how human rights, established and ratified at a global level, can gradually filter down to the national, local, and even domestic spheres.

AFRICA

South Africa became a signatory of CEDAW in 1993. One year later, South Africa's Women's National Coalition adopted the "Women's Charter for Effective Equality" and presented it to the political parties that were negotiating an end to apartheid at that time. The Charter represented the outcome of extensive participatory research and widespread consultation on the demands and requirements of women. In 1995, one year after the dramatic change of government, South Africa ratified CEDAW. In 1998, the provisions of the 1927 Black Administration Act were superseded by a much-reformed Recognition of Customary Marriages Act, which established the legal environment to support equality between husbands and wives. Under the earlier provisions of the Black Administration Act,[28] a woman living with her husband had been considered a legal minor with her husband as her guardian. The Recognition of Customary Marriages Act changed her status by providing that "a wife in a customary marriage has, on the basis of equality with her husband and subject to the matrimonial property system . . . full status and capacity." This new status gave wives the right to acquire and dispose of assets as well as the right to enter into and litigate contracts. Furthermore, a woman was granted all powers and rights to customary law by these means. The leap from 1927 to 1998 was huge for the women of South Africa.

In *Ethiopia*, the Family Code, in place since 1960, was finally revised in the year 2000. The reform in these laws was of direct economic benefit to women, for it annulled a husband's right to deny his wife permission to work and required the consent of both spouses, not only that of the husband, in the administration of marital property. Although it was first introduced in three regions and two charter cities only, the reform has now been implemented throughout Ethiopia. Two nationally representative surveys, one before the reform took place and the other five years later, allowed researchers to estimate its impact. Wherever the reform had been implemented, women's labor force participation and work outside the home increased. Women were also more likely to work full-time and in higher-skilled jobs as a result.[29] This is a clear example of the importance of establishing legal instruments to promote gender equality.

FAR EAST

South Korea affords another example of change through long and sustained efforts by women's groups to reform the law. In a revealing 2006 paper about the politics of family law in contemporary Korea, author Ki-Young Shin discusses why it took so long to abolish the gender hierarchy of Korea's family law and what made the so-called house head system so entrenched. The decision to eliminate discrimination toward women in South Korea first began in 1974, when sixty-two women's groups, led by the Korean YWCA and the Legal Aid Center for Family Law, came together and organized the Pan-Women's Group for the Revision of Family Law. The Pan-Women's Group instituted a widespread lobbying campaign at that time as well as a thorough media outreach strategy through TV, radio, and print. Its primary aim was to raise awareness of the need to reform the *Ho-jue jae-do*, or "house head" system. Shin describes the Korean cultural tradition in which the family was conceived as a collective with the husband at its center. The leadership of this collective household passed down through the male line, recording all future *male* descendants as heads of their own households in a family register. According to the system, a woman who married into a family would be automatically removed from her birth family's register and recorded in that of her husband. The sixty-two women's groups under the Pan-Women's Group realized that unless this fundamental concept of male-dominated family registers could be changed, discriminatory laws against women would persist in Korean society.

According to Shin, the first reform campaign encountered strong opposition from conservative elements, who felt that the family law was the embodiment of Confucian principles and the cornerstone of traditional Korean family structures. In 1977, the campaign by the Pan-Women's Group succeeded in producing a few amendments to the family law, but they had no impact on the family head system. As civil society slowly gained strength, progress was made toward greater democratization in South Korea. After South Korea finally ratified CEDAW in 1994, the increased process of democratization toward the end of the decade led to further reform of the family law, giving women more rights within the family structure and overturning the earlier inheritance provision that provided for married daughters to receive, under certain circumstances, only a one-fourth share of what their brothers inherited.[30] But the "house head" system remained doggedly in place.

Finally, in 2005, a decade after South Korea had become a signatory of CEDAW and after three unsuccessful attempts to change the "house head" system, the Constitutional Court of South Korea declared unconstitutional several provisions of the Civil Code that were not compatible with equality, overturning the provisions which held that only men could assume the position of legal head of household. This was an unprecedented, landmark victory. In its statement, the Court declared that "the house head system is discrimination based on stereotypes concerning sexual roles. This system, without justifiable grounds, discriminates [between] men and women in determining succession order to house head, forming marital relations, and forming relations with children."[31] The Court further stated: "The house head system one-sidedly prescribes a system deeply rooted in the ideal of maintaining and expanding a family centered on male lineage regardless of the intention or welfare of the people concerned." After centuries of discrimination against women in South Korea and decades of effort by the Pan-Women's Group, the *Ho-jue jae-do* system was finally recognized in the Constitution as being incompatible with its provisions on gender equality in marriage and family life.[32]

Shin cites a series of other cases in which the Constitutional Court in South Korea struck down other legal provisions that were seen to be discriminatory and to violate the principles of gender equality. For example, the Court decided that children were no longer required to bear their father's family name. It also stated that women were entitled to equal rights with men regarding membership in the patrilineal clan (*jongjoong*). It granted women not only inheritance and ownership rights over clan land but also the ensuing clan responsibilities entailed in its membership.[33] Following these significant decisions, Korea passed the Family Register Act in 2007, according to which the concept of a collective family registration under a male head was abolished entirely, allowing each family member to register individually and receive his or her own record book. These Court decisions, based on the principles of equality enshrined in CEDAW, not only represented an interesting trend but served to equalize women's status within the structures of marriage and family.

South Korea has shown real leadership in reforming the country's legislation in these areas. It has succeeded in eliminating gender bias in labor and employment law as well as in marriage and the institution of the family. According to Chung Bong-Hyup, director general of the Ministry of Gender Equality, "Our strategy has been to change the laws and institutions first so the rest of the society can catch up in changing attitudes and culture in favor of gender equality."[34]

Japan offers us another classic example of how international norms of human rights can influence national legal developments and also how long and how slow this process can be. By following the evolution of the Equal Employment Opportunity Law (EEOL) in Japan and tracking its slow implementation in the workplace, we can identify some of the hurdles that women have had to overcome, long after legislation has been put in place that supposedly was conducive to their empowerment and the exercise of their equal rights.

The Japanese government signed CEDAW in 1980, at the Second World Conference on Women, and ratified it in 1985. Article 2 of CEDAW states that parties must "pursue by all appropriate means and without delay a policy of eliminating discrimination against women" and defines discrimination as

any distinction, exclusion or restriction made on the basis of sex which has the effect or purpose of impairing or

nullifying the recognition, enjoyment or exercise by women,
irrespective of their marital status, on a basis of equality of
men and women, of human rights and fundamental
freedoms in the political, economic, social, cultural, civil or
any other field.

Given this requirement, the Japanese government proceeded the very next year to implement its EEOL, in order to bring its domestic legislation in line with its international obligations under CEDAW.

Thus, it appeared, at least on paper, that within the span of six years the Japanese government had granted women equality in employment. But this was merely the first step in a lengthy process of evolution toward real equality. According to Professor M. Christina Luera (2004), despite the prohibitions against gender-based discrimination in vocational training, benefits, and retirement in Japan's 1986 EEOL, the only recourse women had when facing various forms of discrimination was voluntary mediation by the mutual consent of both parties. Moreover, the EEOL only *recommended* that employers "endeavor to give women equal opportunity with men" in recruitment, hiring, job assignments, and promotions.[35] Such stipulations made any voluntary mediation highly unlikely.

Interpretation of the EEOL fell within the purview of the Japanese Ministry of Health, Labor and Welfare, which decided that "equal opportunity for women" meant that women should be offered the same avenues for advancement as men rather than being excluded outright from employment.[36] Whereas in the past companies had advertised certain jobs for men only and others just for women, all jobs were now, in theory, open to both genders.[37] To get around the EEOL requirement, Japanese companies then began to hire according to a two-tier system, distinguishing between a "management" track—which offered opportunities for advancement and higher pay—and a "general" track, which offered no such chances.[38] Thus, women were supposedly given equal opportunity upon hiring but in actuality were blocked in the lower tier and rarely reached the higher one. In their analysis of the hiring methods in Japan in 2001, authors Liu and Boyle also note that, according to surveys, in companies that adopted the two-track system hiring policy, only 3.7 percent of women, as opposed to 99 percent of men, were on the management track.

Between 1986 and the end of the century, women began to push back against this glaring discrimination by launching a series of legal actions. In 1995, female employees at Sumitomo Electric sued their employers for discrimination in wages and promotions. As Liu and Boyle report, these women claimed that only 19 among them (0.8 percent of female employees), compared to 2,400 men (19 percent of male employees), were on the management track in 1994. Two of the plaintiffs even sought voluntary mediation under the EEOL. Sumitomo admitted that it had used the existing hiring classifications but argued that the current laws permitted this. The women's request for mediation was refused, because, according to the company, women were not totally excluded from the management track. The plaintiffs then took the unusual action of suing Sumitomo Electric for wage discrimination and the government for failure to mediate.

Luera writes that in 1997, the EEOL was finally revised by the Japanese Diet and its recommendations were finally turned into explicit prohibitions regarding antidiscrimination in recruiting, hiring, assignments, and promotion. But it was only in 2004, seven years later, that the Sumitomo Electric case was eventually settled. Under the terms of the agreement, both plaintiffs received promotions to managerial positions.[39] Although there is no record of what this decade-long battle may have cost these women, psychologically or even physically, it certainly paved the way for others who joined the workforce after them.

The troublesome EEOL was further revised in 2006 to prohibit various forms of indirect discrimination. This second revision, put into effect a full two decades after the Japanese government implemented the EEOL, also prohibited discrimination against women for reasons of pregnancy and childbirth. Such factors, according to data from the Ministry of Health, Labor and Welfare, had classically accounted for 90.8 percent of retirement and dismissal cases brought by women against their employers under the mediation provisions of the EEOL.[40] Only when the second set of revisions was in place did the EEOL come closer to the stipulations of the Convention, which the Japanese government had signed twenty years earlier, in 1986.

Thus, a quarter of a century had to pass between the time that Japan first became a signatory of CEDAW and when it finally brought its domestic legislation into proper alignment with its international obligations. Clearly, the habits and attitudes toward the laws established to protect women's rights had proven much more difficult to change than the actual laws themselves.

WHAT LIES BEHIND THE LAWS?

Laws can be changed, but underlying them are deeply entrenched attitudes and behaviors discriminatory toward women, which the Japanese story vividly highlights. In order to confront the challenge of implementing human rights in general and laws protecting women's rights in particular, the government of Japan has had to make concerted efforts to change old cultural models. One way to do this has been to use a new language and find new words to highlight what is at stake in effecting this change. It has called its new policy "womenomics," a word first coined by Prime Minister Abe and his team.[41]

According to the old Japanese model, economics had nothing to do with women. Husbands were expected to devote themselves to long working hours in return for lifetime job security in a single company, and wives were responsible for running the household and caring for the children. It was unthinkable for a married woman to compete with a man for his job;[42] doing so would have been tantamount to threatening the whole fabric of society. As a result, firms naturally hired new graduates, whom they expected would remain with the firms for the duration of their working lives. This explains why wages and promotions were traditionally age-based[43] and why companies that hired young female graduates often assumed that they would leave upon marriage or with the birth of their first child.[44]

As a result of this employment model, female participation in the Japanese workforce typically reflects a pattern known as the M-curve. Women enter the workforce on graduating from college, after which their employment peaks and begins to drop off in their late twenties and early thirties. This is when they leave their jobs to marry and have children, and this drop represented the nadir of the M in the curve. But Robbi Louise Miller describes the process by which Japanese married women in their mid-forties begin reentering the workforce once their children reach school age. This results in a second spike in the curve, which diminishes once again at retirement age. The M-curve pattern of women's participation in the workforce, marked by these twin peaks of entry and exit from paid employment, makes it very difficult for women to find full-time jobs once the children have grown and they feel ready to reenter the labor force. The lifetime tenure model of Japanese employment and women's heavy family responsibilities thus effectively undermine equal employment opportunities technically granted by law.

In fact, a particular characteristic of women's employment in Japan, and one that is starkly detrimental to their equal opportunities, has been the phenomenon of nonregular, temporary, short-term contract and part-time work. According to author Wei-hsin Yu (2002), these jobs are not usually taken on by young mothers who need flexible working arrangements while they raise their children but by older married women trying to reenter the job market. Such women accept lower-paid positions that lack benefits and security, because they cannot find anything else. Yu goes on to state that the concentration of middle-aged married women in nonstandard employment in Japan is best explained as a "mismatch" between an excess supply of older married women and overly rigid full-time employment. As yet, no laws have addressed this issue.

In fact, as authors Houseman and Abraham explain, employers often use the overavailability of Japanese female workers, who have been excluded from the lifetime male employment model, as a buffer in times of labor shortages and economic downturns to allow for flexibility in hiring and firing.[45] For example, Houseman and Abraham show that in 1988 women accounted for 79 percent of temporary workers and 75 percent of day laborers in manufacturing; they also accounted for over 90 percent of part-time workers in this domain. In the wake of the EEOL, companies gradually began to remove some of the requirements that prevented women from being hired or from advancing in their professions. Some companies went so far as to eliminate the requirement that unmarried women commute from their parental home or quit work once they married.[46] But even with these changes, there was still considerable pressure on women to leave the labor force when they had children. In fact, many married women with young children chose not to work outside the home simply because of the impediments they faced.[47]

The example of one forty-five-year-old university-educated woman, who describes with bleak irony her attempts to reenter the job market, illustrates the relentless discrimination experienced by women in an environment dominated by the traditional Japanese employment model:

> I went to a Belgian bank in Tokyo for a job interview. The middle-level manager, who was a Japanese middle-aged man, kept asking me questions about my family, how I was going to take care of my kids since they were too young to be at school, whether I had anybody to help me if my kids got sick, etc. He went on and on.[48]

She then goes on to explain how the higher-level manager who was interviewing her and was clearly a foreign national made the point that, since she was applying for the job, one could safely assume that she must have taken care of such family considerations. "I almost laughed," she allegedly added. "That was really funny."

CONCLUSION

As this story makes clear, even when international treaties are in place and laws have been ratified, we must look beyond the courts to effect change in society. As indicated in Chapter 4, hidden patterns of patriarchy and entrenched habits of behavior in relation to gender tend to clog, curb, and encumber the implementation of laws protecting women's rights. Although the Universal Declaration of Human Rights paved the way for equality in the world as no other legal instrument had done before it, the fact remains that translating these ideals into practice is supremely difficult where women are concerned. The process has been slow and the setbacks many, due to the age-old customs and domestic roles attributed to men and women. This is true in Japan. It was true in Korea and South Africa, and it is true of many other countries, such as those under sharia law today. When the traditional roles and old cultural patterns clash with women's rights, change seems painful.

But if new laws are to replace the old ones effectively, these patterns do need changing. When laws created for the harmonious development of society become the source of its stagnation and decline, change is not only necessary but inevitable. Indeed, to resist such change marks the death of that society. It is an age-old conundrum. As the Bible famously puts it, "The Sabbath was made for man and not man for the Sabbath," and as has been more recently stated, in even plainer language, "[L]egal standards, political and economic theories are solely designed to safeguard the interests of humanity as a whole, and not humanity to be crucified for the preservation of the integrity of any particular law or doctrine."[49] At the end of the day, if we are to survive at all, human rights must meet the needs of an evolving human community. And if we are to evolve, if civilization is to enhance rather than impede and undermine the well-being of the human race, its social laws must include women's rights rather than exclude women from the rights enshrined in law.

How can this be done? In what ways can countries ensure gender equality as long as the function and cohesion of patriarchal patterns of behavior are maintained and remain resistant to change? How can a revolution of understanding and its implementation in social norms be effected through nonviolent, nonconfrontational, and evolutionary means?

As already stated, the empowerment of women must take place at two levels simultaneously: global and personal. As shown, laws need to be changed internationally as well as implemented nationally and regionally; they too need to evolve at global as well as local levels. Indeed, empowerment is a two-way street, because the traffic of influence runs in both directions: Denial of full equality between the sexes not only "perpetrates an injustice against one half of the world's population [but] promotes in men harmful attitudes and habits that are carried from the family to the workplace, to political life, and ultimately to international relations."[50] Women must therefore find their place in the human family as well as in the family unit.

But the roots of inequality go deep. They reach beyond even these grass roots, of family and society. Although a world vision confirms women's equal rights with men in principle, and a home environment protected by legal instruments gives them the confidence to exercise those rights in practice, it is impossible to implement either principle or practice if the hearts and minds of individuals remain impervious. International legislation can only promote change at the national, the regional, and indeed the local and domestic levels of society, if personal attitudes do not block and impede these attempts. However refined the wording of new laws, and however many revisions are applied to the articles and conventions they entail, however many treaties and acts are ratified or methods of compliance are devised for their more rapid implementation, gender equality will never be understood as a basic human right unless we embrace it at an individual level; it will never become a fundamental belief system in society unless change also takes root in our minds and understanding, unless our ability to use reason and deploy language enables us to grasp the relationships between cause and effect, between policy and its consequences. In other words, the implementation of laws depends on the enhancement of education in society.

The next chapter addresses the relationship between human rights and education, knowing that age-old habits and cultural traditions regarding gender quality can be changed only incrementally, organically, generation by generation, through the development of the mind. And the role of women is vital in this regard.

6

EDUCATION FOR EQUALITY

*Let women then go on, not asking favors, but claiming
as a right the removal of all hindrances to her elevation in the
scale of being. Let her receive encouragement for the proper
cultivation of all her powers so that she may enter profitably
into the active business of life.*
—LUCRETIA MOTT, 1849

*Educating girls is one of the most powerful things we can do,
not just for girls and their families, but for their communities and
their countries. We need parents to actually believe that their
daughters are as worthy of an education as their sons and that
sending girls to school is a good investment for their future.*
—MICHELLE OBAMA, 2014

THE ULTIMATE BARRIER

Changes in legislation, institutional reforms, and labor incentives, however partial and incomplete, all demonstrate a commendable will and a laudable, if so far limited, intention among certain governments, institutions, and corporations to alleviate the burden of poverty from women. These changes are all vital components of an irresistible and profoundly organic progress that has been set in motion to ensure the gradual dismantling of barriers to gender equality in the world.

But as long as legislation lags in many countries, hundreds of millions of people are being born into absolute wretchedness and poverty. As long as governments continue to delay or simply ignore the vital role that women play in relation to the health of economies and the stability of society, more and more of the earth's inhabitants are growing up in failed states, doomed to restricted lives, crippling impediments, and deeply unjust circumstances. This can lead only to more and more frustration, despair, and violence in civil society. It can culminate only in increased insecurity all over the planet, the consequences of which will affect everyone.

The fact is that none of the attempts to solve the problem of gender inequality through legislation, reform, and even various political incentives is, in and of itself, enough. None of them can be implemented, none can produce concrete results or resolve these grave problems without radical changes of another kind, urgent reforms of a different sort. There has been a vital element missing in the discussion so far: education. And by education is not just meant bare literacy, how to read and write, how to add and subtract. Education enables us to recognize patterns in the past and project our thoughts into the future. It shows us how to deploy the deductive method and exercise the imaginative faculty, which is our birthright. It trains the mind to distinguish between essentials and nonessentials, to evaluate what is true from what is false; it gives us the tools and the fresh incentives to define and to resolve our problems. In a word, education is essential if we are to avoid the waste of human potential caused by gender inequality.

And women themselves are the means of ensuring this. Women determine prosperity for all. When women are denied access to education, human capital is lower than its potential. When human capital is lower, economic growth inevitably sinks too. And when inadequate economic growth leads to patterns of endemic poverty, domestic and social violence, lagging health care services, dysfunctional government, and a deteriorating social fabric, rampant insecurity ensues. This is a fair description of many failed and failing states today, cursed by the poisoned waters of the Sphinx, whose riddle can be solved only by our attitude toward the education of girls.

GOOD AND BAD NEWS

Let's begin by looking at the data.

There are some who feel encouraged by the global progress made in the field of education in recent decades. Just as there has been a dramatic increase in average life expectancy and a decline in infant mortality across the world, improvements on the literacy front have also appeared to be positive.[1] Adult literacy rates rose from 47 percent in 1960 to 85 percent in 2015.[2] According to the World Bank (2012), gender gaps in participation in education "have shrunk dramatically at all levels." In 1980, girls' primary school enrollment was 75 percent on average across the world; boys' enrollment was slightly higher, at 80 percent. But by 2014, even this gap had almost disappeared, and 89 percent of girls were enrolled in primary schooling as against 90 percent of boys. It all looks like very good news.

The evolution is even more striking for secondary and tertiary education. In 1980, secondary school enrollment was 44 percent for girls and 50 percent for boys. But by 2014, girls had closed the gap with 65 percent enrolled for both sexes. At the tertiary level, enrollment used to be 11 percent for girls and 14 percent for boys, but by 2014, the ratio had actually tipped and the numbers had completely changed in favor of girls, with 36 percent of girls registered in schools as compared to only 33 percent of boys. Furthermore, the fact that these rates are rising more rapidly for women than for men in tertiary education highlights the encouraging prospect of barriers being removed to women's future participation in the labor market.

Notwithstanding these glowing statistics, however, there are still a number of serious problems when it comes to the education of girls. The global average enrollment figures just quoted disguise a much more dire situation than might appear at first glance. A very sad story about girls' education is to be told in several individual countries, particularly those in Central and West Africa. In many other places as well, there are underprivileged populations when it comes to equality of education for girls. Beyond Africa, and for somewhat different reasons, girls are also at a serious disadvantage as compared with boys in India, Pakistan, Afghanistan, Turkey, and Cambodia, for example. So why are we not hearing more about the bad news?

When we examine the data more carefully, we find five negative factors that significantly influence equality of gender in the education field. These can be masked by such statistics as were just presented and require a different set of questions if they are to reveal themselves for what they are. They concern cultural attitudes toward the education of girls, literacy levels among women, a lower rate of female enrollment at secondary and tertiary levels of education in many countries, the widening gap in the education of the rich and the poor, and finally the stream divergence that channels girls very early on into lower-paying jobs. Each of these negative factors will be addressed in turn, in the following pages, in order to assess the bad news as objectively as possible.

ATTITUDES TOWARD GIRLS' EDUCATION

In the first place, there are still many countries—some with sizable populations—where people's opinions and expectations impose a clear disadvantage for girls. Sub-Saharan Africa, for example, stands out in the world for its generally negative attitudes toward the education of women, and the statistics show a correspondingly low participation of girls in schools in this region. As events in Afghanistan and northern Nigeria also attest, the negative attitude toward female education has actually hardened in recent decades in these countries too. Furthermore, in twenty-seven of the sixty countries covered in the World Values Survey of 2010 to 2014, at least a quarter of the population still think that university education is more important for a boy than for a girl (see Figure 6.1). With such attitudes, it is easy to see how challenging it would be for women and girls to reach the same level of human capital as that of their male counterparts. It would also be more difficult for them to enter the labor force.

As a result, it would also be very difficult for girls to benefit from the advantages of economic autonomy. Reduced levels of education diminish a woman's potential of finding a better-paying job. Research confirms over and over again that this has grave consequences long-term and, at a national scale, for society as a whole. Klasen (1999) finds that between 0.4 and 0.9 of a percentage point of the differences in economic growth rates between East Asia on one hand and sub-Saharan Africa, South Asia, and the Middle East on the other can be attributed to large gender gaps in education prevailing in the latter regions. Inequality in education by gender, he categorically states, has a substantial impact on the economy.

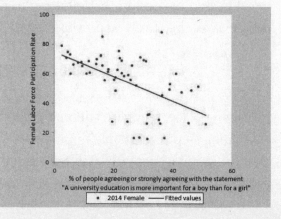

Figure 6.1: People's perceptions on education and women labor force participation.

LITERACY LEVELS

In the second place, there are still millions in the world who cannot read and write, the majority of whom are women. A closer look at the statistics reveals the dismal details.

As the next table illustrates, the number of illiterate persons in the world fell from 878 million in 1990 to 758 million in 2015, with the share of women in the total remaining broadly unchanged over this period, at around 63 percent. Further, it is clear that more than 100 percent of this reduction can be explained by a large drop in China alone.[3] The illiteracy headcount has actually *increased* significantly in Africa, due to population growth and the rise of radicalism, civil unrest, and high levels of corruption in many of these countries, creating conditions that impair the state's ability to prioritize education as a tool for economic and social development.

In this respect, the illiteracy data closely resemble the headcount of extreme poverty published by the World Bank, with much of the progress made over the past couple of decades being attributed to the impact of high economic growth in China. The largest contingent of illiterate persons is still located in Asia—mainly India, Pakistan, and Bangladesh—where 65 percent, or 317 million of the 490 million illiterate persons, are women. This is not to say that people who cannot read or write are unable to support themselves or make some kind of contribution to the informal economy. Indeed, such persons often carry the heaviest burden of low-paid, unskilled jobs precisely because they are women. But illiteracy is a hugely limiting factor to the development of human potential. People without knowledge and information are being systematically excluded from our increasingly complex global economy and are being denied access to prosperity. Such exclusion and segregation will inevitably spill over into the social and political realm and will become a catalyst for frustration and unrest. The depressing corollary to this fact is that the frustration is

NUMBER OF ILLITERATE POPULATION (15+ YEARS) BY REGION (IN MILLIONS)

	WOMEN		MEN		BOTH SEXES	
	1990	2015	1990	2015	1990	2015
World	556.5	479.1	321.2	279.2	877.7	758.3
of which: Less-developed regions	547.2	465.2	317.1	271.2	864.3	736.3
Africa	110.2	138.4	68.0	86.6	178.2	225.1
Asia	416.4	316.7	231.6	173.0	648.0	489.8
of which: India, Pakistan, Bangladesh	218.8	225.6	145.2	130.9	364.0	356.5
China	128.1	30.8	54.5	10.7	182.6	41.5
Europe	7.4	3.0	2.5	1.7	9.9	4.7
Latin America and the Caribbean	20.4	18.3	17.2	14.5	37.7	31.9
Other	2.1	2.7	1.9	3.4	3.9	6.8

*Source: UNICEF, 2018.

frequently directed toward young women and girls who are attempting to acquire an education.

Most discouraging of all, according to the UN's latest prognosis, is that given current trends, it looks as if little further progress can be expected in reducing the absolute number of illiterate women over the medium term. Indeed, a rise is projected for sub-Saharan Africa, and virtually no change can be envisaged in South Asia. If hostilities continue in the Middle East, moreover, we can anticipate negative consequences in illiteracy there, too, and a general shrinking of educational possibilities accompanied by a rise in psychological problems, antisocial behavior patterns, and endemic violence in Syria, Iraq, and Libya.

LOW RATES AT HIGHER LEVELS

The third piece of bad news is that while primary school enrollment rates are fairly high for both girls and boys, the same is not true for secondary schools, where attendance remains quite low in many countries in Africa, South Asia, and elsewhere. More generally, in UN member countries, the data on the highest level of educational attainment reached by women provide a sobering perspective of just how inadequate it can be and how limiting its lack. In middle-income countries, the data on women's educational attainment are depressing. In Brazil, for example, 42 percent of women twenty-five years or older have no more than a primary school education. The situation in Thailand is even worse, with 61 percent of women over twenty-five having no more than primary schooling; in Turkey, it is 53 percent; in Indonesia, 56 percent. Even high-income countries are not exempt from low educational attainment for women; for example, in Portugal the corresponding figure is 48 percent. A wide chasm remains to be bridged if deeply entrenched historical legacies of female disadvantage in education and training are to be overcome.

The data on secondary and tertiary education for women are equally sobering.[4] In 50 countries, out of 160 countries for which data was available, the percentage of women with secondary or tertiary attainment is below 50 percent, sometimes substantially so. In Bangladesh and Pakistan—countries with a combined population of close to 340 million people—the figure is around or less than 25 percent. Furthermore, in Algeria, Bangladesh, Burkina Faso, Chad, Ethiopia, Ghana, Guinea, Malawi, Mali, Pakistan, Senegal, and Togo anywhere from 43 to 93 percent of women over the age of twenty-five have received no schooling whatsoever.

Even when girls do reach tertiary-level education, as is apparently the case for 64 percent of university students in Iran, this does not guarantee, as will be discussed later, that the quality of education they are receiving is worth the same as that in developed countries or that they will necessarily enter the labor force afterward. According to a recent interview with Shirin Ebadi, the Iranian Nobel Peace Prize winner, in spite of there being far fewer male university graduates, three times more Iranian women find themselves unemployed after leaving university than men.[5]

POOR AT ALL LEVELS

The fourth negative factor to consider in world education data is that the rich are better educated than the poor and that children in developing countries are being taught considerably less than their counterparts in high-income countries. This is a well-established and dangerous fact. According to the World Bank (2012, p. 113), "[O]nly 27 percent of children ages 10 and 11 in India can read a simple paragraph, do a simple division problem, tell the time, and handle money. This low learning is not an Indian problem; it recurs in nearly all low- and middle-income countries." In Argentina, 64 percent of fifteen-year-old children tested by the Program for International Student Assessment 2012 were unable to reach the most basic level of proficiency in mathematics (level 1); in Brazil, the figure was 70.3 percent; in Indonesia, 68.6 percent; in Thailand, 53.8 percent. Inadequate skills will, of course, sharply limit the ability of developing countries to successfully integrate with the global economy. This is particularly disturbing at a time when "brain" skills are essential for survival and a growing proportion of better-paid jobs are shifting to the knowledge economy, due to globalization. According to a 2015 BBC article, "[T]he developing world is about 100 years behind developed countries" in educational achievement.[6] Since 95 percent of the increase in population by 2050 is expected to take place in the developing world, governments will have to invest heavily to prevent emerging masses of poorly educated youth from joining the ranks of the unemployed.

But while it is important to boost the quality of education and pass on to children vital twenty-first-century skills, it is equally crucial that the curricula and pedagogy employed to this end should not reinforce prevailing stereotypes and inequities. This is true in relation to race, religion, cultural stereotypes, and above all gender prejudice. If the lesson plans used and subject matter taught in schools merely reinforce inequities, no amount of literacy and education will serve to close the gender gap. Curricula must change; pedagogy must be redesigned; teachers must be retrained; the priorities of school administrations must be redefined; and governments need to readjust budgets and reallocate resources to cover these radical new developments. In the section of this chapter titled "Barometers of Progress," some of these changes will be analyzed more closely and the values consistent with gender equality will be discussed in greater detail. Our educational systems should be imparting appropriate knowledge and skills to our children that will enable them to advance civilization. Girls deserve not only to be literate but to receive the kind of training and education that is relevant to the needs of the age.

STREAM DIVERGENCE

The fifth problem with regard to worldwide data on education is that women and men tend to opt for different fields of study. This is true in both the developing and the developed world, and has a significant impact on their respective occupational choices and subsequent productivity and earnings. According to the World Bank (2012, p. 115), "[G]ender differences in occupation and sector of employment account for 10–50 percent of the observed wage gap in 33 low- and middle-income countries (of 53 [with data])." These differences are pervasive; they manifest themselves early on and become more entrenched as women and men acquire higher education. For instance, in 109 out of 172 countries, more women choose general education as opposed to vocational secondary education, where there are much larger numbers of men. These differences are accentuated even more at the tertiary level, where, all over the world, women tend to be overrepresented in education and health and underrepresented in engineering, manufacturing, construction, and science.

There is, of course, no credible evidence of systematic gender differences in ability at any level of education. A number of studies—see, for instance, Flabbi (2011) and Giles and Witoelar (2011)—show similar test scores from standardized high school graduation tests for both girls and boys. In fact, in Indonesia and Italy, test scores for women with a college education are slightly higher. But so-called stream divergence is driven by cultural attitudes and social expectations. Boys choose male-dominated fields of study because that is what they are "supposed" to do, and girls likewise. The World Bank's *World Development Report* on gender notes (2012, p. 116) that in some countries, school textbooks "depict women in a limited range of social roles and present stereotyped images of women as weaker and operating primarily in domestic domains." The authors thoughtfully add that "countries pay a heavy cost when the average quality of every field is reduced because of the mismatch between training and ability." Stream divergence, then, is also linked to the quality of education, about which more will later be said.

THE IMPORTANCE OF GIRLS

In both East and West, it was only in the nineteenth and twentieth centuries that women were generally given access to education. The reasons for this stark denial of what we now recognize to be an essential human right have not yet been fully admitted by the rank and file of the population; the deep-seated fears that initially provoked and have sustained such discrimination for millennia have not been resolved, either, for such attitudes are still evident in our own times. Even today, extremist groups and reactionary movements motivated by these same fundamental fears are resorting to the abduction of young girls from schools and are punishing them with death and disfigurement solely on the grounds of their pursuit of education. Such reactions, by those determined to resist change, are a tacit recognition that women are its fundamental agents. Even if certain governments and corporations have not wished to admit the fact to themselves, such groups are fully aware that there is, as one journalist has characterized it, "no force more powerful to transform a society"[7] than an educated young woman.

In her 1792 treatise *A Vindication of the Rights of Women*, Mary Wollstonecraft blamed women's lack of education for their perceived inferiority and centuries-old suppression. It is hardly surprising that women invariably limited themselves to the roles of mother and wife when they were unable to gain access to primary sources of knowledge and understanding on a comparable basis to men; it is no wonder that so few achieved the intellectual and scientific distinction in the past that would have made stateswomen and business leaders of them. Although few people now question the fact that higher levels of educational attainment are a fundamental prerequisite for empowering women in all spheres of life, it is a sad truth that a not-insignificant share of the world's population still remains deprived of one of the most essential means of self-improvement even today. As the statistics in the previous pages have proven, 500 million of the total of close to 800 million illiterate people in the world are women.

A VICIOUS CYCLE

The education of girls, when effectively implemented, would appear to hold special promise for the future. If a young woman is empowered to gain such skills as would enable her to join the workforce, she could contribute to changing undesirable attitudes and long-standing prejudices against women. If she were given access to higher education herself, she could play a far more effective part as the role model and primary educator of the next generation. But this promise has not yet been fulfilled. We are still trapped in a vicious cycle. Lawrence Summers (1992), former chief economist at the World Bank, noted:

[U]nderinvestment in girls is not an ineluctable consequence of poverty, nor is it made necessary by any religious or cultural tradition. It is an economic problem that results from a vicious cycle caused by distorted incentives. The expectation that girls will grow to do little other than serve their husbands reduces parents' incentive to invest in their daughter's human capital. Uneducated women then have few alternatives and so the expectation becomes self-fulfilling, trapping women in a continuous circle of neglect. (p. 1)

This vicious cycle has both a microhousehold and a macroeconomic dimension. To the extent that women are expected to play a limited role, bound by cultural and religious traditions that restrict them to motherhood, housekeeping, and the care of others, girls will receive less education and, as the mortality data suggest, inadequate health care and poorer nutrition than boys. Raised and equipped to limit themselves to caregiving roles of both husbands and children and, increasingly, the elderly, women find their choices correspondingly constrained; they are either forced or else choose to marry early, with the result that they are trapped by their large families and have a reduced earning potential outside the household. Their contribution to national productivity thus becomes correspondingly low.

As has been already stated, education needs to be given the highest level of priority by governments, but this is certainly not the case right now. And as long as this state of affairs continues, the vicious cycle cannot be broken. Let us contrast, for example, the wasteful misapplication of resources in the world with the emphasis placed on education. Many governments, instead of prioritizing education to alleviate radical poverty around the world and to ensure literacy levels of close to 800 million people, are pouring hundreds of billions of dollars every year into energy subsidies. The sums allocated to these wasteful subsidies are enormous in relation to the size of total government expenditure; they often exceed total spending on education and in some countries are larger than the budgets for health and education combined.

Previous chapters have alluded to the adverse distributional implications of these subsidies, the bulk of the benefits going to those segments of the population well-endowed with cars and larger houses to light and heat. According to the International Energy Agency, removing fuel subsidies would by 2030 cut carbon dioxide emissions in an amount equivalent to the current emissions of the entire European Union. Marcelo Giugale (2017, p. 133) states that "a dollar spent on public infrastructure or on cash transfers to the poor generates more private investment and consumption than a dollar spent subsidizing gasoline or electricity." But, unfortunately, we are still pouring money into gasoline, diesel, and coal rather than the human mind.

Lack of education reinforces women's view of themselves as playing a limited role in both the family and society at large. This contraction of the imagination is itself another aspect of the vicious cycle. Such attitudes give no incentive to parents to invest in the education of their girls, and as a result, societies in which such patterns of educational inequality are the norm tend to have a large burden of dependency. Since families are often large, broadly half of the population in such societies is under eighteen, requiring a considerable share of public resources to be allocated to maintain minimum levels of schooling and health care. As a result, a country like India, for example, with its relatively less educated population, will have higher poverty levels, higher fertility rates, and higher child mortality, representing a vicious cycle at the macro level that is an impediment to productivity and higher economic growth.

A HEALTHIER CYCLE

Provided that they utilize some of the wide range of remedies to keep children, especially young and adolescent girls, in school,[8] countries can, of course, make the transition to a healthier developmental cycle in which women and men are expected to have broadly equal options in life, in which girls and boys will receive equivalent educational opportunities, and in which both have equal access to health care and food. When women and men have similar human capital endowments for highly productive work, they will tend to marry later; they will have smaller families and healthier, better educated children; and they will be more likely to join the labor force.

According to Barbara Herz et al. (1991), such societies will, in contrast to societies where girls do not have equal access to education, health care, and food, have a smaller burden of dependency. Only about a third of the population will be under eighteen; other things being equal, this, in turn, will mean that there will be more resources available for schooling and better health care. Beyond the household, at the macro level, more educated societies—that is, those societies where women have been relatively more empowered through a higher human capital endowment—tend to be more prosperous and have lower rates of child mortality.

Recent experience shows that various public interventions can be quite successful in spurring the integration of children into the educational system, and some of these have been particularly successful with girls. One such intervention has to do with the role of incentives. When parents perceive that the returns on girls' education increase, they will willingly spend more in educating their daughters. For instance, the growth of outsourcing in India and the opening up of new information technology–enabled service centers has had a beneficial impact on school enrollment rates, particularly in English-language schools. According to Hoyos and Narayan (2011), business processing outsourcing opportunities have had a tangible impact on the education of women. After information about employment opportunities in this field was disseminated at the village level, it was found that girls aged between five and fifteen who had been exposed to the recruiting services were still in school three years later, had a higher body mass index, and were more likely, if they were among the older ones, to be already employed in paid work. Once the information about these improved returns for education was disseminated, it was enough to boost female school enrollment and open other opportunities for girls.

The price of schooling is singularly important to parents, in light of such incentives. Reduced school fees would make it less necessary for them to consider the gender of their children when deciding whether or not to invest in their education. In Africa, the introduction of free primary education across the continent significantly boosted student enrollment rates, and the effects were more favorable to girls than boys.[9] The price of schooling also has an impact on the relative attractiveness of child labor, whether in the formal economy or at home; this is important because there is ample evidence to show that higher rates of child employment are associated with lower rates of school enrollment. Not surprisingly, reducing the distance from the village to the school also boosts enrollment, as data from Pakistan and Afghanistan clearly prove. On a related point, Kabubo-Mariara and Mwabu (2007) have shown that reducing the distance from the village to a water source in Kenya by two kilometers would boost educational attainment twice as much for girls as for boys, since it is typically the former who have the primary task of fetching water.

Likewise, increases to household income clearly have a beneficial effect on children's participation in school, with the positive impact being greater for girls than for boys, as noted by the World Bank (2012, p. 111): "Increases in maternal income have a greater impact on girls' schooling than increases in paternal income." The work done by Fiszbein, Schady, and others (2007) also presents compelling evidence that conditional cash transfers—money given to families on condition that the children attend school for a minimum number of days—are an effective way to protect children's education in difficult times.

There are signs that it could happen. There are examples where it does work. But the changes need to be more radical, more rapid, and wider-ranging if girls' education is to be protected and promoted in more countries. Education is empowering, but it also needs to be empowered as a national policy. It needs to become a top priority of nations all over the world.

EMPOWERMENT

The education and empowerment of women go hand in hand. Just as low levels of physical capital endowment can exacerbate or perpetuate low levels of human capital, so too a positive change in one type of capital can trigger positive results in another. For instance, Geddes, Lueck, and Tennyson (2012) found that the expansion of women's economic rights in the United States resulted in higher rates of relative school attendance by girls. The authors studied the period between 1850 and 1920, when most of the states in America had already passed laws increasing the rights of married women to own and control property and earnings. They tested the hypothesis that a change in women's rights would produce higher returns on the investment in girls' education. The data clearly confirmed higher schooling rates for girls after laws gave women control over their property and earnings.

This principle appears to hold true no matter what the scale of earnings or education might be. According to Amartya Sen (1999), the state of Kerala, though one of the poorest in India, not only showed some of the highest average life expectancies in the country and above-average educational and health facilities, but property inheritance actually passed through the female line for an important part of the population, the Nairs. The sex ratio in Kerala was well within the natural norm. A number of researchers have noted that most households are the locus of intricate interactions of collaboration and power. Sen believes not only that working mothers would be good examples to their daughters, creating in them a higher sense of ex- pectation about the range of legitimate activities to aspire to, but that a woman's own power will be boosted by her participation in the labor market. This, in turn, would enhance her daughter's access to the ed- ucational system, improving her skills and the human capital en- dowment of the whole country.

After the two states of Karnataka and Maharashtra, in India, re- formed the Hindu Succession Act in 1994, giving both sexes equal rights to inherit joint family property, women and girls were the im- mediate beneficiaries. The control of assets in families was automat- ically altered, and there was increased parental investment not only in the acquisition of sanitary latrines, which improved the health and welfare of the family, but in the education of daughters as well.[10] The impact of the change in the law was even greater in the second gen- eration. Mothers who benefited from the reform doubled their spend- ing on their daughters' education and made sure their children had greater opportunity to acquire skills and knowledge than they had been given themselves. As a result, women were more likely to have bank accounts, developed greater intrahousehold bargaining power, and gained autonomy.[11]

Wherever girls have received education, they have ultimately risen to ranks of influence and had an impact on the laws of the land. Whenever the legal environment has enabled women to exert them- selves and acquire financial independence, they have achieved greater agency. When women are empowered, society can progress.

BAROMETERS OF PROGRESS

Economists and social scientists have identified general attitudes that characterize progressive societies and specific values that help shape constructive systems of education within them. These attitudes stim- ulate gender equality by greatly influencing patterns of development in any given society. The core values on which they are based provide a barometer by which to measure the progress of that development,[12] as will be explored next.

Knowledge

First and foremost among these signs of progress is a society's basic attitude toward education. Knowledge, to paraphrase David Landes (2000, p. 2), "makes almost all the difference" to development, and education, training, and skill acquisition are key drivers of competitiveness. As the global economy becomes more complex, it is essential to boost the human capital endowments of the labor force, and in order to maintain a competitive edge in global markets, therefore, people need access to new knowledge. They must have the opportunity to learn how to operate the latest technologies and need to be retrained in these new processes. The experience of Finland, Korea, Taiwan, and Israel clearly proves that emphasis on education has been particularly important in the areas of technological innovation.[13]

Conversely, lack of such basic skills, which have become the contemporary form of literacy, severely limits the participation of citizens in development. When education is not considered an asset in society and its importance is undermined by inadequate budgets, by risible salaries, and by lack of funding, poor incentives, and inadequate qualifications, a society is effectively on a slippery slope as far as its own future prosperity is concerned. But wherever coverage of primary education has expanded rapidly, as it has done in the developing world, higher education has gained corresponding importance. Thus, countries that have invested heavily in creating a well-developed infrastructure for tertiary education have reaped enormous benefits in terms of growth.

But for people to be gainfully employed, well informed regarding government policies, good judges of politicians, and impervious to demagogic manipulation, they need levels of education that go far deeper and reach much further than technological expertise. This degree of conscious awareness may not be to the short-term benefit of those who hold the reins of power, but it is vital for the long-term development and security of their societies.

It may be salutary to remember in this regard that the teaching profession, like the other service industries referred to in Chapter 3, is invariably dominated by women. There was a time when education was considered a vocation and respected. Today, when there are more female teachers than male ones, teachers, the world over, are generally undervalued, poorly paid, and overworked. If education is not given the importance it deserves, if the teaching profession is not better validated in financial terms, not only the millions of women who teach but the billions of children they teach and therefore society as a whole will suffer.

Time

Our attitude toward time also has a significant influence on developmental patterns in society. Time management and a systematic approach toward work, for example, are crucial for economic progress. In this regard, Landes (1998) characterizes the invention of the mechanical clock as "the greatest achievement of medieval mechanical ingenuity" (p. 49), both for its revolutionary conception and, equally important, for how it permitted the ordering of life in the cities in ways that had a major impact on productivity. "Indeed, the very notion of productivity is a by-product of the clock: once one can relate performance to uniform time units, work is never the same" (pp. 49–50). The invention of the mechanical clock led to one of Adam Smith's seminal insights: Wealth and prosperity depend directly—to use Smith's language—on the "productive powers of labor."[14]

But we have suffered from myopia in ordering time in the past. Work can become an important organizing principle of life and productivity an engine of prosperity in the future only if the mechanical clock respects the rhythms of female as well as male biology. One of the negative aspects of the Industrial Revolution was that it set the clock ticking to suit only half the human race. If women are to join the labor force effectively, if they are to play their part in enhancing productivity, the clock has to be adjusted to allow for pregnancy, for parental leave, and for childcare, and it must respect the return to the workforce of women who have chosen to stay out of it during their childbearing years. The fact that this has already been achieved in several countries, such as Finland, for example, proves that if policy makers look forward rather than back at old models of ordering time, huge strides can be made in society.

Temporal orientation and whether a particular culture is forward-looking or unduly focused on the past also make big differences to its prosperity. It has been found to be much more helpful to an economy, for example, to confront challenges by asking, "How can we set this right?" rather than by reacting with the statement, "Who did this to us?" Home Minister Okubo Toshimichi in 1870s Japan opted for the future. He believed that instead of undertaking punitive military expeditions and adventures in neighboring countries, a better way to engage the creative energies of the Japanese people was through the acquisition of technological know-how and the emulation of best practices from the developed world. This choice led to a century of rapid economic growth and a steady convergence to rich-country standards of living.

Interestingly enough, temporal orientation also has consequences for the way gender roles are perceived. A conservative society that leans toward old customs and traditions is invariably going to fall back into entrenched habits of patriarchal power, as seen in Chapter 4. The psychology of blame, moreover, which prefers the default reaction of "Who did this to us?" rather than the proactive one of "How can we set this right?" is much more inclined to the misogynist attitudes which blamed women for centuries for the sins of the world. One of the greatest challenges facing those who try to rectify and calibrate the injustices of the past is to avoid falling into the same backward-looking patterns of victimization and accusation today.

Ethics

The often unspoken code of ethics and moral values underpinning a society are likewise among the barometers of change characterizing a progressive system of education within it. Amartya Sen (2009) reminds us that Adam Smith "talked about the important role of broader values for the choice of behavior, as well as the importance of institutions" in *The Wealth of Nations*. But, Sen adds, it was in his first book—*The Theory of Moral Sentiments*, published some 250 years ago—that Smith "extensively investigated the powerful role of non-profit values." While Smith stated that "prudence was of all virtues that which is most helpful to the individual," he went on to argue that "humanity, justice, generosity and public spirit, are the qualities most useful to others." Harvard professor Benjamin Friedman (2005) corroborates this point by arguing that "economic growth not only relies upon moral impetus, it also has positive moral *consequences*" (p. 18), as "the predominant tendency is for economic growth to render a society more inclined toward openness, tolerance, mobility, and democracy" (p. 101).

A related value, closely associated with ethical standards and their absence, concerns the criteria of advancement used by societies. Do such criteria operate through meritocratic systems where rewards are linked to excellence of performance in any given field, of labor, law, or government? Or, as previously mentioned in Chapter 4, do they depend on factors such as friendship, ethnic kinship, family connections, or party affiliation, where corruption can easily abound? Productivity is invariably enhanced when resources are allocated according to efficiency rather than to subjective considerations unrelated to performance. A paper by Bertrand and Schoar (2006) shows that those countries in which kinship ties and family loyalty prevail "have lower levels of per capita GDP, smaller firms, a higher fraction of self-employed, fewer publicly traded firms, and a smaller fraction of total market value controlled by families, on average" (p. 82). These "tribal" criteria of advancement, if they could be so delineated without offense, have been notoriously unjust toward anyone who does not have the "right" connections, who does not belong to the "right" caste or club, who is peripheral to the centers of power. In such countries, a tiny minority of women may be the beneficiaries of various forms of nepotism, but the vast majority are penalized, and society as a whole suffers.

Trust

The common thread linking ethics, time management, and education together is trust. The role of trust as a barometer of progress in economic and financial development has received increased attention in the recent academic literature. It is a concept that has a significant impact on prosperity in terms of both its depth and its breadth, the levels of trust reached depending on the largeness of its circle. It also serves as a barometer of whether women are in or out of that circle.

From the point of view of economic theory, trust can be defined as the degree of probability that an individual assigns to any specific event. One example is a business partner's compliance with the contract terms. Another is an employer's adherence to an agreed rate of pay. And a third could be a government's decision to invest in the education of girls. All such transactions depend on probability outcomes, and as empirical evidence abundantly demonstrates, trust is always accompanied by risk. It is also affected by a wide range of cultural influences, such as religion, ancestral origins, and ethnic roots. Although the impact of inherited culture is attenuated for individuals with higher levels of education,[15] these deep-seated influences still exist and play an important role in who and how we do or do not trust.

The survey Eurobarometer questions the bilateral trust between individuals from different countries, for example, and asks how much the Swedes trust other Swedes, or Germans, or Italians. The answers reveal that this trust is affected not only by historical and linguistic features, such as the number of years countries have been at war between AD 1000 and 1970, or the commonality of linguistic roots, but also by the genetic distance between two populations.[16] Economic literature has further proved that people who are more positively inclined and more willing to trust are also more likely to become entrepreneurs. It is clear, therefore, that the level of trust between two countries affects the level of trade, of foreign direct investment, and of portfolio investment between them.[17]

The radius of identification in a society, and, in particular, whether the circle of trust is narrow or wide, is also likely to make a difference to the economy. It is noteworthy that the fast pace of growth in India and China over the past several decades has coincided with an opening up of their economies to international trade, foreign investment, and the rigors of international competition. India spent the first four decades after its 1947 independence mired in poverty and lack of opportunity, largely isolated from the global economy. Similarly, during the Ming dynasty in China (1368–1644), the country turned inward, trade with the outside world collapsed, and the economy came to a standstill; China fell rapidly behind Europe at this time, which, by contrast, had set a course of vigorous development, having "discovered" the New World with its resulting commercial advantages. If our primary identification is with the family or the tribe, there may be problems in fruitfully engaging with the rest of the world. And by the same token, if we exclude women from the "club" by denying girls education, there are immediate consequences for society. Trust thrives on inclusion.

Gender

The most important barometer for progress and the one that most dramatically helps to shape constructive systems of education concerns gender—in other words, the way in which women are included in society. As we have argued throughout this book, there is a close connection between national economic performance and the degree to which societies have succeeded in integrating women into the economy. There is a vital link between financial prosperity in any particular society and whether women have been allowed to participate in decision-making, particularly in the case of representation in parliaments, cabinets, and other executive bodies. But such progress and prosperity depend entirely on whether the attitude that characterizes any particular society makes it possible for a woman to avail herself of education and has the opportunity to build up her human capital.

International competitiveness and productivity have much to do with the efficient allocation of resources, including, of course, human resources. The efficient operation of our increasingly knowledge-based economy is not only a function of adequate levels of available finance and a reasonably open trade regime for goods and services; more and more, it is dependent on our ability to tap into a society's reservoir of talents and skills. And that depends on whether women as well as men, girls as well as boys have equal access to quality education at all levels.

When—because of tradition or a misunderstanding of the purpose of religion, social taboos or blind prejudices—half of the world's population is prevented from making its contribution to the life of a nation by being deprived of education, the economy will suffer. The skills that the private sector can tap will be necessarily narrower and shallower, and productivity, the engine of sustainable growth, will be impaired. It is indeed no surprise that the most competitive countries in the world, those that have been better able to operate on the boundaries of the technology frontier, are also those where women have been given the greatest opportunities to be equal partners with men.[18] When corporate boards or other groups of people appointed to formulate policies, design programs, or undertake some other specific task are all male-dominated, the decisions arrived at will tend to be suboptimal because they will inevitably reflect the priorities and biases of men, who have a particular way of looking at the world and analyzing its problems. Thus, gender equality does not have a purely ethical or moral dimension but is, in fact, an issue of economic efficiency and educational opportunity and, thus, is fundamental to the creation of a more prosperous, more informed, and more educated world.

Education and the acquisition of knowledge and skills are desirable development objectives everywhere, in all countries, and under all conditions, but traditions and social norms will certainly affect a sociodemographic group's "capacity to aspire."[19] Cultural norms naturally affect women's ability to improve themselves and ultimately to contribute to the economy. Within the limits allowed by availability of data of this nature, economic literature shows that women's participation in economic activities is profoundly affected by culture. For example, cultural heritage affects living arrangements[20] and women's labor force participation; fertility rates are affected by those prevailing in the country of origin of women's ancestors.[21] The World Bank's 2016 *Women, Business and the Law* data and report also show the close connection between the law and restrictions embedded in the law that can impose various limitations on women's agency in 173 countries, including labor force participation, ownership of firms, and access to the financial system. All these factors impinge on the quality and accessibility of education.

This reality is true not only for women but also for minority groups. Several studies, however, have shown that the performance on standardized tests becomes worse when participants are told that the tests are targeted to minority groups or when they are asked to disclose their membership in such groups.[22] So whatever efforts are made to enhance educational opportunities and level the playing field for girls to participate in society, these should in no way target a particular cultural bias or be directed at a particular religious tradition or linked to one set of values, Western or otherwise. Education is vital in many different regions of the world; it is relevant to all contemporary societies and cultures; it is urgently needed as much in northern China as it is in Siberia, in central London, or in the Bolivian Andes. The progress of science and technology in years to come is only likely to make the universality of this need even more apparent.

These core values, related to gender, trust and ethics, time and knowledge, affect all societies and are the direct consequences of globalization. They are a fundamental proof of the gradual emergence of a common language across national and cultural frontiers. They are a universal barometer by which to measure the progress of development in society and they provide the key criteria that are accepted internationally as the foundations for economic development. Of course, societies will differ in the ways and the extent to which they have internalized some of these values in their policies, their traditions, and their institutions. Acceptance of gender equality, for instance, as a critical element of a progressive development strategy does not mean that inequalities and injustices based on gender will suddenly disappear. The desirability of trust and a common foundation of ethics necessary for inclusive models of prosperity does not imply that utopia is round the corner. But few would disagree with the thesis that gender disparities are out of step with modernity and that their presence retards human progress. Development is not only about reducing poverty and expanding opportunities against the background of rising incomes. It is also about adopting a set of values that are compatible with humanity's moral development and that can only be encouraged through education.

CONCLUSION

Changes that have long-lasting effects and far-ranging consequences in the world have to take place at the microcosmic level. They occur slowly, secretly, at the seemingly least significant scale of society. In fact, if we have seen an escalation in efforts to restrict and curtail the education of girls in sub-Saharan Africa in recent years, it is precisely because the secret is finally out in the open. Radicalized groups intent on maintaining the status quo in such countries have realized how fundamental the education of girls is to seismic change in society.

As we have seen, gender disparities and inequality matter hugely because the subjugation of women has brought untold ills to humanity. Not only has it led to the great injustices associated with the oppression of half of the world's population, but it has also imposed a heavy cost on human welfare everywhere. The denial of girls' right to education has pernicious consequences on the economy and on demographics; it leads to rising violence, endemic corruption, and political instability. In other words, whenever and wherever women suffer injustice, society as a whole is jeopardized; its progress is impeded. Health care suffers. The environment is jeopardized. Epidemics ensue. And civilization erodes dramatically.

In these circumstances, traditional societies frozen in custom and dependent on timeworn patterns between the sexes become very vulnerable; they can be paralyzed in the face of these crises and cut off for decades from engagement with the outside world. But as soon as women are sufficiently empowered to enter the workforce, processes of change are set in motion, which can lead to rapid shifts of behavior and expectation even in these societies. There are potentially large rewards for policy interventions that reallocate the rights and responsibilities between the sexes, that encourage women to receive higher education, that enable them to enter the labor force, and that encourage them to assume decision-making roles in government. Women's presence in society at large invariably creates mutually reinforcing mechanisms to the benefit of others as well as themselves.

Education is a powerful engine not only for women's advancement but for the amelioration and betterment of social conditions in general. Whenever mothers are educated, there is a higher probability that their daughters will be too. Whenever girls are given education, there is a greater chance that the children of both sexes will be healthier. Empirical evidence that is both substantial and compelling shows that the literacy and education of girls can reduce mortality rates of children—especially of female children; it can help to reduce fertility rates, which in turn has important consequences for demographics, with its train of social issues. Education of girls will have a direct impact on the household and beyond. Not only will educated girls be able to contribute effectively to family income, but they will have a greater say over household finances as they grow older; they will begin not only to engage productively in the workplace but to have their voices heard in society at large.

For whenever an educated woman enters the labor market, the balance of power in society begins to shift and change. A woman with a well-paid job in the formal sector will be far more likely to participate and be represented in government; she will be more empowered to have political influence and be better able to help change the negative social attitudes impeding economic progress. She could become the driving force behind implementing new legislation in society. She could be at the vanguard of environmental protection, human rights, and higher social standards. Above all, she would surely be the advocate for raising the quality of education everywhere, and this, in turn, shall ensure global prosperity, increased security, and economic growth, and shall promote peace. As the great Persian sage and Baha'i teacher 'Abdu'l-Bahá stated in the course of his public talks in America, just before the outbreak of World War I:

> When all mankind shall receive the same opportunity of education and the equality of men and women be realized, the foundations of war will be utterly destroyed. Without equality this will be impossible because all differences and distinction are conducive to discord and strife. Equality between men and women is conducive to the abolition of warfare for the reason that women will never be willing to

sanction it. Mothers will not give their sons as sacrifices upon the battlefield after twenty years of anxiety and loving devotion in rearing them from infancy, no matter what cause they are called upon to defend. There is no doubt that when women obtain equality of rights, war will entirely cease among mankind.[23]

7

THE COSTS OF INEQUALITY

Leveling the . . . playing field for women holds real promise for the world—in both human and economic terms. Unfortunately, that promise remains largely ignored and its potential untapped. In too many countries, too many . . . restrictions conspire against women.
—Christine Lagarde, 2015

WHO IS THE BOTTOM LINE?

We usually ask "what" rather than "who" in relation to the bottom line, and we generally come up with the same answer each time: *money*. In fact, as soon as the subject of economics is raised in connection with gender, the popular assumption is that we are talking, first and foremost, about salaries. We think the debate is about wages, about equal pay for equal work. This is certainly a serious issue, as previous chapters have attempted to show. But the real bottom line has to do with much more than cash. It concerns people as well as paychecks, human as well as monetary resources. Women are the bottom line because that is where they usually end up: at rock bottom.

It is obvious that as long as women are relegated to the bottom rungs of society, we will all pay. Gender inequality is very expensive to sustain and has incalculable economic as well as social and political dimensions. Gender-based disparities in education and legal rights, as well as in employment prospects and pay, radically undermine global prosperity. They result in societies where poverty, violence, and paranoia prevail. They give rise to individual frustration, civic instability, and increasing cultural disaffection. And although the correlation between gender-based disparities and global prosperity has not often been examined in the academic literature, these factors all contribute to the heightened sense of collective insecurity we are currently facing. The dangerous disparities in society created by the unequal treatment of girls and boys, of women and men, in the fields of labor and the law, culture and education, may well be a primary cause of the sense of insecurity that defines our times. As long as we do not look at "who" as well as "what" is at that bottom line, we are at risk.

Gender inequality has not generally been perceived to be that significant as far as national security is concerned. The majority of governments in the world would not normally consider women's rights to be among the top ten priorities for the defense of their countries. Military research and acquisition of arms, certainly; surveillance methods, immigration control, protection against cyber and other attacks, definitely. Even food safety and security would figure prominently on the agenda, together with natural and unnatural disasters, epidemics, and environmental catastrophes, of course. But women's rights are usually low on the list; most often they are not even on it. Departments of finance and homeland security have not yet grasped how much it is costing them to ignore women.

The fact is that the denial of equal opportunities for health, education, legal protection, and employment to women and girls is costing the world as much as an estimated $9 trillion per year,[1] or close to 12 percent of the world's gross national product. We need to grasp the international ramifications of these figures, but for some reason we resist doing so. Despite the heavy price that humanity has paid over the centuries for having men run the world alone, despite the fearful waste of resources, raw materials, money, and lives in the course of the last blood-soaked century, few have seen the link between these concrete losses and the absence of enough women in decision-making positions. Few have correlated the rising costs of insecurity in society today with the fact that women comprise 60 percent of the world's working poor and two-thirds of its close to 800 million illiterate people. We have not yet put two and two together. We have not done our math in order to understand that inequality for women = poverty for all.

A hundred years ago, we thought that science and technology, coal and steel, and colonial expansion were the long-term answers to economic development and human prosperity. Seventy years ago, after two world wars, we favored the stockpiling of armaments, not only as a political deterrent but also as an economic incentive to growth. The military establishment employed a sizable share of the postwar population in Europe, in the United States, and in the Soviet Union, and it was supposed to keep that shrinking elite safe. Today, however, as proxy wars fueled by the sale of arms bring terrorists ever closer to home and internet leaks as well as cyberattacks render conventional warfare obsolete, as the world's flawed financial systems begin to threaten the very economies they were meant to sustain and the gap between rich and poor expands by the nanosecond, we need to look for other reasons for our predicament.

The preceding chapters explored, among other issues, the legal and cultural causes of our predicament as well as its demographic implications. This chapter highlights the heavy price that is being paid for the destabilization of economies as a result of gender discrimination. As already stated in the introduction, one of the vital resources providing a map of the multiple factors undermining prosperity today can be found in the research garnered by the Women, Business and the Law (WBL) project of the World Bank. Some of its findings will now be analyzed in order to see how much it costs society, in security and stability, when governments continue to deny women their full and equal rights.

RESTRICTIONS AGAINST WOMEN: THE *WBL* REPORT

In the 2016 report, the WBL project highlights three significant sets of factors affecting women, business, and the law that have a broad impact on the security and stability of society. The first compares the conditions in some countries that impose a variety of legal restrictions on women with conditions in some that do not. The second provides examples of job limitations that exist in certain countries and the gender pay gap that results. And the third analyzes the legal impediments that exist in those countries curtailing women's access to equal economic rights and the impact these laws have on labor force participation. When seen in conjunction with each other, the WBL indicators provide something like a diagnosis of our current ills.

It is interesting to note that of the 173 economies covered in the 2016 *WBL* report, 90 percent have at least one restriction against women embedded in the law. Only eighteen of the economies examined are free from gender discriminations or differences. They comprise an interesting and at times unexpected group, including certain countries that one would expect to find in such a list, such as Canada, the Netherlands, and New Zealand, but others one would not, such as Armenia, the Dominican Republic, and Peru. Only five members of the European Union are among the restriction-free nations on this list: Estonia, Hungary, the Netherlands, the Slovak Republic, and Spain.[2]

Of course, even in those countries, where women are seemingly privileged, a gender gap still exists. Although discrimination against them is not embedded in the law, they still experience significant social and financial differences from men. Women in these economies are subjected to restrictions of political empowerment, to various forms of discrimination when it comes to participation in the labor market, to lack of equal economic opportunities, and other limitations that put them at a disadvantage with respect to men. Legal restrictions are only the tip of the iceberg, it would seem.

Not all of these eighteen restriction-free economies are high-income nations either. This is revealing and suggests that income levels are not a determining factor in terms of the presence or absence of legal restrictions against women. One line of argument sometimes put forward, when it comes to the lack of equal gender rights before the law, is that we need only wait two hundred or so years for all the countries of the world to become rich and prosperous, that gender equality will be a natural response to rising prosperity. But the existence of middle- or lower-middle-income countries on this list of the top eighteen countries seems to fly in the face of such theories. Furthermore, the many high-income countries where women suffer considerable restrictions sometimes make it clear that the issue is far more complex than has been assumed. Prosperity may not inevitably lead to gender equality.

Conversely, there are 30 among the 173 economies studied that have at least ten or more—and sometimes many more—restrictions on women. Not surprisingly, twenty-six of these are located in the Middle East and North African regions and in sub-Saharan Africa. The WBL data are quite powerful, rather like a magnifying glass, in fact; once the law has been codified in this manner, the reader is free to look in considerable detail at individual country circumstances and able to make some startling comparisons.

In the Democratic Republic of the Congo, for example, there are thirteen restrictions against women. A married woman there cannot get a job or pursue a trade or profession in the same way as a man: She needs her husband's authorization to sign a contract, to register a business, to open a bank account, and even to establish a place of residence. Married women cannot be the legal heads of household either, in the same way as married men, and female and male spouses have unequal ownership rights to property. In Chile, a country at a high level of development, there are still seven restrictions embedded in the laws that are disadvantageous to women in some way. There is no nondiscrimination clause that includes gender as a protected category in the Chilean constitution; the mandatory retirement age for women is sixty while for men it is sixty-five; and only husbands can legally administer property during marriage under the default marital property regime. Just as in the Democratic Republic of the Congo, women in Chile cannot be heads of household.

In the Islamic Republic of Iran, however, there are twenty-three restrictions against women embedded in the law. In several areas, married women are expressly forbidden to do what married men can do, such as apply for a passport, travel outside the home without authorization, choose where to live, or be heads of household. They cannot get a job or pursue a trade or profession in the same way as men; they cannot be ensured of equal remuneration for work of equal value like men, and there are no laws to protect them from gender discrimination in hiring. Iranian women are required by law to obey their husbands. They cannot generally convey citizenship to their children or to their spouse in the way that men can. They have no legal protection from domestic violence or sexual harassment inflicted by anyone, including their husbands. Their mandatory retirement age is lower than that of men, and there are restrictions on their agency and autonomy at every level. An Iranian woman's testimony does not generally carry the same weight in court as a man's either, and the constitution has no nondiscrimination clause with gender as a protected category. Nor are there any laws penalizing or preventing the dismissal of pregnant women from work, or providing rights for paternity or parental leave, or ensuring flexible schedules for employees with minor children, or tax-deductible payments for childcare. And no quotas exist for women in parliament, or in local government, or on corporate boards. Instead, there are gender-differentiated inheritance rights for sons and daughters and unequal inheritance rights for female and male surviving spouses. Article 1117 of Iran's Civil Code, moreover, states that a husband can prevent his wife from undertaking any occupation, even if unpaid, that he considers is "incompatible with the family interests or the dignity of himself or his wife." Needless to say, the Civil Code does not include a reciprocal clause giving a woman the right to prevent her husband from undertaking occupations she considers incompatible with family interests or the dignity of herself or her husband.

Although these lists for the Democratic Republic of the Congo, Chile, and Iran are not comprehensive, they do highlight areas in which women are typically at a disadvantage, often in ways that place considerable limitations on their ability to contribute to national prosperity.

JOBS AND THE GENDER PAY GAP

A second insight that comes from the WBL data is that in one hundred of the economies examined, laws restrict the types of jobs that women can do. The most extensive set of restrictions can be found in Eastern and Central Europe and in Central Asia. In Russia, for instance, there are a total of 456 jobs that are off-limits to women. There a woman cannot be a truck driver in agriculture, she cannot be a bulldozer machinist, she cannot be a controller of speed of train wagons, and she cannot be an operator or a driver in the Metro. In Kazakhstan, there are 299 similar restrictions, including, among dozens of others, limits on a woman's right to be a lumberjack or a snowmobile driver.

In many of these examples, one might sense a kind of well-meaning paternalism, a patronizing attitude of protection assumed by those who for the most part control the political bodies that made the rules. In many countries, too, there is a deep-seated belief, however ill founded, that certain forms of work are harmful to women's reproductive organs. Sometimes these jobs are physically demanding, and the intention of the law may have been to protect women from the strain involved. Other times this is not the case at all. For example, while brute force might have been required in earlier times to justify the fact that only men were allowed to drive trucks in Chilean copper mines, this is not necessarily true today. Some gender restrictions have sometimes failed to catch up with technological change. But many such jobs are also very well paid and highly coveted, which makes it easy to understand why men would prefer to exclude women from such fields. The fact that women in Russia cannot work on oil rigs, for example, or hold jobs in several other highly paid positions in the energy sector contributes to a very large wage gap between men and women.

Indeed, the primary reason why one should be concerned about job restrictions such as those that are pervasive in Russia and other countries has little to do with whether women would actually enjoy driving trucks in mines or operating oil rigs. But it has everything to do with the ability of women to participate in the labor market at comparable levels of remuneration. It also has to do with ways in which the gender wage gap undermines the incentive to work, with consequences for the potential economic benefits derived by women. On this front, the global data are not very reassuring. There is convincing evidence, as already stated, that women often earn less than men for comparable effort and tend to be less well represented in the high-paying and prestigious occupations.

The indicator most often used to track the gender pay gap is the ratio of female to male average earnings, expressed on a 0–100 scale. This is usually compiled by the International Labour Organization on the basis of statistics from the manufacturing sector. The data are patchy and not particularly up-to-date, and country coverage is not as comprehensive as one would like. And it is well to bear in mind that even the limited basis of comparison provided by this dataset is not above criticism. Some researchers argue that an indicator using data of average earnings is likely to disguise the important differences in occupations, in qualifications, and in the hours actually worked. They claim that many factors are not easily observable in these sorts of statistics, such as job performance and effort level, which could also explain lower wages. Nevertheless, while it may be a crude gauge in terms of earnings differentials, the consensus seems to be that the indicator still provides a useful measure of the gender pay gap. However much disagreement there might be about the means and methods of acquiring this information, all studies agree with its conclusions. The data provide overwhelming evidence that women on average earn less than men for performing a similar job.

A review of the statistics gathered over the past twenty years leads to two main conclusions, one good and the other bad. The good news is that the pay gap has been narrowing in a large number of countries. The bad news is that it still remains wide nearly everywhere else. The only possible exception to this conclusion can be found in countries like Sweden and Denmark, where the gap has been reduced to 15 percent or less in a relatively short period.

A closer look at the gender discrepancy in pay for thirty countries in Europe—for which the data on earnings in manufacturing are of a better quality and more comparable across countries—shows a gap ranging from 6.6 percent in Sweden to 29 to 33 percent in Slovakia, Cyprus, and Estonia. Furthermore, the data show that this gap increases with age, with level of education, and with years of service. For instance, as of 2008, the gap in earnings between men and women was above 30 percent for the fifty to fifty-nine age group, as compared to just 7 percent for those under the age of thirty.[3] In other words, the older women get, the less equal they become.

It is important to note that the gender wage gap is not the same across all earnings levels. At the higher earning levels, the gender wage gap appears to be even larger than at other levels. In fact, a study by the Organisation for Economic Co-operation and Development on the wage gap shows that top-earning females are paid 21 percent less than their male counterparts. The results presented in Blau and Kahn (2001) and other studies further emphasize this dismal pattern. Using microdata for twenty-two countries over ten years, for instance, they find that in sectors where there is less variability in wage, the gender wage gap is smaller, but where the variability is higher, the gender pay gap is correspondingly larger too. In other words, wherever there is more money, you find more men.

LAWS AND THE LABOR FORCE

The third finding revealed by the 2016 WBL data is that there is an inverse relationship, over the sample of countries analyzed, between the number of restrictions embedded in the law and the labor force participation rates. This result is perhaps not surprising, given all that has already been discussed. The more constraints the law imposes on women's freedoms, the less women will participate in the labor market; the more women are discouraged to enter the labor force, the weaker and more prone to instability will be the long-term economic health of a nation.

Amartya Sen (1999), who has devoted considerable time to the issue of gender equality, claims that reducing or ameliorating gender inequalities not only contributes to the empowerment of women but also enhances the well-being of society as a whole. He insists that we should look on women not so much as passive recipients of help but as capable and dynamic promoters of social change. He points to the body of persuasive evidence indicating that the education, employment, and ownership rights of women have a direct influence on their ability both to control their own environment and to contribute meaningfully to their economies. In his 1992 paper titled "Missing Women," Sen ascribed considerable importance to public policies that facilitate female participation in the labor market, since paid employment enhances women's social standing, in part through the contributions they make to family income. Indeed, in a large sample of countries, the data show a high positive correlation between women's gainful employment (relative to that of men) and female life expectancy (relative to that of males). Public policies that encourage the incorporation of women into the labor force and that are supported by greater efforts to advance the education and training of women will, therefore, be central to the creation of conditions in society where discrimination against women is the exception rather than the rule.

There is a similar correlation when it comes to the ownership of firms that are run by women. The greater the number of restrictions on women's property rights, the fewer the number of such firms. It is therefore clearly to the benefit of national economies to change these laws in order to enable more women to participate in activities of this kind. The marital property regime is also critical to the financial autonomy of women and their ability to make decisions about family spending because it can determine whether the law allows for bank accounts to be held jointly by both spouses or owned individually by one. Generally, under a full or even partial community property regime, bank accounts are held jointly by both spouses as marital property; under a separation of property regime, they belong solely to the spouse who opened the account. The WBL data show that in economies with a full community property regime, there are on average 8 percent more women with an account at formal financial institutions than in economies with a default separation of property regime.

Two further correlations that emerge from the WBL data show that the higher the number of restrictions imposed by the law, the lower the number of girls there are (relative to boys) who attend secondary school. And the larger the number of restrictions embedded in the law, the larger, too, is the pay gap between women and men. These insights are all very interesting, but none of them comes as a surprise. To live in an environment where entrenched discrimination is part of a country's public policies invariably discourages women and girls and has damaging ramifications across a broad range of other areas. Restrictive laws and failing economies are directly linked to women's rights and lead to many disparities.

DISPARITIES

Disparities can be dangerous. As previously discussed, gender disparities in demographics can lead to violence. Disparities arising from culture can curtail women's rights. Disparities in relation to the law not only affect women but can also have a negative impact on their families and the wider community. This last section will focus on the disparities that affect the learning potential of girls, the earning capacity of women, and the difference in spending patterns between the sexes. Although most gender-related disparities pose a threat to the overall prosperity and security of society, this last one may offer some hope.

Learning

One of the recent areas of research on the costs of inequality concerns the learning process. It relates to the relationship between equal educational opportunities for girls and boys and their subsequent employment opportunities. Inequalities of education impose an artificial limit on the pool of talent from which societies can draw skills and manpower. By excluding qualified girls from the educational stream and promoting less qualified boys, the average amount of human capital in a country is impaired. This has an adverse impact on economic performance. In other words, unequal educational opportunities for girls and boys leads to a less qualified workforce, with the result that economic progress slows. People become poorer.

Another aspect of recent research highlights the link between the promotion of female education and lower births rates, since educated women have greater knowledge of family planning. As a bonus, lower fertility levels help reduce child mortality. Furthermore, education offers women a range of choices beyond childbearing and can expand opportunities for the next generation. Indeed, it is known that lowered fertility has long-lasting effects and delivers a "demographic dividend" some decades down the line, since the working-age population grows more rapidly than the overall population and this boosts per capita economic growth.[4] In other words, equal education for girls results in lower birthrates and child mortality, which in turn allows for higher income. These factors combine to boost economic growth.

An equally powerful driver of economic growth associated with the narrowing of educational gender gaps may be related to what economists call the "bargaining power within families." Not surprisingly, when women earn a better income as a result of better education, they can be more empowered within the home. Beyond direct personal benefits, this provides them with a number of other favorable effects, identified in the economics literature as higher savings, more productive investments, and better use and repayment of credit. Other studies have shown that equal education plants the seeds for accumulating human capital for the next generation.[5] In other words, higher education for girls leads to better employment opportunities for them; better income for women gives them greater power within the household; greater female power in the family in turn leads to higher investments in health, in education, and in future employment for the next generation, all of which are beneficial for long-term economic growth.

As education spreads and a growing share of the population partakes of its benefits, one might expect a leveling off of income and other disparities. There is evidence that this is exactly what happened in England in the nineteenth century: the disparities of income widened rapidly at first as the process of industrialization got under way and then leveled off before the end of the century.[6] But there is no guarantee that such leveling will be permanent or that it will affect women and men in the same way. The fact that it does not immediately eradicate gender disparities should remind us that there are "more things in heaven and earth," as Hamlet tells his friend, Horatio, than measurable statistics: there is only so far that education and training can go in protecting women's rights.

Earning

Disparities in learning between the sexes are unfortunately paralleled by those in earnings, because income levels also play an important role in maintaining gender inequality in the world. However, unlike the links between economic growth and poverty, which are reasonably unambiguous, the interaction between a country's economic growth and income inequality is a complex one. It depends on multiple factors, not all of which are easy to identify. Although its relationship to gender inequality has only recently begun to be assessed, income disparity has been the subject of considerable study since the 1950s,[7] and some factors that have been shown to sharpen such disparities have now begun to be better understood.

The first has been our gradual shift away from agriculture in societies everywhere. This has been a universal characteristic of development over the past century and has affected both the rich, developed countries and the developing world.[8] As people moved from the villages to the cities, from agriculture to industry, they also moved from a sector of low productivity to a higher one. This heightened many income disparities in society, especially in relation to gender. Incomes tended to be more equal in agriculture than in the urban areas, but as people moved to the cities, the share of the population whose income was more unequal increased. Women and children were the first to suffer the consequences.

The second factor leading to income disparity that has had significant implications for gender inequality over the past several decades is technology and the dynamic forces associated with industrialization, particularly during its early phases. The introduction of new technologies and their accompanying processes has meant that those with the skills to handle new machinery or to read instruction manuals—the vast majority of them men—could command much higher wages. This in turn inevitably led to a widening of income disparities, which was self-reinforcing, because those whose skills and training—again, overwhelmingly men—commanded higher wages could afford to get loans to start new ventures. In fact, far from having a leveling effect, the arrival of new technologies resulted in exactly the same sorts of income disparities as occurred with simpler technologies during earlier stages of social development. In other words, inequality of income once again intervenes on the basis of skills-based wage differentials, and this inequality invariably penalizes women.

The third disparity between men and women is the direct consequence of the second. Since men can earn more, they accumulate more of the country's wealth, which obviously provides them with more chances for profitable investment and more opportunities to enter into new business ventures, create new companies, and so on. But there is a dismaying reversal on the other side of this divide arising from its strong gender component. As a result of this phenomenon, women earn less, accumulate less of the country's wealth, and have less chance for profitable investment and consequently less opportunity to enter into business. The concentration of savings in the upper-income groups is, therefore, in men's hands, for the most part. In the United States, for example, the richest 5 percent of the population, among which independently wealthy women are still a minority,[9] accounts for about 72 percent of total savings. (The top 1 percent accounts for 64 percent of total savings.)[10] According to Nobel laureate Simon Kuznets, "[T]he cumulative effect of such inequality in savings would be the concentration of an *increasing* proportion of income-yielding assets in the hands of the upper groups—a basis for larger income shares of these groups and their descendants."[11] Further evidence of this phenomenon can be found in Oxfam's latest report on inequality, which indicates that "just 62 people own as much wealth as the 3.5 billion people in the bottom half of the world's income scale." Since "the gap between rich and poor has continued to widen at an alarming rate," the report adds, "the fortunes of 388 billionaires were needed to reach that halfway mark" just five years ago.[12] Not surprisingly, fifty-four out of these sixty-two billionaires are men.

In countries with weak institutions, with ineffective regulations and poor law enforcement, this self-reinforcing phenomenon has often increased financial and economic leeway for the unscrupulous. What is particularly worrisome is that wealth accumulation has also translated into the language of politics, providing access and leverage of power to men who assume prime positions of control. The amount of wealth stemming from corruption, which was endemic in the past and is still a familiar feature of the present, has assumed astronomical proportions. And wherever growing income disparities arise from corruption and the abuse of power, growing social tensions and political instability are often the result. As already stated, there is a fatal logic leading inexorably from gender inequality to general insecurity.

Spending

Despite the inequalities in education and income, discussed earlier, a third disparity also exists that might offer some hope in redressing the balance of gender inequality. Unlike the discrepancies in learning and earnings between the sexes, the disparity in spending patterns between the sexes is encouraging. Research repeatedly shows that women use money differently from men; they have a different relationship to household finances and by extension to economic policies from men. They basically tend to have different priorities, and perhaps this disparity holds the key to reducing the costs of gender inequality in society.

In many parts of the world, men are very much at the center of decision-making regarding the use of family earnings, which they are more likely to spend on liquor, on sweets, and on lavish celebrations. Many of them consider alcohol or gambling essential.[13] They throw money at luxury items of which they alone are the primary beneficiaries. But when women are in control of funds or earn money themselves, spending patterns in the family appear to change radically. With women holding the purse strings, fewer resources are wasted and more are spent on buying nutritious foods, on education, and on family health. A commonly quoted figure is that women spend up to 90 percent of their earnings on health and education, whereas men spend just 30 to 40 percent in these areas.[14] The divergent spending patterns between men and women have been verified by numerous studies across a diverse range of countries.[15]

So, once again, it seems that women use their "bargaining power within families" to concentrate their means on gender-specific spending patterns that have a long-term impact on the priorities of society as a whole. Esther Duflo (2006, p. 14), who has studied consumption patterns of women and men, summarizes the tendency in this way:

> *When women command greater power, child health and nutrition improves. This suggests that policies seeking to increase women's welfare in case of divorce or to increase women's access to the labor market may impact outcomes within the household, in particular child health . . .*
> *Increasing women's control over resources, even in the short run, will improve their say within the household, which will increase . . . child nutrition and health.*

The life experience of women seems to give them a radically different and vitally important perspective on the needs of the community, as compared with that of men. Indeed, evidence for this difference in male and female spending patterns has been so frequently confirmed that all women's organizations—from the politically savvy in developed countries to fledgling nongovernmental organizations in the developing world—are making demands for a change in priorities on its basis.

For example, a study in three widely differing countries—Bolivia, Cameroon, and Malaysia—makes it indubitably clear that were women to have a greater say in spending priorities, they would be far more likely to use hard-earned family and community resources for improving health and education, for building up community infrastructures, and for eradicating poverty in society rather than on guns, alcohol, or gambling.[16] Indeed, the tendency of men to allocate income toward alcohol comes as no surprise, given what is known about its consumption pattern. Ample evidence indicates that alcohol is more often than not a male problem. By and large, its use by men is far greater than by women in a wide range of countries, from India and China to Brazil and Mexico. Consequently, men contribute significantly to the global burden of disease attributable to alcohol abuse.[17]

Another aspect of the disparity between men's and women's attitudes toward money lies in the growing evidence that women workers are less prone to corruption and nepotism than men. Confirmation of this fact comes from a number of sources. The criminology literature, for instance, has long established that "the most consistent pattern with respect to gender is the extent to which male criminal participation in serious crimes at any age greatly exceeds that of females, regardless of the source of data, crime type, level of involvement or measure of participation."[18] A 2015 survey looking at the gender composition of 6,500 companies in the United Kingdom showed clear evidence that those with greater female participation on governing boards were less likely to be hit by scandals involving bribery, fraud, and other factors likely to depress business confidence.[19]

In other words, by boosting women's spending power, we see improvements in the quality of management and hence better allocation of funds; we see a more effective deployment of scarce resources to activities that are far more likely to improve productivity as well as economic growth. So there is clearly a dynamic relationship among education, training, and enhanced labor skills on one hand and gender inequality, income disparity, and endemic poverty on the other. And most important, this relationship extends beyond the circle of individual families to reach the community as a whole. Civil society benefits from gender equality.

CONCLUSION

The previous six chapters identified several ways in which gender inequality might be gradually mitigated in the world. In addition to the different spending patterns between men and women that counteract inequality at regional as well as national levels, certain governments are now attempting to bridge the gap between inequality in *living standards* and inequality in *incomes* by redistributing budgets so as to give women greater benefits at the national level too. Some of them have even tried to implement policies to reduce gender disparities of skills, training, and income through changes in inheritance taxes, or through the gradual introduction of various mechanisms of social protection, or through publicly financed education to large segments of the population, including girls, for example. All these efforts as well as developments in technology, in and of themselves, can to some extent diminish income disparities, stimulate rapid economic growth and convergence, and greatly influence employment opportunities for both men and women. Finally, we have noted that countries which integrate women into the workforce significantly improve their international competitiveness.

Such changes have had an incremental, if slow, impact on the disparities between men and women. But the operative word is "slow," and in the meantime, the costs of inequality continue to rise alarmingly fast. In fact, these costs are quite simply too expensive to sustain. If girls cannot enjoy equal education or grow up to have access to equal employment opportunities, the costs will mount calamitously. If women cannot be politically empowered to participate

in structures of governance and influence public discourse, spending decisions will be out of their hands and opportunities for growth
will be shamefully squandered. And when it is predominately men
who take up space on the budget committees, who lobby in parliaments and control ministries of finance, spending decisions will reflect their particular priorities and biases.[20] At best, this lack of
political empowerment will merely contribute still further to growing
disparities between men and women; at worst, it will lead to the
proliferation of failed states and collapsing economies. And it is
precisely in these conditions, when economies collapse and states
begin to fail, that civil society comes under huge strains and the cost
of that can sometimes be incalculable.

Of course, it has become customary for pundits of doom to brood
on the end of the world. Latter-day prophets have summoned the
spectral Horsemen of the Apocalypse before our eyes time and again,
trailing clouds of economic crises, environmental catastrophes, wars,
and epidemics in their wake, and on a scale that was unimaginable
until recent events have proven them altogether too possible. It would
not be foolish to question the likelihood or indeed the actual presence in our midst of such imminent disasters, given our propensity
as a human race to miss our opportunities, mistake our priorities, and
fail, at the eleventh hour, to rise to the challenges we ourselves have
created. Nor would it be useful to diminish the urgency of the problems that need to be addressed if we are to emerge from this critical
period with anything like our humanity intact. But it might be helpful to focus on solutions and to realize that the longer we avoid them,
the more devastating the costs for all of us will be.

Economists love to talk about efficiency in resource allocation
when it comes to looking for solutions. But much depends on how
we define "efficiency," and even more depends on the recognition of
our true resources. The extent to which a country can nourish and
provide for the participation of women in civil society and the
workplace is vital to this recognition. The degree to which their

participation could be more "economically efficient" in certain areas and the opportunities given to them more readily available is equally important. The increased presence of qualified women at the higher levels of the professions, of political leadership, and of intellectual creativity will have a salutary influence on society and is urgently needed. The resource that women symbolize is critical, not only to the economy but also to security.

Although the ramifications for international security cannot be the direct focus of this book, there is no question that it is directly linked to the question of gender equality. The stability of our societies and the health of our economies depend on gender equality. The shifting of social attitudes, the evolution of cultural mores, and the replacement of old taboos by new laws are all rooted in gender equality. In the last several decades this issue has unleashed a crisis, aroused a new awareness in human society. And this awareness, whose early signs first emerged in the nineteenth century, is now spreading all over the world. It has forced us to face dilemmas, political, social, cultural, and even environmental, that were unimaginable fifty years ago. And the only way to cure these crises, to resolve these dilemmas is through gender equality.

The riddle of the Sphinx can no longer be ignored. The curse we turned our backs on for more than a century is now staring us in the face. And the need to address it has never been so urgent, the consequences of ignoring it have never been so costly. But since riddles are always ambiguous, we must find answers now that are different from those of the past. We have to interpret the riddle differently from Oedipus, if the curse of our times is to be lifted, not just for Thebes but for the security of the whole planet. The patriarchal answer that may have been valid 2,500 years ago is unable to resolve the complex problems of contemporary society. What walks with four legs in the morning, two legs at noon, and three in the evening is no longer just "man," even generically. For we need both arms to be strong if we are to crawl; we need both legs to be of equal length and strength if we are to walk and to run. And in old age we all need the additional support of society, whether we are men or women.

It has become evident, even to economists today, even to those of us who do not normally deal in riddles, who prefer facts and figures and the evidence of the bottom line, that the answer to this particular riddle is women. The cost of the curse has become too high and can only be lifted by the equality of women. And gender equality is vital for us all, and essential for a more just and prosperous world.

NOTES

INTRODUCTION

1. Yeats, 1919.
2. Kipling, 1889.
3. Wollstonecraft and Mill, 1792.
4. See, for instance, the paper by Klasen and Lamanna (2009), among others.
5. Following is a condensed sampling of the forty-seven questions: Can a woman, whether married or single, apply for a passport in the same way as a man? Can she travel outside the country, in the same way as a man? Can she sign a contract? Can she register a business? Does she have the right to confer citizenship on her children? Are married women required by law to obey their husbands? Is there a nondiscrimination clause covering gender in the country's constitution? Do men and women, whether married or not, have equal ownership rights to property? If one spouse dies, does the other have equal inheritance rights to the marital home? Can women work in the same industries as men? Do laws or constitutional provisions exist mandating equal pay for equal work? Are there specific tax deductions or tax credits that are applicable only to men? Does a woman's testimony carry the same evidentiary weight in court as a man's? Do adult married women need their husband's permission to initiate legal proceedings? Are there criminal sanctions for sexual harassment?

1. THE PEOPLE PROBLEM

1. In a 1991 article, Coale estimated the number of missing females in the world at 60 million, lower than the 100 million figure initially provided by Sen. Coale argued that the low masculinity ratios in Europe, North America, and Japan were an "inappropriate standard" because of "past male war losses and . . . an age composition that reflects past low fertility, as well as the absence of excess female mortality." His lower estimate, however, "confirms the

enormity of the social problem brought to wide public attention by Professor Sen" (p. 522).

2. See, for instance, Waldron, 1983, 1998, 2003.

3. *The Economist,* 2015.

4. Guilmoto, 2012.

5. In this study from the year 2000, Hank and Kohler note that when Europeans are asked for the preferred sex of their first child, "there is some indication for a predominance of sons over daughters . . . Is there any possible explanation for the persistence of a slight son preference in some modern societies? Although the 'structural' conditions in which son preference was originated have eroded, the related 'cultural' idea of boys providing higher utility for the family, etc., may have survived."

6. Traditionally, sons and daughters in India did not have equal inheritance rights. Although the passage of the Hindu Succession Act in 1956 abolished women's "limited owner" status, it still denied women the right to inherit ancestral property. Instead, inheritances were left only to sons. There are several theories, but many believe that this history of no female inheritance contributed to the dowry system. Because daughters had no rights to their families' wealth, they brought economic and financial security into their marriages through movable goods (i.e., dowries). A 2005 amendment to the Hindu Succession Act gave daughters and sons of the deceased equal rights to property. Despite the amendment, the practice of dowry has continued.

7. For a reasonably comprehensive compendium in 173 countries see World Bank Group, 2016, which shows gender-differentiated inheritance rights to be widespread in at least thirty-four countries. These include all eighteen countries covered in the Middle East and North Africa, eight in sub-Saharan Africa (Guinea, Mali, Mauritania, Senegal, Sudan, Swaziland, Tanzania, and Uganda), four in South Asia (Afghanistan, Bangladesh, Nepal, and Pakistan), and four in East Asia and the Pacific (Brunei, Indonesia, Malaysia, and Tonga).

8. *International Herald Tribune,* 21 September 2010. "A Boy's Life for Afghan Girls: Freedom and Status."

9. Littauer, 2012. "While homosexuality is considered a sin and crime punishable by death, transsexuality is categorized as an illness subject to cure (i.e., gender reassignment). Iran has between 15,000 and 20,000 transsexuals, according to official statistics, although unofficial estimates put the figure at up to 150,000."

10. See Vlassoff, 1990.

11. In India, for instance, female mortality rates are much higher than male mortality rates at all age groups between the ages of one and twenty-four. In China, the same is particularly true for those under four. In sub-Saharan Africa, female mortality is higher than male mortality for females between the ages of one and thirty-four. See Anderson and Ray, 2010, Table 2, p. 1272.

12. Ebenstein, 2006, p. 9, quotes a 2006 study for India that estimates that "10 million fetuses have experienced early termination in the past two decades." The reader may be surprised to know that the study indicates that the higher the level of education of the woman, the higher the probability that she will practice sex selection (Jha et al., 2006).

13. According to Das Gupta et al. (2003, p. 3), in South Korea and China "sex ratios at birth began to rise sharply around 1985, when sex-selective technology began to become widespread."

14. These are commonly defined as family planning, safe abortion, cervical cancer screening, skilled attendance in pregnancy and childbirth, care of the newborn, emergency obstetric intervention, and counseling regarding prevention and treatment of sexually transmitted infections.

15. See G. Sen et al., 2002, p. 9.

16. Ibid., p. 10.

17. Ibid., p. 48.

18. Hartigan et al., 2002, p. 46.

19. Cottingham and Myntti, 2002, pp. 83–109.

20. Disability-adjusted life years (DALYs) are derived by considering various grades of disability equal to certain periods of loss of healthy life. For instance, medical professionals at the WHO might hypothesize that three years in full paralysis is equivalent to two years of healthy life. These estimates can then be used, for example, to calculate a disability-adjusted (or health-adjusted) life expectancy.

21. Cottingham and Myntti, 2002, p. 96.

22. Ibid., pp. 94–96.

23. Sedgh et al., 2007.

24. Obstructed childbirth occurs when, notwithstanding normal contractions of the uterus, the baby does not exit the pelvis during childbirth due to some physical blockage.

25. United Nations, 2013a, Chapter 6, pp. 93–97.

26. Planned Parenthood, 2000, citing Alan Guttmacher Institute findings, 1997.

27. Shah and Ahman, 2009, p. 1149.

28. *South China Morning Post*, 2013.

29. According to the authors of this study, a 0.01 increase in the sex ratio increased the rate of violent and property crime by some 3 percent.

30. *The Economist*, 2015.

31. Jacobs, 2015.

32. Livingston, 2013.

33. According to the UN's *World's Women 2015* report: "After reaching its peak around 1990–1995, the sex ratio at birth in that country progressively declined to expected levels by 2010. Changes in social norms and societal development driven by increases in education, together with legislation against sex-selective

abortions, are among the main forces driving the reversal of the trend in the sex ratio at birth. In contrast, in India, while sex-selective abortions have been technically illegal since 1996, the law has had little effect so far on the sex ratio at birth" (p. 7).

34. *The Economist*, 2017. "Too Many Single Men: The Legacy of Gender-cide." 21 January 2017. Available at: https://www.highbeam.com/doc/1G1 -478128085.html.

35. Hewlett, 2002.

36. McQuillan et al., 2012.

37. Pew Research Center Analysis of Current Population Surveys.

38. Scott, 2013.

39. For an insightful discussion of some of the flaws of our system of national accounts, with particular reference to the exclusion of women's work, see Waring, 1988.

40. The World Bank's 2008 *World Development Report* confirms this: "Many women will declare themselves as not in the labor force if they consider their main activity as being responsible for household care, even if they are active on the farm or in the household business."

41. Family Caregiver Alliance, 2003.

42. Rosenblatt, 2013.

43. Euthanasia is currently (2016) legal in Colombia, the Netherlands, Belgium, and Luxembourg. Assisted suicide is legal in Switzerland, Germany, Japan, and Canada, and in the US states of Washington, Oregon, Colorado, Vermont, Montana, and California, and in the District of Columbia. There is increasing support to legalize it in France too, where in January 2016 France's parliament approved a measure that, while stopping short of euthanasia, would allow doctors to keep terminal patients sedated until death.

44. Ebenstein and Sharygin (2009) used the 2002 Survey of Rural Households in China, published by the China National Bureau of Statistics, to estimate that some 62 percent of households in China expect that their children will be the primary source of income in old age.

45. Subsidies, for instance, often lead to smuggling, to shortages, and to the emergence of black markets and corruption. The mechanisms are generally trivially simple. One example is in Bolivia. Substantial subsidies on LPG lead to a thriving smuggling business on the border with Peru, as Bolivians respond to the incentives provided by a three-to-one price difference between the two markets. Putting aside the issue of the opportunity cost associated with wasteful consumer subsidies (how many schools could be built with the cost of one year's LPG subsidy?), and the environmental implications associated with high (and often wasteful) consumption because of artificially low prices, subsidies can often put the government at the center of corruption-generating schemes, hardly a desirable outcome. Initially intended to cushion the im-

pact of high international prices, subsidies mainly help to boost consumption, to weaken the budget, and to distort incentives and in many countries they end up perverting public policy. Because subsidies accustom the public to low prices, leaders are often unwilling to eliminate them owing to (at times violent) public protest and riots. They therefore have a tendency to become entrenched and greatly diminish the ability of the government to spend in more productive areas. .

46. Among the worst offenders on subsidies on petroleum products are Angola, Bangladesh, Bolivia, Cameroon, Ecuador, Ghana, India, Indonesia, the Kyrgyz Republic, Malaysia, Myanmar, Nigeria, Sri Lanka, Trinidad and Tobago, Turkmenistan, Venezuela, and the vast majority of countries in the Middle East and North Africa. The list of countries where subsidies account for a large share of government revenues is much longer when one accounts for subsidies on electricity, natural gas, and coal. In Iran, according to the IMF, these subsidies account for 70 percent of total government revenue.

47. Kristof and WuDunn, 2010, pp. 221–229.

48. Ibid.

2. THE VIRUS OF VIOLENCE

1. Nelson, 2013.
2. Thakur, 2015.
3. Sally Kohn (2013) writes in *More Magazine* that "in India, a country of over 1.2 billion people, 24,206 rapes were reported in 2011. The same year in the United States, a nation of 300 million, 83,425 rapes were reported."
4. Carter, 2015.
5. Udwin, 2015.
6. Berkowicz, 2012.
7. "Feminism is hated because women are hated. Anti-feminism is a direct expression of misogyny; it is the political defense of women hating." Dworkin, 1983, p. 195.
8. Palermo et al., 2014.
9. Iaccino, 2014.
10. "Conflict Assessment" by Anke Hoeffler, Research Officer at Oxford, and James Fearon, Professor of Political Science at Stanford University, for the think tank Copenhagen Consensus Center, 2014.
11. Malkin, 2013.
12. Hoeffler and Fearon, 2014.
13. Hudson and den Boer, 2007.
14. Jacobs, 2015.
15. Ibid. Interestingly enough, as a result of the uproar created by this particular event in the media, the Chinese authorities released the women on bail on

April 13, 2015, a surprise move that seems to indicate that international pressure does have some influence when it comes to issues of gender.

16. Chowdhury, 2013.

17. Malkin, 2013, p. 135.

18. M. Seiff, 2017.

19. *The Guardian*, 2013.

20. In 2010, Swedish police recorded the highest number of offenses, about 63 per 100,000 inhabitants. According to rape crisis advocates, one-third of Swedish women have been sexually assaulted by the end of their teens.

21. The *International Business Times* of January 29, 2014, reports that "a group of boys targeted . . . underage teenage girls, plied them with alcohol and then gang-raped them. The videos of the sexual assaults were then uploaded to social media sites." The article reports that in 2012, sexual assaults rose 15 percent, and at schools the number doubled. It also indicates that UN statistics show that the prevalence of rape cases per 100,000 inhabitants was thirty in 2011.

22. The General Assembly adopted four resolutions in the period 2006 to 2009 on intensification of efforts to eliminate all forms of violence against women, thus emphasizing Members' concern about the issue.

23. *First Post,* 2017.

24. Hancock, 2006.

25. This is the informal title for Brazil's federal law, enacted in 2006, that regulates violence against women in various aspects of domestic life and is regarded as an important milestone in Brazilian legislation on gender.

26. Saul, 2014.

27. Amnesty International and Kvinfo, a Danish interest organization, referenced in: https://www.thelocal.dk/20180308/denmarks-female-politicians-subjected-to-online-harassment.

28. Krook, 2016. http://paperroom.ipsa.org/papers/paper_53875.pdf

29. A recent article by Lomborg and Williams in the 22 February 2018 edition of the *Washington Post* discusses this fact at length, highlighting that 54 percent of the mass shootings between 2009 and 2016 in the United States were conducted by close relatives of the victims, and that "more than 4 million women were assaulted" in this manner over the past year. According to the authors, "The Centers for Disease Control and Prevention estimates that in the United States about 1 in 4 women and 1 in 7 men have experienced severe physical violence from a partner in their lifetimes."

30. Ortiz-Barreda and Vives-Cases, 2013.

31. Shaikh, 2013.

32. Hajjar, 2004.

33. Interested readers can go to https://www.zoominfo.com/p/Shahnaz-Bokhari

/1499404399 to see some data updates and recent stories on violence against women in Pakistan. The Progressive Women's Association Facebook page also contains additional information, including some harrowing photography.

34. Quoted in Terzieff, 2002. For more information about Shahnaz Bokhari, see *The Independent*, 1999.
35. Shepard and Pence, 1988.
36. Hoeffler and Fearon, 2017, p. 20.
37. Parent-Thirion et al., 2007.
38. Moore, 2017.
39. McFarlane et al., 1999.
40. Anderson and Ray, 2010.
41. Hoeffler and Fearon, 2017, p. 20.
42. Begikhani, 2005.
43. Araji and Carlson, 2001.
44. Sheeley, 2007.
45. Rubin, 2015.
46. Shears, 2005.
47. Open Doors International, 2013.
48. International Labour Organization, 2007.
49. S. Smith, 2015.
50. Hoeffler and Fearon, 2017, p. 21.
51. Ortiz-Barreda and Vives-Cases, 2013.
52. Lomborg and Williams, 2018.
53. Lomborg and Williams's article in the *Washington Post* draws attention to significant studies about these two factors, by Jacqueline M. Golding (1999) and Jacquelyn C. Campbell (2002).
54. Day et al., 2005.
55. United Nations, 2010, p. 131.
56. Duvvury et al., 2013. The nine countries are the US, Australia, the UK, Nicaragua, Chile, Uganda, Morocco, Bangladesh, and Vietnam.
57. Psytel, 2009.
58. Ribero and Sanchez, 2004.
59. Khumalo et al., 2014.
60. Lomborg and Williams, quoting from Hoeffler and Fearon's findings.
61. According to Lomborg and Williams, "more than 4 million women were assaulted in the United States in the past 12 months."
62. Lomborg and Williams, 2018.
63. This is in contrast to entertainment, sports, or election campaigning: the 2010 FIFA World Cup cost around US$3 to 5 billion.
64. The #MeToo movement, the #NeverAgain movement, and the increased mobilization of women and students marching in protest across the country

over the past year seem to indicate a change of mood in response to endemic sexual abuse and escalating violence in the United States in particular.

65. Associated Chambers of Commerce and Industry of India, 2013.

66. This fear is not gender neutral: less than a quarter of men were fearful of traveling under the same circumstances.

67. Associated Chambers of Commerce and Industry of India, 2013.

68. "The danger of the practice of violence, even if it moves consciously within a non-extremist framework of short-term goals, will always be that the means overwhelm the end. If goals are not achieved rapidly, the result will not merely be defeat but the introduction of the practice of violence into the whole body politic. Action is irreversible, and a return to the status quo in case of defeat is always unlikely. The practice of violence, like all action, changes the world, but the most probable change is a more violent world" (Arendt, 1969).

69. According to the World Economic Forum's 2017 Gender Gap Report.

70. Clark et al., 2002. Other reviews on this subject can be found in Day et al., 2003.

71. Tiefenthaler, 2000.

72. Demirguc-Kunt et al., 2013.

3. WOMEN AND WORK

1. Describing misogyny, historian Gerda Lerner (1993, p. 3) states that "once established as a functioning system of complex hierarchical relationships, patriarchy transformed sexual, social, [and] economic relations and dominated all systems of ideas."

2. In *Women and Men: A Philosophical Conversation*, Françoise Giroud and Bernard-Henri Lévy (1993) suggest that this applies to literature as well. In their fascinating conversation, Giroud writes: "Here, it's very hard to talk about women, in the plural. How am I supposed to know what all women's inner thoughts are? Who can? They've never talked about themselves . . . except rarely, or little. Everything we know about their feelings, their thoughts, their inner workings (to use a phrase I dislike), comes from what men have imputed to them. Men of genius, sometimes, but really . . . It's a man who tells us about Anna Karenina, about Mathilde de la Mole in *The Red and the Black*, about Emma Bovary" (p. 19).

3. In some cultures, while men are considered prototypically "human," women have been mythologized as being allied to alien powers. From Circe and Medusa to Lilith and Morgane le Fay, from the queen of the Black Isles in the *Arabian Nights* to Galadriel and Princess Leia in more recent examples, legendary women, whether perceived as embodiments of absolute good or evil, have always been linked to otherworldly powers.

4. The figures on labor force participation are for 2016, as published in the World Bank's World Development Indicators Database (% of population ages 15+,

modeled ILO estimate, last updated April 27, 2017). Regional aggregates are for all income levels.

5. Fernández, 2013.

6. See, for instance, Esteve-Volart (2000, 2004).

7. Not to be confused with the "plow theory," according to which new settlers pushing West onto the Great Plains in the late 1800s persuaded themselves that they were the agents of increased precipitation if they simply broke the prairie sod and allowed rainfall to be absorbed more quickly into the soil.

8. Brewer, 2013.

9. Given the importance of soil in agriculture, and the considerable time spent cultivating the land in cultures that have used the plough, it is not hard to see the strong connections that developed in "plough culture" between the seeding of fields and the insemination of women. Both types of harvest, after all, confirmed social survival: one through grain, the other through sons. It is hardly surprising, therefore, that the symbol of woman as earthly and man as heavenly has colored patriarchal myths from ancient times. In classical terminology, men were engaged in "transcendent" activities, while women, like lower-class people of both sexes, were to be engaged in that which is "immanent" and perishable.

10. Guthrie, 2004.

11. Hegeman, 2007, p. 43.

12. United Nations Food and Agriculture Organization.

13. Gneezy et al. (2009) present interesting evidence that further underlines the role of patriarchy in perpetuating social perceptions of gender roles. A stylized finding in many studies is that men and women differ in their propensities to engage in competitive activities, with men tending to compete more often than women, even in tasks where women are more able. The implication is that this may provide a rationale for why, for instance, a higher fraction of men are CEOs, while a higher fraction of women are grammar school teachers. To investigate whether patriarchy has a role in this, Gneezy et al. use experimental games to explore whether there are gender differences in selecting into competitive environments across two distinct societies: the Maasai in Tanzania and the Khasi in India. The Maasai represent a textbook example of a patriarchal society, whereas the Khasi are matrilineal. Maasai men opt to compete at roughly twice the rate of Maasai women. However, this result is reversed among the Khasi, where women choose the competitive environment more often than Khasi men, and even choose to compete weakly more often than Maasai men.

14. The fact that this opinion is borne out, as we shall see in the following pages, by statistics in certain developing countries where childcare has been institutionalized to allow women to join the workforce, only highlights the crucial underlying problem, which is that women are penalized by guilt as well as

economics, their role as mothers and as salaried workers both undermined by social norms.

15. Woolf, 1973, p. 43.

16. Thibos et al., 2007, p. 3.

17. See World Bank, 2013.

18. June 6, 2015. Regarding firm performance, *The Economist* cites studies that indicate no relationship between gender diversity and performance or that uncover a negative relationship. One study actually has a more nuanced finding: Improvement in gender diversity of the board in US firms leads to board effectiveness and leads to a negative effect on performance only for firms that already have strong governance. For firms with weak governance, gender diversity does have a positive effect on performance. Even one of the most prominent studies uncovering a negative relationship between female board representation and performance due to quotas in Norway (Ahern and Dittmar, 2012) notes that the mechanism triggering the effect is potentially the small pool of female talent available to fill boardroom positions. The policy argument in this case is that any boardroom quota system should go hand in hand with policies promoting female participation and experience in the private sector.

19. Lee et al., 2015

20. Credit Suisse Research Institute, 2014.

21. Lee et al., 2015.

22. One study found that countries with specific targets, quotas, and penalties for not meeting regulations, including Norway, Iceland, Finland, and Sweden, had nearly double the average percentage of women on boards (about 34 percent) of countries without those measures (about 18 percent) (see Association for Psychological Science, 2016).

23. Japan also fits in this category with 5 percent of women on its boards of directors (Harvard Law School Forum on Corporate Governance and Financial Regulation, 2017).

24. Jacobsen, 2011.

25. Amin and Islam, 2015.

26. The Gini coefficient is a variability measure designed to represent the income or wealth distribution of a group of people, such as a nation's inhabitants. It is the most commonly used measure of inequality. It was developed by the Italian statistician Corrado Gini in 1912. The coefficient is typically normalized to be between 0 and 1, with higher scores signifying higher levels of inequality.

27. For further evidence on how difficulties in accessing inputs and market failures can lower agricultural productivity for women, see Palacios-López and López (2014) and Kilic et al. (2015).

28. The data on mandatory paid maternity leave comes from the Women, Busi-

ness and the Law database at the World Bank Group, 2015, and United Nations, *The World's Women*, 2015.

29. Geiger and Kent, 2017.

30. UN Women calculation based on Stockholm University and Interparliamentary Union, Global Data Base of Quotas on Women (United Nations Women, 2016).

31. Chen, 2010.

32. Chattopadhyay and Duflo, 2004.

33. Beaman et al., 2012.

34. Hewlett, 2002.

35. Researchers have also pointed out an additional dimension that has hampered the progress of women in gaining better jobs. The issue is the recent surge in hours worked by both women and men. The pressure of a round-the-clock work culture, in which emails are answered late at night and phone calls are taken on weekends, may affect the career progress of women more than men, given the former's socially assigned role of primary caretaker of children (Cain Miller, 2015).

36. United Nations Human Rights, 2010.

4. THE CULTURE QUESTION

1. See, for instance, the generally low rankings of countries in the Middle East and North Africa region in the Innovation Capacity Index featured in López-Claros (2010).

2. Temin, 1997, p. 268.

3. Murdock (1965, p. 116) claims that "increases or decreases in population, changes in the geographical environment, migrations into new environments, contacts with peoples of differing culture, natural and social catastrophes such as floods, crop failures, epidemics, wars, and economic depressions, accidental discoveries, and even the death or rise to power of a strong leader" are all among the classes of events that can precipitate cultural change.

4. Murdock also observes that modern American culture provides a good example of the extent to which borrowing or diffusion shapes the underlying culture. Its language comes from England, the alphabet from the Phoenicians, the numerical system from India, and paper and printing from China. Its system of real property is derived from medieval Europe and its religion is a composite of pieces brought together from the ancient Hebrews, Egyptians, Babylonians, and Persians. Paper money is from China, metal coinage from Lydia, checks from Persia, the banking system (including credit, loans, discounts, mortgages) in its modern version comes from Italy and England. Domesticated plants and animals, virtually without exception, are borrowed from other cultures, and vanilla and chocolate, the favorite American ice cream flavors, were borrowed from the Aztecs.

5. K. Armstrong, 2014.

6. Richard Dawkins (2015) fulminates: "Tradition is fine where it amounts to songs or literature, styles of dress or architecture. But tradition is a terrible basis for ethics, or beliefs about the origin of the universe or the evolution of life."

7. Landes (1994, p. 641) invites us to contrast this with "the bulimic appetite of European sailors, their greed cloaked with missionary virtue, ready to venture on unknown seas in small boats and to put up with months of verminous crowding and famine to get their hands on the riches of the Indies, nothing deterred by failure or disappointment, each voyage a stepping stone to the next. Once they caught the whiff of wealth in their sails, no change in government policy, no want of official support, was going to stop them."

8. Balazs, 1964, pp. 13–27.

9. Goldstone, 1996.

10. De Long (1988, p. 1147) makes the additional point that Protestantism is correlated with other factors, such as specialization in manufacturing, a high investment ratio, and northern latitude. And, of course, neither Japan nor Italy, two countries that successfully converged in the twentieth century to the upper ranks of the rich, had much connection with the Protestant ethic.

11. "In the age of hand-crafted products, Protestants and Catholics were economic equals. But when it became necessary to invest in factories and machinery to exploit a new technology, then the culture of Protestantism was a decided advantage" (Temin, 1997, p. 269).

12. Hudson, 2011. "Female employment in the 1850s, 60s and 70s appears to have been higher than any recorded again until after World War II. Family budget evidence suggests that around 30–40 percent of women from working class families contributed significantly to household incomes in the mid-Victorian years. This might have been even higher during the decades of the industrial revolution, before the rise of State and trade union policies regulating female labor and promoting the male breadwinner ideal."

13. A recent historical example of the power of demonstration effects is provided by the opening (glasnost) set in motion by Mikhail Gorbachev in the waning days of the Soviet Union. Glasnost may well have accelerated the collapse of internal Communist Party control in the second half of the 1980s, which had previously been based on censorship, travel restrictions, limitations on the access to information, and other constraints that fed the myth that central planning was a functioning engine of human prosperity and a viable alternative to the market economy.

14. The list also includes such elements as bodily adornment, calendars, cooperative labor, eschatology, ethics, food taboos, greetings, incest taboos, joking, language, law, luck superstitions, medicine, mythology, numerals, penal sanctions, property rights, religious ritual, status differentiation, surgery, tool making, trade, and more.

15. Marshall, 2017: "The role of religion at the intersection of women's rights and the family is both highly controversial and poorly understood. For secular critics, faith traditions are at the foundation of patriarchal norms that underwrite the subordination of women. Many religious conservatives counter that civic equality for women is compatible with traditional family structures. Religious progressives stake out a third position, supporting full gender equality within the family as well as society as an expression of the equal dignity of sons and daughters of God. As controversy within and across these groups and perspectives has grown more visible and polarized, our knowledge of how women's rights, religion, and the family interact in practice has lagged behind."

16. United Nations Security Council Resolution 1267 refers to the Council's "deep concern over the continuing violations of international humanitarian law and of human rights, particularly discrimination against women and girls."

17. Gibbon, 1776 (1983 edition), p. 250.

18. Coomaraswamy, 1997.

19. This is how the Grand Inquisitor addresses the Captive, upon his return to the streets of Seville in Dostoyevsky's (1880) *Brothers Karamazov*: "There is for man no preoccupation more constant or more nagging than, while in the condition of freedom, quickly to find someone to bow down before. But man seeks to bow down before that which is already beyond dispute, so far beyond dispute that all human beings will instantly agree to a universal bowing-down before it. For the preoccupation of these miserable creatures consists not only in finding that before which I or another may bow down, but in finding something that everyone can come to believe in and bow down before, and that it should indeed be *everyone*, and that they should do it *all together*. It is this need, for a community of bowing-down that has been the principal torment of each individual person and of mankind as a whole since the earliest ages. For the sake of a universal bowing-down they have destroyed one another with the sword. They have created gods and challenged one another. 'Give up your gods and come and worship ours or else death to you and to your gods!'" (p. 292).

20. According to the World Bank's 2016 *Women, Business and the Law* report, 90 percent of all the countries in the world have at least one form of discrimination against women embedded in their laws.

21. Lerner, 1993, p. 4.

22. The interpretation of the Judaic texts has always been a male prerogative. According to such interpretations, a wife is a "man's chattel." Women are property, alongside cattle and slaves, and intercourse with a menstruating woman is comparable to incest with one's mother, punishable by death (Babylonian Talmud, Tractate Keritoth 2b Soncino, 1961 ed., p. 1). According to the Talmudic law of Niddah, a woman is unclean for the week she is menstruating and for another week afterward too. During this time she

pollutes all she touches until she takes a ritual bath. If she violates this law, she is subject to arrest and punishment, but if she obeys it, she will certainly be hard-pressed to maintain a career.

23. "Tertullian told women to shroud their bodies in veils and make themselves as unattractive as possible. He blamed them for the sin of Eve: 'You are the devil's gateway . . . because of you the Son of God had to die!' . . . Some of the fathers of the church seemed totally unable to deal with women, and attacked them in vicious, immoderate and, indeed, unchristian language. Because they believed that celibacy was the prime Christian vocation, they projected their own frustration on to women, whom they castigated as evil temptresses."

24. Tallan and Taitz, n.d.

25. S. Armstrong, 2014, pp. 60–61. Sally Armstrong claims that these statements, which illustrate how the social destiny of women was "sealed" in Christianity, are taken from epistles to the Ephesians, Titus and Timothy, and all signed in the name of St. Paul. Armstrong believes that this was done as a mark of respect toward St. Paul and, perhaps, as an attempt to appropriate his authority, but that in fact they were all written decades after his death.

26. Al-Hashimi (1996): "Do not stop your women from going to the mosque, although their houses are better for them" (Chapter 1).

27. New Family, 2017.

28. Laws related to the use of drugs and alcohol, for example, can be routinely ignored when applied to those men who impose strictures of dress and constraints of liberty on their womenfolk.

29. This point is made abundantly clear by analyzing the Women, Business and the Law dataset.

30. Armstrong, 2009.

31. Armstrong claims that if Christ distinguished between Caesar and God, it was merely to emphasize that everything belonged to God and nothing should be given to Caesar. According to her, faith and politics were always one in the past and the separation between church and state is a European invention; the secularism to which it has given rise, in her opinion, is partly responsible for the fundamentalisms it provokes.

32. According to Donald Read (1994, p. 38), in spite of the fact that "a queen reigned at the apex of Victorian society, wife-beating constituted a major Victorian social problem." See also Doggett (1992) for a bibliography and examples of similar cases of domestic brutality.

5. RIGHTS AND WRONGS

1. Milani, 2011, pp. 118–119.
2. G. Miller, 2008.
3. Chen, 2010.

4. Chattopadhyay and Duflo, 2004.

5. World Bank, 2012, p. 336.

6. Geddes, Lueck, and Tennyson, 2012.

7. Singapore Women's Charter, 2017. This allowed a married woman to acquire, hold and dispose of property, to be liable for contracts, debts or obligations, to sue and be sued in her own name, to be entitled to remedies and redress as well as subject to the laws of bankruptcy and the enforcement of judgments, etc.

8. Demirguc-Kunt et al., 2013.

9. See Deere and Doss, 2006; Deere and León, 2003; Quisumbing and Hallman, 2005.

10. Gonzales et al., 2015.

11. 1981 in the case of Spain and only by 1984 in the case of Switzerland.

12. Bosch, 2015.

13. Centre de ressources en Belgique, n.d.

14. See LegiFrance, 2017, re Law 85-1372 (23 December 1985) concerning the equality of spouses in matrimonial regimes and of parents in the management of the property of minor children.

15. Demokratiezentrum, 2008.

16. 1907 Civil Code of Switzerland, Articles 195, 200, and 201.

17. United Nations, available at: http://www.un.org/en/documents/udhr/

18. Consisting of the Universal Declaration of Human Rights, the International Covenant on Civil and Political Rights with both of its optional protocols, and the International Covenant on Economic, Social and the Cultural Rights.

19. See General Comment No. 18 in United Nations Compilation of General Comments, 2008, p. 134, para. 1.

20. ECHR Article 14, ACHR Article 24.

21. Article 3(1) and (2).

22. Primarily in Articles 1(3), 55(c), and 56.

23. Interights, 2011.

24. UN Women, "Declarations, Reservations, and Objections to CEDAW."

25. Human Rights Watch, 2011.

26. Details of the committee's proceedings, along with all of the relevant documents, are available at Office of the High Commissioner for Human Rights, "The Right to Equality and Non-Discrimination in the Administration of Justice."

27. Byrnes and Freeman, 2012.

28. The BAA was set up as a separate legal system for the administration of African Law, subject to a separate political regime from the rest of South Africa. These areas were ruled by proclamation, not parliament, and their laws were independent of both civil and common law practices. The imperative behind the act was to establish a strong system of "native administration" to contain the political pressures resulting from territorial segregation.

29. Hallward-Driemeier and Gajigo, 2010.

30. Cho, 1995.

31. Constitutional Court of Korea, 2007, p. 101.

32. "Marriage and family life shall be entered into and sustained on the basis of individual dignity and equality of the sexes, and the State shall do everything in its power to achieve that goal." Constitution of South Korea, Article 36(1).

33. Kim, 2006.

34. Quoted in Choe, 2010.

35. R. L. Miller, 1998.

36. Lam, 1992.

37. R. L. Miller, 2003.

38. Liu and Boyle, 2001.

39. International Women's Rights Action Watch Asia, 1999.

40. Nakakubo, 2007.

41. *The Economist*, 2014.

42. Sasaki, 2002.

43. Yu, 2002.

44. R. L. Miller, 2003.

45. Houseman and Abraham, 1993.

46. R. L. Miller, 1998.

47. According to the 1995 Population Census conducted by the Japanese Ministry of Public Management, Home Affairs, Posts, and Telecommunications, 45 percent of married women are considered full-time housewives. The fraction of full-time housewives among the age group fifteen to thirty-four is 55 to 68 percent, while the fraction of full-time housewives among the age group thirty-five to fifty-nine is 33 to 45 percent. See Sasaki, 2002.

48. Yu, 2002.

49. Effendi, 1977, p. 30.

50. Universal House of Justice, 1985.

6. EDUCATION FOR EQUALITY

1. Between 1950 and 2015, world GDP per capita expanded at an annual average rate of 2.1 percent and this expansion—although with considerable regional variations—was associated with a remarkable evolution in three key indicators of human welfare. In the half-century between 1960 and 2015, infant mortality fell from 122 to 32 per 1,000 live births; average life expectancy at birth rose from 52 to 71 years, a 36 percent increase, which is nothing short of spectacular; and adult illiteracy fell from 53 to 15 percent. Equally impressive was the sharp drop in the incidence of poverty: data from the World Bank show that between 1990 and 2013—a period that includes the globalization phase of the twentieth century—the number of poor people liv-

ing on less than $1.90 per day (the poverty line used for the definition of extreme poverty) fell from about 2 billion to slightly less than 800 million. (See the World Bank's World Development Indicators.)

2. United Nations Educational, Scientific, and Cultural Organization (UNESCO) Institute for Statistics.

3. This is possible because while the reduction in the total number of illiterate persons over the period 1990 to 2015 has been about 120 million, the reduction in China alone has amounted to 141 million, which implies that there has been an *increase* in the number of illiterate persons in other regions.

4. See, for instance, World Bank, 2014.

5. Ebadi, 2015.

6. Winthrop, 2015.

7. Kristof, 2014.

8. See Kristof and WuDunn, 2010 (pp. 171–173), for a discussion of some of the less costly remedies for keeping the 115 million children (57 percent of whom are girls) who have begun school but dropped out, including deworming, helping girls to manage menstruation, iodizing salt, and paying parents to keep children in school.

9. World Bank, 2012, p. 110.

10. See Deininger et al., 2010.

11. See Deininger et al., 2014.

12. See, for instance, Harrison, 2000.

13. On the role of education in the emergence of Israel as an ICT power, see López-Claros and Mia (2006).

14. A. Smith, 1994, p. 5.

15. Guiso et al., 2006.

16. Guiso et al. (2009) use a linguistic measure proposed by Fearon and Laitin (2003), and a measure of genetic distance developed by Cavalli-Sforza et al. (1996).

17. Guiso, Sapienza, and Zingales, 2009.

18. The relationship between an economy's level of development and women's labor market participation is, however, not a linear one: Mammen and Paxson (2000) use cross-country data from 1970 to 1985 to show that the percentage of women in the labor force first decreases and then increases as the GDP per capita increases.

19. Appadurai, 2004.

20. Giuliano, 2007.

21. Fernández et al., 2004, and Fernández and Fogli, 2009.

22. Steele and Aronson, 1995; Hoff and Pandey, 2006.

23. 'Abdu'l-Bahá, 1912, pp. 174–175.

7. THE COSTS OF INEQUALITY

1. See ActionAid, 2015. ActionAid estimates the additional income women could earn if their wages and employment rates were the same as men's. This is achieved by first calculating the total income of men and breaking it down into its components: employment, wages, and labor share in the economy. Thus the gender pay gap, the gender employment gap, and the gender population gap can be applied to the components of men's total income to uncover the income forgone by women due to inequality. The gender pay gap data are obtained from International Labour Organization data, which indicates that women in developing countries on average earn 14.9 percent less than men. The gender employment gap data are obtained from the World Bank and the UN, and indicate that 36.8 percent fewer women than men are employed in developing economies. The authors of the report acknowledge that there are potential limitations in these estimates, but consideration of some of these limitations, especially the reliability of wage data, may lead to a higher estimate than $9 trillion for the costs of gender inequality.

2. The full set includes Armenia, Canada, the Dominican Republic, Estonia, Hungary, Kosovo, Malta, Mexico, Namibia, the Netherlands, New Zealand, Peru, Puerto Rico, Serbia, the Slovak Republic, South Africa, Spain, and Taiwan.

3. These figures are discussed in greater detail in United Nations, *The World's Women 2015.*

4. See Friedman, 2005; Klasen and Lamanna, 2009; Lagerlof, 2003.

5. See A. Sen, 1990; World Bank, 2001.

6. Friedman (2005) argues that "Karl Marx's claim that capitalism inevitably leads to ever increasing misery of the working classes, and hence to an explosive polarization of society, resulted from Marx's myopic extrapolation of the widening inequality that accompanied England's economic growth in the first half of the nineteenth century" (p. 349).

7. A substantive early contribution was by Simon Kuznets, who tackled some of the more difficult issues directly in his presidential address to the American Economic Association given in December of 1954 and published in 1955.

8. Between 1991 and 2001, for instance, more than 8 million people left agriculture in India. Between 1965 and 2000, the share of the labor force employed in agriculture fell from 49 to 21 percent in Brazil, from 26 to 5 percent in Japan, from 55 to 11 percent in Korea, from 81 to 47 percent in China, and from 5 to 2 percent in the United States.

9. This does not include the "poor little rich woman" syndrome, the wives of powerful men running hedge or private equity funds, described by Martin (2015).

10. Saez and Zucman, 2016.
11. Kuznets (1955, p. 7) was prescient in anticipating trends in the concentration of income and wealth. According to the latest data, 70 percent of the world's population receives less than 15 percent of the world PPP dollar income, while the top 10 percent of the population receives close to 58 percent of total world income. Comparing incomes not at PPP exchange rates but at actual market exchange rates, the top 10 percent receive an even larger share of world dollar income. Another indicator of overall inequality is the comparison between the average income of the top decile and the average income of the bottom decile: this ratio was 95 using PPP exchange rates and well in excess of 300 using market exchange rates, huge numbers by any definition.
12. Cohen, 2016.
13. Duflo and Udry, 2004.
14. Lagarde, 2014.
15. For example, in Côte d'Ivoire, Hoddinott and Haddad (1995) find that raising wives' share of cash income increases the budget share of food, and reduces the budget shares of alcohol and cigarettes. In Bangladesh and South Africa, women's assets increase expenditure shares on education (Quisumbing and Malucci, 2003). In Brazil, unearned income in the hands of a mother has a bigger effect on her family's health than income under the control of a father; for child survival probabilities the effect is almost twenty times bigger (Thomas, 1990). In Nepal, children of mothers who own land are significantly less likely to be severely underweight (Allendorf, 2007). In Ghanaian households where women have more bargaining power, a larger share of the household budget is spent on education, while alcohol and tobacco expenses are negatively related to the percentage of assets held by urban women (Doss, 2006). In Mexico, using Progresa data, Attanasio and Lechene (2002) find that a higher share of income for the wife is associated, on average, with significantly higher budget shares of expenditures on clothing for children of both genders and with significantly lower shares of alcohol.
16. Bahá'í International Community, 1993.
17. According to the World Health Organization 2005 report "Alcohol, Gender and Drinking Problems: Perspectives from Low and Middle Income Countries," in the South Asia B sub-region (which includes Bangladesh and India), the percentage of male drinkers is 26 percent while the corresponding figure for female drinkers is a mere 4 percent. Similarly in the Western Pacific WHO sub-region B (e.g., China, Philippines, Vietnam) there are 84 percent male drinkers and just 30 percent female. In the Americas WHO sub-region B (e.g., Brazil, Mexico) male drinkers account for 73 percent while female drinkers account for 58 percent. Furthermore, the WHO study reports the global burden of disease in 2000 attributable to alcohol. Overall, the disability-adjusted

life year (DALY), a measure of overall disease burden, expressed as the number of years lost due to ill-health, disability, or early death, is globally 8,926,000 for females, and 49,397,000 for males.

18. From a study conducted by the National Academy of Sciences of the United States, cited in Swamy et al. (2001).

19. S. Smith, 2015.

20. To take a recent example, in Russia, in the 1990s, these priorities reflected the need to protect the financial interests—usually through very expensive tax exemptions—of cronies and an emerging oligarchic class, rather than to protect the eroding incomes of close to 40 million pensioners or to safeguard the real value of children's allowances and other social benefits to the population, including millions of women.

BIBLIOGRAPHY

Abdalla, R. 1982. *Sisters in Affliction: Circumcision and Infibulation of Women in Africa.* London: Zed Press.

'Abdu'l-Bahá. 1912. Paris Talks. London: Baha'i Publishing Trust.

———. 1982. The Promulgation of Universal Peace: Talks Delivered by 'Abdu'l-Bahá during His Visit to the United States and Canada in 1912. Wilmette, IL: Baha'i Publishing Trust.

Abramovitz, M. 1986. "Catching-Up, Forging Ahead and Falling Behind." *Journal of Economic History* 46(2): 385–406.

ActionAid. 2015. *Close the Gap! The Cost of Inequality in Women's Work.* Available at: https://www.actionaid.org.uk/sites/default/files/publications/womens _rights_on-line_version_2.1.pdf

Agüero, J. 2013. "Causal Estimates of the Intangible Costs of Violence Against Women in Latin America and the Caribbean." IADB Working Paper Series No. IDB-WP 414.

Ahern, K., and Dittmar, A. 2012. "The Changing of the Boards: The Impact on Firm Valuation of Mandated Female Board Representation." *Quarterly Journal of Economics* 127(1): 137–197.

Akumu, C. O., Amony, I., and Otim, G. 2005. *A Study of Sexual and Gender Based Violence (SGBV) in Pabbo Camp, Gulu District, Northern Uganda.* Gulu District Sub Working Group on SGBV. Available at: https://reliefweb.int/sites /reliefweb.int/files/resources/BEFB77D29CC17FE74925702200095601 -unicef-uga-15jun.pdf

Al-Adili, N., Shaheen, M., Bergstro, S., and Johansson, A. 2008. "Deaths Among Young, Single Women in 2000–2001 in the West Bank, Palestinian Occupied Territories." *Reproductive Health Matters* 16(31): 112–121.

Alberta Federation of Labour. April 2009. *Domestic Violence Is a Workplace Issue.* Available at: https://d3n8a8pro7vhmx.cloudfront.net/afl/pages/2414/attachments

/original/1257262582/Domestic%20Violence%20is%20a%20Workplace%20
Issue.pdf?1257262582

Alesina, A., Giuliano, P., and Nunn, N. 2013. "On the Origins of Gender Roles:
Women and the Plough." *Quarterly Journal of Economics* 128(2): 469–530.

Al-Hashimi, M. A. 1996. *The Ideal Muslimah*, 3rd ed., translated by Nasiruddin
Al-Khattab. Riyadh, Saudi Arabia: International Islamic Publishing House.

Allendorf, K. 2007. "Do Women's Land Rights Promote Empowerment and Child
Health in Nepal?" *World Development* 35(11): 1975–1988.

Amin, M., and Islam, A. 2014. "Are There More Female Managers in the Retail Sector? Evidence from Survey Data in Developing Countries." Policy
Research Working Paper No. 6843. Washington, DC, World Bank. License:
CC BY 3.0. Available at: https://openknowledge.worldbank.org/handle/10986
/18328

———. 2015. "Does Mandating Nondiscrimination in Hiring Practices Influence
Women's Employment? Evidence Using Firm-Level Data (English)." *Feminist
Economics*, 26 February. Available at: http://documents.worldbank.org/curated
/en/228751467987848955/Does-mandating-nondiscrimination-in-hiring
-practices-influence-womens-employment-Evidence-using-firm-level-data

Anderson, S., and Ray, D. 2010. "Missing Women: Age and Disease." *Review of
Economic Studies* 77: 1262–1300.

Annan, K. 2005. Quotes on Human Rights. Fonds des Nations Unies pour la Population. Available at: https://www.unfpa.org/fr/node/9207

Appadurai, A. 2004. "The Capacity to Aspire: Culture and the Terms of Recognition." In *Culture and Public Action: A Cross-Disciplinary Dialogue on
Development Policy.* Edited by Rao, V., and Walton, M. Palo Alto, CA: Stanford University Press.

Araji, S., and Carlson, J. 2001. "Family Violence Including Crimes of Honor in
Jordan: Correlates and Perceptions of Seriousness." *Violence Against Women*
7(5): 586–621.

Arendt, H. 1969. "Reflections on Violence." *New York Times*, 27 February. Available   at: http://www.nybooks.com/articles/archives/1969/feb/27/a-special
-supplement-reflections-on-violence/

Armstrong, K. 1987. *The Gospel According to Woman: Christianity's Creation
of the Sex War in the West.* Norwell, MA: Anchor Press.

———. 1993. *A History of God.* New York: Random House.

———. 2004. "The Eve of Destruction." *The Guardian.* 15 January. Available
at: https://www.theguardian.com/world/2004/jan/15/gender.religion

———. 2006. *The Great Transformation: The World in the Time of Buddha,
Confucius, Socrates and Jeremiah.* New York: Random House.

———. 2009. "Karen Armstrong Builds a 'Case for God.'" National Public Radio.
21 September. Available at: http://www.npr.org/2009/09/21/112968197/karen
-armstrong-builds-a-case-for-god

————. 2014. "The Myth of Religious Violence." *The Guardian*. 25 September. Available at: https://www.theguardian.com/world/2014/sep/25/-sp-karen -armstrong-religious-violence-myth-secular

————. 2014. "Religion Gets a Bad Rap on Women. But There's More to the Story." *On Faith*. 26 March. Available at: https://www.onfaith.co/onfaith/2014 /03/26/religion-gets-a-bad-rap-on-women-but-theres-more-to-the-story /31437

Armstrong, S. 2014. *Ascent of Women*. Toronto, Canada: Vintage Random House.

Asquith, C. 2015. "Turkish Men Get Away with Murder." *New York Times*. 23 February. Available at: https://www.nytimes.com/2015/02/24/opinion /ozgecan-aslan-and-violence-against-women-in-turkey.html

Assemblée Nationale de France. "La Conquête de la Citoyenneté Politique des femmes." Available at: http://www2.assemblee-nationale.fr/decouvrir-l-assemblee /histoire/le-suffrage-universel/la-conquete-de-la-citoyennete-politique-des -femmes

Associated Chambers of Commerce and Industry of India. 2013. "Women-Workforce Productivity Impacted by 40% in Delhi-NCR: ASSOCHAM." Available at: http://www.assocham.org/prels/shownews.php?id=3843

Association for Psychological Science. 2016. "Putting Corporate Quotas to Work for Women." Available at: http://www.psychologicalscience.org/news/minds -business/putting-corporate-quotas-to-work-for-women.html

Attanasio, O., and Lechene, V. 2002. "Tests of Income Pooling in Household De-cisions." *Review of Economic Dynamics* 5(4): 720–748.

Averett, S., Peters, E. H., and Waldman, D. M. 1997. "Tax Credits, Labor Supply and Childcare." *Review of Economics and Statistics* 79(1): 125–135.

Baha'i International Community. 1993. "Traditional Media as Change Agent." *One Country* 5(3). Available at: https://www.bic.org/statements/traditional -media-change-agent

Baker, M., Gruber, J., and Milligan, K. 2008. "Universal Childcare, Maternal Labor Supply, and Family Well-Being." *Journal of Political Economy* 116(4): 709–745.

Balazs, E. 1964. *Chinese Civilization and Bureaucracy: Variations on a Theme*. New Haven, CT: Yale University Press.

Banville, J. 2014. "Too Many Woman Are Victims in TV Dramas." *Daily Mail*. 19 May. Available at: http://www.dailymail.co.uk/news/article-2633273/Too -woman-victims-TV-dramas-says-Booker-prize-winning-author-John -Bannville.html

Barkindo, A., and Wesley, K. C. 2014. "Our Bodies, Their Battleground: Boko Haram and Gender-Based Violence Against Christian Women and Children in North-Eastern Nigeria Since 1999." *World Watch Monitor*. 25 April. Available at: https://www.worldwatchmonitor.org/2014/04/article_3113594.html

Barry, E. 2017. "In Rare Move, Death Sentence in Delhi Gang Rape Case Is Upheld." *New York Times.* 5 May. Available at: https://mic.com/articles/22405 /jyoti-singh-pandey-live-updates-on-india-gang-rape-case#.4VziNkC0j

Beaman, L., Duflo, E., Pande, R., and Topalova, P. 2012. "Female Leadership Raises Aspirations and Educational Attainment for Girls: A Policy Experiment in India." *Science* 335 (6068): 582–586. Available at https://doi.org/10.1126 /science.1212382

Begikhani, N. 2005. "Honour-Based Violence Among the Kurds: The Case of Iraqi Kurdistan." In *"Honour": Crimes, Paradigms and Violence Against Women.* Edited by Welchman, L., and Hussain, S. London: Zed Books, 209–229.

Berkowitz, E. 2012. "How Frightened Patriarchal Men Have Tried to Repress Women's Sexuality Through History." *AlterNet.* 29 May. Available at: http:// www.alternet.org/story/155645/how_frightened_patriarchal_men_have _tried_to_repress_women's_sexuality_through_history

Bertrand, M., and Schoar, A. 2006. "The Role of Family in Family Firms." *Journal of Economic Perspectives* 20(2): 73–96.

Bialik, H. N., and Ravnicki, Y. H., eds. 1948. *Sefer Haaggadah* (The book of legends), 3rd ed. Tel Aviv: Dvir (in Hebrew).

Birdsall, N. 1993. "Social Development Is Economic Development." World Bank Policy Research Working Paper Series 1123. Washington, DC.

Blau, F. D., and Kahn, L. M. 2003. "Understanding International Differences in the Gender Pay Gap." *Journal of Labor Economics* 21(1): 106–144.

———. 2007. "The Gender Pay Gap: Have Women Gone as Far as They Can?" *Academy of Management Perspectives* 21(1): 7–23. Available at: http://www .jstor.org/stable/4166284

Blumel, D., Gibb, G. L., Innis, B. N., Justo, D. L., and Wilson, D. W. 1993. *Who Pays? The Economic Costs of Violence Against Women.* Brisbane: Womens' Policy Unit, Office of the Cabinet, Queensland.

Bokhari, S. 1999. "A Week in the Life: Fighting the Wife Burners of Pakistan: Fighting Fire with Ire to Rescue Wives." *The Independent,* 17 April. Available at: https://www.independent.co.uk/news/world/a-week-in-the-life-fighting-the -wife-burners-of-pakistan-fighting-fire-with-ire-to-rescue-wives-1087737 .html

Bosch, E. 2015. *The Policy on Gender Equality in Germany.* European Parliament: Directorate General for Internal Policies, Policy Department: Citizens' Rights and Constitutional Affairs. Available at: http://www.europarl.europa.eu /RegData/etudes/IDAN/2015/510025/IPOL_IDA(2015)510025_EN.pdf

Brewer, P. 2013. "On the Origins of Women's Oppression." *Links: International Journal of Socialist Renewal.* Available at: http://links.org.au/node/159

Brown, S. 1962. "Okubo Toshimichi: His Political and Economic Policies in Early Meiji Japan." *Journal of Asian Studies* 21(2): 183–197.

Burn-Murdoch, J. 2013. "69,000 Female, 9,000 Male Rape Victims per Year." *The Guardian.* 11 January. Available at: http://www.theguardian.com/news /datablog/2013/jan/11/male-female-rape-statistics-graphic

Byrnes, A., and Freeman, M. 2012. "The Impact of the CEDAW Convention: Paths to Equality." University of New South Wales Faculty of Law Research Series. Paper 7. Sydney, Australia: University of New South Wales.

Campbell, J. C. 2002. "Health Consequences of Intimate Partner Violence." Available at: https://jhu.pure.elsevier.com/en/publications/health-consequences-of -intimate-partner-violence-3

Carter, C. 2015. "Student, 20, Is Stabbed and Clubbed to Death for Fighting Back Against Bus Driver Rapist: Thousands Protest in Turkey after Woman's Burned Body Is Found in Woodland." *Daily Mail.* 16 February. Available at: http://www .dailymail.co.uk/news/article-2955748/Thousands-protest-Turkey-woman-s -burned-body-woodland.html

Catalyst. 2018. Women in S&P 500 Companies. 2 February. Available at: http:// www.catalyst.org/knowledge/women-sp-500-companies

Cavalli-Sforza, L., Menozzi, P., and Piazza, A. 1996. *The History and Geography of Human Genes.* Princeton, NJ: Princeton University Press.

Centre de Ressources en Belgique. n.d. "Garçon ou fille: un destin pour la vie? Belgique, 1830–2000." Available at: http://www.avg-carhif.be/media/d_Carhif _dossierpdagogique_frlight_76967.pdf

Chandramouli, C. 2011. "Gender Composition of the Population." In *Census of India 2011, Provisional Population Totals*, Paper 1 of 2011, Chapter 5. Office of the Registrar General & Census Commissioner, India. Available at: http:// censusindia.gov.in/2011-prov-results/prov_results_paper1_india.html

Chattopadhyay, R., and Duflo, E. 2004. "Women Policy Makers: Evidence from a Randomized Policy Experiment in India." *Econometrica* 72(5): 1409–1443.

Chen, J. 2010. "Do Gender Quotas Influence Women's Representation and Policies?" *European Journal of Comparative Economics* 7(1): 13–60.

Chinese Academy of Social Sciences. 2010. Available at: http://news.bbc.co.uk/2 /hi/asia-pacific/8451289.stm

Cho, M.-K. 1995. "Korea: The 1990 Family Law Reform and the Improvement of the Status of Women." *University of Louisville Journal of Family Law* 33: 431.

Choe, S.-H. 2010. "Korean Women Flock to Government." *New York Times.* 1 March. Available at: http://www.nytimes.com/2010/03/02/world/asia/02iht -women.html

Chowdhury, D. R. 2013. "Deadly Demographics: Women Face Grim Odds in Male-Heavy Societies like China, India." *South China Morning Post.* 29 January. Available at: http://www.scmp.com/news/china/article/1138110/deadly -demographics-women-face-grim-odds-male-heavy-societies-china-india

Clark, K. A., Biddle, A. K., and Martin, S. L. 2002. "A Cost-Benefit Analysis of the Violence Against Women Act of 1994." *Violence Against Women* 8: 417–428.

Clements, M. B. J., Coady, D., Fabrizio, M. S., Gupta, M. S., Alleyne, M. T. S. C., and Sdralevich, M. C. A. 2013. *Energy Subsidy Reform: Lessons and Implications.* 28 January. International Monetary Fund.

Coale, A. 1991. "Excess Female Mortality and the Balance of the Sexes in the Population: An Estimate of the Number of 'Missing Females.'" *Population and Development Review* 17(3): 517–523.

Cohen, P. 2016. "Wealth Inequality Rising Fast, Oxfam Says, Faulting Tax Havens." *New York Times.* 18 January. Available at: https://www.nytimes .com/2016/01/19/business/economy/wealth-inequality-rising-fast-oxfam-says -faulting-tax-havens.html?_r=0

Collier, P. 2007. *The Bottom Billion: Why the Poorest Countries Are Failing and What Can Be Done About It.* Oxford: Oxford University Press.

Constitutional Court of Korea. 2005. "Decisions of the Constitutional Court (2005)." Available at: http://goodofall.org/archive/General/%EC%97%B0%EC %86%8D%EA%B0%84%ED%96%89%EB%AC%BC/DECISIONS%20 OF%20THE%20CONSTITUTIONAL%20COURT%20KOREA/decision _2005.pdf

Constitution of the Republic of Korea. Available at: http://english.ccourt.go.kr /cckhome/images/eng/main/Constitution_of_the_Republic_of_Korea.pdf

Coomaraswamy, R. 1997. "Reinventing International Law: Women's Rights as Human Rights in the International Community." Edward A. Smith Lecture, Human Rights Program, Harvard Law School. Available at: http://library.law .columbia.edu/urlmirror/11/ReinventingInternationalLaw.htm

Cottingham, J., and Myntti, C. 2002. "Reproductive Health: Conceptual Mapping and Evidence." In *Engendering International Health: The Challenge of Equity.* Edited by Sen, G., George, A., and Östlin, P. Cambridge, MA: MIT Press, 85–109.

Credit Suisse Research Institute. 2014. "The CS Gender 3000: Gender Diversity and Company Performance." Available at: https://www.calpers.ca.gov/docs /diversity-forum-credit-suisse-report-2015.pdf

Cruz, A., and Klinger, S. 2011. "Gender Based Violence in the World of Work: Overview and Selected Annotated Bibliography." ILO Working Paper 3/2011. Available at: http://www.ilo.org/wcmsp5/groups/public/—-dgreports/—-gender /documents/publication/wcms_155763.pdf

Das Gupta, M. 2005. "Explaining Asia's 'Missing Women': A New Look at the Data." *Population and Development Review* 31(3): 529–535.

Das Gupta, M., Chiang, W., and Shuzhuo, L. 2009. "Is There an Incipient Turnaround in Asia's 'Missing Girls' Phenomenon?" World Bank Policy Research Working Paper Series 4846. Available at: https://doi.org/10.1596/1813-9450 -4846

Das Gupta, M., Zhenghua, J., Zhenming, X., Bohua, L., Chung, W., and Hwa-Ok, B. 2003. "Why Is Son Preference So Persistent in East and South Asia? A Cross-Country Study of China, India, and the Republic of Korea." *Journal of Development Studies* 40(2): 153–187.

Dawkins, R. 2015. "Don't Force Your Religious Opinions on Your Children." Available at: https://www.richarddawkins.net/2015/02/dont-force-your-religious-opinions-on-your-children

Day, T., McKenna, K., and Bowlus, A. 2005. *The Economic Costs of Violence Against Women: An Evaluation of the Literature.* London, ON: University of Western Ontario. Available at: http://www.un.org/womenwatch/daw/vaw/expert%20brief%20costs.pdf

Deere, C. D., and Doss, C. R. 2006. "The Gender Asset Gap: What Do We Know and Why Does It Matter?" *Feminist Economics* 12 (1,2): 1–50.

Deere, C. D., and León, M. 2003. "The Gender Asset Gap: Land in Latin America." *World Development* 31 (6): 925–947.

Deininger, K., Goyal, A., and Nagarajan, H. 2010. "Inheritance Law Reform and Women's Access to Capital: Evidence from India's Hindu Succession Act" (English). Policy Research working paper no. WPS 5338. Washington, DC: World Bank. Available at: http://documents.worldbank.org/curated/en/36406 1468283536849/Inheritance-law-reform-and-womens-access-to-capital-evidence-from-Indias-Hindu-succession-act

Deininger, K., Xia, F., Jin, S., and Nagarajan, H. K. 2014. "Inheritance Law Reform, Empowerment, and Human Capital Accumulation : Second-Generation Effects from India" (English). Policy Research Working Paper no. WPS 7086. Washington, DC: World Bank Group. Available at: http://documents.worldbank.org/curated/en/855241468043453527/Inheritance-law-reform-empowerment-and-human-capital-accumulation-second-generation-effects-from-india

Deloitte. 2017. "Missing Pieces Report: The 2016 Board Diversity Census of Women and Minorities on Fortune 500 Boards." Available at: http://progresomicrofinanzas.org/en/missing-pieces-report-the-2016-board-diversity-census-of-women-and-minorities-on-fortune-500-boards/

De Long, J. B. 1988. "Productivity Growth, Convergence, and Welfare: Comment." *American Economic Review* 78(5): 1138–1154.

Demirguc-Kunt, A., Klapper, L., and Singer, D. 2013. "Financial Inclusion and Legal Discrimination Against Women: Evidence from Developing Countries" (English). Policy Research Working Paper no. WPS 6416. Washington, DC: World Bank. Available at: http://documents.worldbank.org/curated/en/801311 468330257772/Financial-inclusion-and-legal-discrimination-against-women-evidence-from-developing-countries

Demokratiezentrum. 2008. "Familienrechtsreform." May.

Doggett, M. E. 1992. *Marriage, Wife-Beating and the Law in Victorian England.* Columbia: University of South Carolina Press.

Dollar, D., and Gatti, R. 1999. "Gender Inequality, Income, and Growth: Are Good Times Good for Women?" Policy Research Working Paper no. 1. Washington, DC: World Bank. Available at: http://documents.worldbank.org/curated/en/251801468765040122/Gender-inequality-income-and-growth-are-good-times-good-for-women

Doss, C. R. 2006. "The Effect of Intrahousehold Property Ownership on Expenditure Patterns in Ghana." *Journal of African Economies* 15(1): 149–180.

Dostoyevsky, F. 1993. *The Brothers Karamazov.* Translated by David McDuff. London: Penguin Books.

Duflo, E. 2006. "Gender Equality in Development." BREAD Policy Paper No. 011. Available at: http://www.econ.yale.edu/growth_pdf/cdp857.pdf

———. 2012. "Women's Empowerment and Economic Development." *Journal of Economic Literature* 50(4): 1051–1079.

Duflo, E., and Udry, C. 2004. "Intrahousehold Resource Allocation in Côte d'Ivoire: Social Norms, Separate Accounts and Consumption Choices." Yale University Economic Growth Center Discussion Paper No. 857. Available at: https://doi.org/10.3386/w10498

Duhart, D. 2001. *Violence in the Workplace.* 1993–99, Bureau of Justice Statistics Special Report. Available at: https://www.bjs.gov/content/pub/pdf/vw99.pdf

Duvurry, N., Callan, A., Carney, P., and Raghavendra, S. 2013. *Intimate Partner Violence: Economic Costs and Implications for Growth and Development.* World Bank Participation and Research Series No. 3 I. Available at: http://documents.worldbank.org/curated/en/412091468337843649/Intimate-partner-violence-economic-costs-andimplications-for-growth-and-development

Dworkin, A. 1983. *Right Wing Women.* London: Women's Press, p. 195.

Ebadi, S. 2015. "Iranian Nobel Peace Prize Laureate Shirin Ebadi on Nuclear Deal, Islamic State, Women's Rights." Interview, *Independent Global News.* 28 April. Available at: https://www.democracynow.org/2015/4/28/iranian_nobel_peace_prize_laureate_shirin

Ebenstein, A. Y. 2006. "Sex Selection and Fertility Choices: Analysis and Policy." Available at: http://paa2007.princeton.edu/papers/70655

Ebenstein, A. Y., and Sharygin, E. J. 2009. "The Consequences of the 'Missing Girls' of China." *World Bank Economic Review* 23(3): 399–425.

Edgerton, Robert B. 2000. "Traditional Beliefs and Practices—Are Some Better Than Others?" In *Culture Matters.* Edited by Harrison, L. E., and Huntington, S. P. New York: Basic Books, 126–140.

The Economist. 2010. "Gendercide: The Worldwide War on Baby Girls." 4 March. Available at: http://www.economist.com/node/15636231

———. 2014. "Holding Back Half the Nation." 28 March. Available at: http://www.economist.com/news/briefing/21599763-womens-lowly-status-japanese-workplace-has-barely-improved-decades-and-country

————. 2015. "The Marriage Squeeze in India and China: Bare Branches, Redundant Males." 18 April. Available at: http://www.economist.com/news/asia/21648715-distorted-sex-ratios-birth-generation-ago-are-changing-marriage-and-damaging-societies-asias

————. 2017. "Too Many Single Men: The Legacy of Gendercide." 21 January. Available at: https://www.highbeam.com/doc/1G1-478128085.html

Edlund, L., Li, H., Yi, J., and Zhang, J. 2008. "Sex Ratios and Crime: Evidence from China's One-Child Policy." Discussion Paper 3214. Bonn: Institute for the Study of Labor.

Effendi, S. 1977. "The Goal of a New World Order." In *Call to the Nations.* Chatham: W. & J. Mackay.

Encyclopedia of Mental Disorders. "Intermittent Explosive Disorder." Available at: http://www.minddisorders.com/Flu-Inv/Intermittent-explosive-disorder.html

Eppig, C., Fincher, C. L., and Thornhill, R. 2010. "Parasite Prevalence and the Worldwide Distribution of Cognitive Ability." *Proceedings of the Royal Society B.* June, 1–9.

Esteve-Volart, B. 2000. "Sex Discrimination and Growth." IMF Working Paper No. 00–84. Available at: http://dx.doi.org/10.5089/9781451850635.001

————. 2004. "Gender Discrimination and Growth: Theory and Evidence from India." LSE STICERD Research Paper No. DEDPS42. Available at: http://ssrn.com/abstract=1127011

Etzioni, A. 1988. *The Moral Dimension: Toward a New Economics.* New York: Free Press.

European Women on Boards. 2016. *Gender Diversity on European Boards: Realizing Europe's Potential: Progress and Challenges.* Available at: http://european.ewob-network.eu/wp-content/uploads/2016/04/EWoB-quant-report-WEB-spreads.pdf

Faley, R., Knapp, D. E., Kustis, G. A., and Dubois, C. L. Z. 1999. "Estimating the Organizational Costs of Sexual Harassment: The Case of the U.S. Army." *Journal of Business and Psychology* 13: 461–484.

Family Caregiver Alliance. 2003. "Women and Caregiving: Facts and Figures." Available at: https://www.caregiver.org/women-and-caregiving-facts-and-figures

Fearon, J. D., and Laitin, D. D. 2003. "Ethnicity, Insurgency, and Civil War." *American Political Science Review* 97: 75–90.

Fernández, R. 2013. "Cultural Change as Learning: The Evolution of Female Labor Force Participation over a Century." *American Economic Review* 103(1): 472–500.

Fernández, R., and Fogli, A. 2009. "Culture: An Empirical Investigation of Beliefs, Work, and Fertility." *American Economic Journal: Macroeconomics* 1(1):146–177.

Fernández, R., Fogli, A., and Olivetti, C. 2004. "Mothers and Sons: Preference Formation and Female Labor Force Dynamics." *Quarterly Journal of Economics* 119:1249–1299. Available at: https://doi.org/10.1162/0033553042476224

Figes, E. 1986. *Patriarchal Attitudes*. London: Macmillan.

First Post. 2017. "Mumbai Gangrape: Justice JS Verma's Recommendations Might Have Helped." 2 June. Available at: http://www.firstpost.com/india /mumbai-gangrape-justice-js-vermas-recommendations-might-have-helped -1060635.html

Fiszbein, A., Schady, N., with Ferreira, F. H. G., Grosch, M., Keleher, N., Olinto, P., and Skoufias, E. 2009. "Conditional Cash Transfers: Reducing Present and Future Poverty." World Bank Policy Research Reports. Washington, DC: World Bank. Available at: https://siteresources.worldbank.org/INTCCT/Resources /5757608-1234228266004/PRR-CCT_web_noembargo.pdf

Flabbi, L. 2011. "Gender Differentials in Education, Career Choices and Labor Market Outcomes on a Sample of OECD Countries." Washington, DC: World Bank. License: CC BY 3.0. Available at: https://openknowledge.worldbank.org /handle/10986/9113

Food and Agriculture Organization. 2011. *The State of Food and Agriculture 2010–11. Women in Agriculture: Closing the Gender Gap for Development*. Rome. Available at http://www.fao.org/docrep/013/i2050e/i2050e.pdf

Franck, T. M. 2001. "Are Human Rights Universal?" *Foreign Affairs* 80(1): 191–204. Available at: https://www.foreignaffairs.com/articles/afghanistan/2001-01 -01/are-human-rights-universal

Freidenvall, L. 2003. "Women's Political Representation and Gender Quotas: The Swedish Case." Working Paper Series 2003, Department of Political Science, Stockholm University.

Friedman, B. M. 2005. *The Moral Consequences of Economic Growth*. New York: Alfred A. Knopf.

Geddes, R., Lueck, D., and Tennyson, S. 2012. "Human Capital Accumulation and the Expansion of Women's Economic Rights." *Journal of Law and Economics* 55(4): 839–867.

Geiger, A., and Kent, L. 2017. "Number of Women Leaders Around the World Has Grown, but They're Still a Small Group." Pew Research Center. Available at: http://www.pewresearch.org/fact-tank/2017/03/08/women-leaders-around -the-world/

Gibbon, E. 1776. *The Decline and Fall of the Roman Empire*. Vol. 1. London: Folio Society, 1983 ed.

Giles, J., and Witoelar, F. 2011. "Indonesian Education and Occupational Segregation and Labor Markets in Indonesia." Background paper for the Women and Development Report 2012. Available at: https://www.gsma.com/mobile fordevelopment/wp-content/uploads/2012/04/2012worlddevelopmentreporto ngenderequalityanddevelopment.pdf

Giroud, F., and Lévy, B.-H., 1993. *Women and Men: A Philosophical Conversation*. New York: Little, Brown.

Giugale, Marcelo. 2017. *Economic Development: What Everyone Needs to Know*. Oxford: Oxford University Press, 2nd ed.

Giuliano, P. 2007. "Living Arrangements in Western Europe: Does Cultural Origin Matter?" *Journal of the European Economic Association* 5(5): 927–952.

Gneezy, U., Leonard, K. L., and List, J. 2009. "Gender Differences in Competition: Evidence from a Matrilineal and a Patriarchal Society." *Econometrica* 77(5): 1637–1664.

Goldin, C. 1994. "The U-Shaped Female Labor Force Function in Economic Development and Economic History." Working Paper No. 4707, National Bureau of Economic Research. In *Investment in Women's Human Capital and Economic Development*. Edited by Schultz, P. T. Chicago: University of Chicago Press, 1995. Available at: http://www.nber.org/papers/w4707.pdf

Goldin, C., and Katz, L. 2002. "The Power of the Pill: Oral Contraceptives and Women's Career and Marriage Decisions." *Journal of Political Economy* 110: 730–770.

Goldstone, J. 1996. "Gender, Work and Culture: Why the Industrial Revolution Came Early to England but Late to China." *Sociological Perspectives* 39(1): 1–21.

Gonzales, C., Jain-Chandra, S., Kochhar, K., and Newiak, M. 2015. "Fair Play: More Equal Laws Boost Female Labor Force Participation." International Monetary Fund Staff Discussion Note SDN/15/02. Available at: https://www.imf.org/external/pubs/ft/sdn/2015/sdn1502.pdf

Guilmoto, C. 2012. "Skewed Sex Ratios at Birth and Future Marriage Squeeze in China and India, 2005–2100." *Demography* 49(1): 77–100.

Guiso, L., Sapienza, P., and Zingales, L. 2006. "Does Culture Affect Economic Outcomes?" *Journal of Economic Perspectives* 20(2): 23–48.

———. 2009. "Cultural Biases in Economic Exchange?" *Quarterly Journal of Economics* 124: 1095–1131.

Guthrie, E. 2004. "A Study of the History and Cult of the Buddhist Earth Deity in Mainland Southeast Asia." Diss. Christchurch, NZ: University of Canterbury.

Hajjar, L. 2004. "Religion, State Power, and Domestic Violence in Muslim Societies: A Framework for Comparative Analysis." *Law & Social Inquiry* 29(1): 1–38. Available at: http://www.academia.edu/4843302/Religion_State_Power_and_Domestic_Violence

Hall. J. 2015. "ISIS fighters are desperately trying to obtain VIAGRA, spending money on kinky underwear for their 'wives' . . . then subjecting them to 'brutal, abnormal' sex acts according to doctors in Syria." *Daily Mail*. 17 February. Available at: http://www.dailymail.co.uk/news/article-2956882/ISIS-fighters-desperately-trying-obtain-VIAGRA-spending-money-kinky-underwear-wives-subjecting-brutal-abnormal-sex-acts-according-doctors-Syria.html

Hallward-Driemeier, M., and Gajigo, O. 2010. "Strengthening Economic Rights and Women's Occupational Choice: The Impact of Reforming Ethiopia's Family Law." Policy Research Working Paper No. 6695. Washington, DC: World Bank. Availableat:http://documents.worldbank.org/curated/en/259861468021600567 /Strengthening-economic-rights-and-womens-occupational-choice-the-impact -of-reforming-Ethiopias-family-law

Hallward-Driemeier, M., and Hasan, T. 2012. "Empowering Women: Legal Rights and Economic Opportunities in Africa." Washington, DC: World Bank. License: CC BY 3.0 IGO. Available at: https://openknowledge.worldbank.org /handle/10986/11960

Hallward-Driemeier, M., Hasan, T., and Rusu, A. 2013. "Women's Legal Rights over 50 Years: Progress, Stagnation or Regression?" Policy Research Working Paper No. 6616. Washington, DC: World Bank. License: CC BY 3.0 IGO. Available at: https://openknowledge.worldbank.org/handle/10986/21474

Hancock, P. 2006. "Violence, Women, Work and Empowerment." *Gender, Technology and Development* 10(2): 211–228. Available at: http://gtd.sagepub.com /content/10/2/211

Hank, K., and Kohler, H. P. 2000. "Gender Preferences for Children in Europe: Empirical Results from 17 FFS Countries." *Demographic Research* 2(1). Available at: http://www.demographic-research.org/volumes/vol2/1/2-1.pdf

Harris, M. 1966. "The Cultural Ecology of India's Sacred Cattle." *Current Anthropology* 7(1): 51–54, 55–56.

Harrison, L. 2000. "Promoting Progressive Cultural Change." In Harrison, L., and Huntington, S. P., Eds., *Culture Matters.* New York: Basic Books.

Harrison, L., and Huntington, S. P., eds. 2000. *Culture Matters: How Values Shape Human Progress.* New York: Basic Books.

Hartigan, P., Price, J., and Tolhurst, R. 2002. "Communicable Diseases: Outstanding Commitments to Gender and Poverty." In *Engendering International Health: The Challenge of Equity.* Edited by Sen, G., George, A., and Östlin, P. Cambridge, MA: MIT Press, 37–61.

Harvard Law School Forum on Corporate Governance and Financial Regulation. 2017. "Gender Parity on Boards Around the World." Available at: https:// corpgov.law.harvard.edu/2017/01/05/gender-parity-on-boards-around-the -world/

Hashmi, T. 2005. "The Shariah, Mullah and Muslims in Bangladesh." Available at: https://gold.mukto-mona.com/Articles/taj_hashmi/sharia_mullah.html

Hegeman, D. B. 2007. *Plowing in Hope: Toward a Biblical Theology of Culture.* Moscow, ID: Canon Press.

Heiskanen, M., and Piispa, M. 2001. *The Price of Violence: The Costs of Men's Violence Against Women in Finland.* Helsinki: Statistics Finland and Council for Equality.

Henderson, M. 2000. *Impacts and Costs of Domestic Violence on the Australian Business/Corporate Sector.* Brisbane: Lord Mayor's Women's Advisory Committee, Brisbane City Council.

Herz, B., Subbarao, K., Habib, M., and Raney, L. 1991. "Letting Girls Learn: Promising Approaches in Primary and Secondary Education." World Bank Discussion Papers No. 133.

Hewlett, S. 2002. "Executive Women and the Myth of Having It All." *Harvard Business Review* 80(4): 66–73.

Hoddinott, J., and Haddad, L. 1995. "Does Female Income Share Influence Household Expenditures? Evidence from Côte d'Ivoire." *Oxford Bulletin of Economics and Statistics* 57(1): 77–96.

Hoeffler, A., Fearon, J. 2014. Benefits and Costs of the Conflict and Violence Targets for the Post-2015 Development Agenda, Copenhagen Consensus Center. Available at: https://www.copenhagenconsensus.com/sites/default/files/conflict _assessment_-_hoeffler_and_fearon_0.pdf

Homer-Dixon, T. 2006. *The Upside of Down: Catastrophe, Creativity and the Renewal of Civilization.* Washington, DC: Island Press.

Houseman, S., and Abraham, K. G. 1993. "Female Workers as a Buffer in the Japanese Economy." *American Economic Review* 83(2): 45–51.

Hoyos, A., and Narayan, A. 2011. "Inequalities of Opportunities Among Children: How Much Does Gender Matter?" Background note for the WDR 2012. Available at: http://siteresources.worldbank.org/INTPOVERTY/Resources/Role _of_Gender_WDR_bground_June_27,_2011.pdf

Hudson, P. 2011. "Women's Work." BBC archive. Available at: http://www.bbc.co .uk/history/british/victorians/womens_work_01.shtml

Hudson, V., and den Boer, A. M. 2005. "Missing Women and Bare Branches: Gender Balance and Conflict." *Environmental Change and Security Program Report* 11: 21–22.

———. 2007. "Bare Branches and Security in Asia." *Harvard Asia Pacific Review.* Winter. Available at: http://www.hcs.harvard.edu/~hapr/winter07_gov /hudson.pdf

Human Rights Watch. 2011. "Tunisia: Government Lifts Restrictions on Women's Rights Treaty." September 6. Available at: http://www.hrw.org /news/2011/09/06/tunisia-government-lifts-restrictions-women-s-rights -treaty

Iaccino, L. 2014. "Morocco: Girl Forced to Marry Her Rapist Has 'Face Disfigured with 50 Razor Cuts' by Him." *International Business Times.* Available at: http://www.ibtimes.co.uk/morocco-girl-forced-marry-her-rapist-has-face -disfigured-50-razor-cuts-by-him-1474504

Institute for Women of Andalusia. 2003. *The Economic and Social Costs of Domestic Violence in Andalusia, Spain.*

Interights. 2011. *Non-Discrimination in International Law: A Handbook for Practitioners*. Available at: http://ilga.org/non-discrimination-in-international -law-a-handbook-for-practitioners-from-interights/

International Covenant on Civil and Political Rights. 1966. Available at: https:// treaties.un.org/doc/publication/unts/volume%20999/volume-999-i-14668 -english.pdf

International Herald Tribune. 2010. "A Boy's Life for Afghan Girls: Freedom and Status." 21 September.

International Labour Organization. 2004. *Decent Work for All Women and Men in Nepal Series*, No. 2. Available at: www.ilo.org/kathmandu/whatwedo /publications/lang—en/docName—WCMS_113780/index.htm

————. 2007. *Forced Labour Statistics Factsheet*.

International Women's Rights Action Watch Asia. 1999. *The Sumitomo Electric Wage Discrimination Case*. Available at: https://www.japantimes.co.jp/news /2004/01/06/national/sumitomo-unit-settles-sex-bias-suit/#.WseMbIWcGUk

Inter-Parliamentary Union. 2018. Women in National Parliaments. Available at: http://www.ipu.org/wmn-e/world.htm

Jacobs, A. 2015. "Taking Feminist Battle to China's Streets, and Landing in Jail." *New York Times*. 5 April. Available at: https://www.nytimes.com/2015/04/06 /world/asia/chinese-womens-rights-activists-fall-afoul-of-officials.html

Jacobsen, J. P. 2011. "Gender Inequality: A Key Global Challenge: Reducing Losses Due to Gender Inequality." Assessment Paper, Copenhagen Consensus on Human Challenges. Available at: http://www.copenhagenconsensus.com/sites /default/files/gender.pdf

Jaspers, K. 2011. *Origin and Goal of History*. New York: Routledge Revivals.

Jaumotte, F. 2003. "Labour Force Participation of Women: Empirical Evidence on the Role of Policy and other Determinants in OECD Countries." *OECD Economic Studies* 37(2).

Jayachandran, S. 2014. "The Roots of Gender Inequality in Developing Countries." NBER Working Paper 20380. Available at: https://doi.org/10.1146/annurev- economics-080614-115404

Jha, P., Kumar, R., Vasa, P., Dhingra, N., Thiruchelvam, D., and Moineddin, R. 2006. "Low Male-to-Female Ratio of Children Born in India: National Survey of 1.1 Million Households." *Lancet* 367(9506): 211–218.

Joy, L., Carter, N. M., Wagner, H. M., and Narayanan, S. 2007. "The Bottom Line: Corporate Performance and Women's Representation on Boards." *Catalyst*. Available at: http://www.catalyst.org/knowledge/bottom-line-corporate -performance-and-womens-representation-boards

Kabubo-Mariara, J., and Mwabu, D. K. 2007. "Determinants of School Enrolment and Education Attainment: Empirical Evidence from Kenya." *South African Journal of Economics* 75(3): 572–593.

Kargar, Z. 2015. "Farkhunda: The making of a martyr." *BBC World News*. 11 August. Available at: http://www.bbc.com/news/magazine-33810338

Keim, B. 2013. Is It Time to Treat Violence Like a Contagious Disease? *Wired*. 18 January. Available at: https://www.wired.com/2013/01/violence-is-contagious/

Kerr, R., and McLean, J. 1996. *Paying for Violence: Some Costs of Violence Against Women in B.C.* Victoria: Ministry of Women's Equality, Government of British Columbia. Available at: http://web.archive.org/web/19980624210511 /www.weq.gov.bc.ca/stv/payingforviolence.html

Khumalo B., Msimang S., and Bollbach K. 2014. *Too Costly to Ignore—The Economic Impact of Gender-Based Violence in South Africa*. Johannesburg: KPMG Services. Available at: https://assets.kpmg.com/content/dam/kpmg/za /pdf/2017/01/za-Too-costly-to-ignore.pdf

Kilic, T., Palacios-López, A., and Goldstein, M. 2015. "Caught in a Productivity Trap: A Distributional Perspective on Gender Differences in Malawian Agriculture." Policy Research Working Paper No. 6381. Washington, DC: World Bank. Available at: http://documents.worldbank.org/curated/en/326491468300553720 /Caught-in-a-productivity-trap-a-distributional-perspective-on-gender -differences-in-Malawian-agriculture

Kim, Y.-H. 2006. "Tradition and Judging: Interpreting the Tradition Pursuant to the Constitutional Value of Gender Equality." Paper presented at International Association of Women Judges Eighth Biennial Conference, 3–7 May, 2006, Sydney, Australia.

Kipling, R. 1889. "The Ballad of East and West." *McMillan's Magazine*. December.

Klasen, S. 1999. "Does Gender Inequality Reduce Growth and Development? Evidence from Cross-Country Regressions." Policy Research Report on Gender and Development Working Paper Series No. 7. Washington, DC: World Bank. Available at: http://documents.worldbank.org/curated/en/612001468741378860 /Does-gender-inequality-reduce-growth-and-development-evidence-from -cross-country-regressions

Klasen, S., and Lamanna, F. 2009. "The Impact of Gender Inequality in Education and Employment on Economic Growth: New Evidence for a Panel of Countries." *Feminist Economics* 15(3): 91–132.

Kluve, J., and Tamm, M. 2009. "Now Daddy's Changing Diapers and Mommy's Making Her Career: Evaluating a Generous Parental Leave Regulation Using a Natural Experiment." IZA Discussion Paper 4500, Institute for the Study of Labor, Bonn. Available at: http://ftp.iza.org/dp4500.pdf

Kohn, S. 2013. "Is India the Rape Capital of the World?" *More Magazine*. Available at: http://www.more.com/news/india-rape-capital-world

KPMG Management Consulting and Tasmanian Domestic Violence Advisory Committee. 1994. *Economic Costs of Domestic Violence in Tasmania*. Melbourne: KPMG Management Consulting.

Kristof, N. 2014. "What's So Scary About Smart Girls?" *New York Times*. 10 May. Available at: https://www.nytimes.com/2014/05/11/opinion/sunday/kristof-whats-so-scary-about-smart-girls.html

Kristof, N., and WuDunn, S. 2010. *Half the Sky: Turning Oppression into Opportunity for Women Worldwide*. New York: Alfred A. Knopf.

Kulczycki, A., and Windle, S. 2011. "Honor Killings in the Middle East and North Africa: A Systematic Review of the Literature." *Violence Against Women* 17(11): 1442–1464.

Kuznets, S. 1955. "Economic Growth and Income Inequality." *American Economic Review* (March).

Lagarde, C. 2014. "Empowerment—The Amartya Sen Lecture." International Monetary Fund. London. 6 June. Available at: https://www.imf.org/en/News/Articles/2015/09/28/04/53/sp060614

———. 2015. "Fair Play—Equal Laws for Equal Working Opportunity for Women." Available at: https://blogs.imf.org/2015/02/23/fair-play-equal-laws-for-equal-working-opportunity-for-women/

Lagerlof, N.-P. 2003. "Gender Equality and Long-Run Growth." *Journal of Economic Growth* 8(4): 403–426.

Lam, A. 1992. "The Japanese Equal Employment Opportunity Law: Its Effects on Personnel Management and Policies and Women's Attitudes." MPRA Paper No. 11559. STICERD—International Studies Paper Series 254, Suntory and Toyota International Centres for Economics and Related Disciplines, London School of Economics.

Lambert, L. D. 1971. "The Role of Climate in the Economic Development of Nations." *Land Economics* 47(4): 339–344.

Landes, D. S. 1990. "Why Are We So Rich and They So Poor?" *American Economic Review* 80(2): 1–13.

———. 1994. "What Room for Accident in History? Explaining Big Changes by Small Events." *Economic History Review* 47(4): 637–656.

———. 1998. *The Wealth and Poverty of Nations*. London: Little, Brown.

———. 2000. "Culture Makes Almost All the Difference." In *Culture Matters*. Edited by Harrison, L. E., and Huntington, S. P. New York: Basic Books, 2–13.

Lee, L.-E., Marshall, R., Rallis, D., and Moscardi, M. 2015. "Women on Boards: Global Trends in Gender Diversity on Corporate Boards." MSCI. Available at: https://www.msci.com/documents/10199/04b6f646-d638-4878-9c61-4eb91748a82b

Leonard, H., and Cox, E. 1991. *Costs of Domestic Violence*. Haymarket, New South Wales: New South Wales Women's Co-ordination Unit.

Lerner, G. 1993. *The Creation of Feminist Consciousness: From the Middle Ages to Eighteen-Seventy*. New York: Oxford University Press.

Lewis, W. A. 1955. *The Theory of Economic Growth*. London: Routledge.

Lindstädt, H., Fehere, K., and Wolff, M., 2011. "Frauen in Führungspositionen— Auswirkungen auf den Unternehmenserfolg" [Women in Executive Positions— Effects on the Company's Success]. German Ministry of Family Affairs. Available at: https://www.bmfsfj.de/blob/93882/c676a251ed4c36d34d640a50905cb11e /frauen-in-fuehrunspositionen-langfassung-data.pdf

Littauer, D. 2012. "Iran Performed over 1,000 Gender Reassignment Operations in Four Years." *Gay Star News*. 4 December. Available at: http://www .gaystarnews.com/article/iran-performed-over-1000-gender-reassignment -operations-four-years041212

Liu, D., and Boyle, E. H. 2001. "Making the Case: The Women's Convention and Equal Employment Opportunity in Japan." *International Journal of Comparative Sociology* 42: 389.

Livingston, G. 2013. "Will the End of China's One-Child Policy Shift Its Boy-Girl Ratio?" *Pew Research Center Fact Tank*. 15 November. Available at: http:// www.pewresearch.org/fact-tank/2013/11/15/will-the-end-of-chinas-one-child -policy-shift-its-boy-girl-ratio

Livingston, G., and Cohn, D. 2010. "Childlessness Up Among All Women: Down Among Women with Advanced Degrees." Pew Research Social and Demographic Trends, 25 June. Available at: http://www.pewsocialtrends.org/files /2010/11/758-childless.pdf

Lomborg, B. and Williams, M. A. 2018. "The Cost of Violence Against Women Is Astonishing." *Washington Post*. 22 February. Available at: https://www .washingtonpost.com/opinions/the-cost-of-domestic-violence-is-astonishing /2018/02/22/f8c9a88a-0cf5-11e8-8b0d-891602206fb7_story.html?utm_term =.c4472c26ffe7

López-Claros, A. 2010. *The Innovation for Development Report 2010–2011: Innovation as a Driver of Productivity and Economic Growth*. Basingstoke: Palgrave Macmillan.

López-Claros, A., and Mia, I., eds. 2006. *Global Information Technology Report 2005–2006*. Basingstoke: Palgrave Macmillan.

López-Claros, A., and Mia, I. 2006. "Israel: Factors in the Emergence of an ICT Powerhouse." *Global Information Technology Report 2005–2006*. Basingstoke: Palgrave Macmillan, 89–105.

López-Claros, A., and Perotti, V. 2014. "Does Culture Matter for Development?" World Bank Policy Research Working Paper No. 7092. Available at: https:// ssrn.com/abstract=2519852

López-Claros, A., and Zahidi, S. 2005. *Women's Empowerment: Measuring the Global Gender Gap*. Special Report, *Harvard Business Review* and World Economic Forum. Available at: http://www.augustolopezclaros.com

Luera, M. C. 2004. "Comment: No More Waiting for Revolution: Japan Should Take Positive Action to Implement the Convention on the Elimination of All Forms of Discrimination Against Women." 13 *Pacific Rim Law and Policy Journal* 611.

Mackay, F., and Bould, C., eds., 1997. *The Economic Costs of Domestic Violence*. Gender Audit 1997. Available at: http://www.wave-network.org/articles/537.htm

Malkin, C. 2013. "Why Do People Stay in Abusive Relationships?" *Psychology Today*. 6 March. Available at: https://www.psychologytoday.com/blog/romance-redux/201303/why-do-people-stay-in-abusive-relationships

Mammen, K., and Paxson, C. 2000. "Women's Work and Economic Development." *Journal of Economic Perspectives* 14: 141–164.

Marshall, K. 2010. Development, Religion, and Women's Roles in Contemporary Societies. "Women and the Family." Berkeley Center for Religion, Peace and World Affairs. *Review of Faith and International Affairs* 8 (4): 35–42. Available at: https://doi.org/10.1080/15570274.2010.528970

Martin, W. 2015. *Primates of Park Avenue*. New York: Simon & Schuster.

McBain, S. 2014. "Gender Inequality Is Costing the Global Economy Trillions of Dollars a Year." *New Statesman*. 12 February.

McFarlane, J., Campbell, J. C., Wilt, S., Sachs, C. J., Ulrich, Y., and Xu, X. 1999. "Stalking and Intimate Partner Femicide." *Homicide Studies* 3(4): 300–316.

McQuillan, J., Greil, A. L., Shreffler, K. M., Wonch-Hill, P. A., Gentzler, K. C., and Hathcoat, J. D. 2012. "Does the Reason Matter? Variations in Childlessness Concerns Among U.S. Women." *Journal of Marriage and Family* 74(5): 1166–1181.

Mernissi, F. 1991. *The Veil and the Male Elite: A Feminist Interpretation of Women's Rights in Islam*. New York: Basic Books.

Midgley, M., and Hughes, J. 1983. *Women's Choices: Philosophical Problems Facing Feminism*. New York: St. Martin's Press.

Milani, F. 2011. *Words Not Swords*. New York: Syracuse University Press.

Mill, J. S. 1869. T*he Subjection of Women*. A. Ryan, Ed. London: Penguin Books.

———. 1869. *The Collected Works of John Stuart Mill*, Vol. XXI—*Essays on Equality, Law, and Education*. John M. Robson, ed. Toronto: University of Toronto Press; London: Routledge and Kegan Paul, 1984. Available at: http://oll.libertyfund.org/quote/399

Miller, C. C. 2015. "The 24/7 Work Culture's Toll on Families and Gender Equality." *New York Times*. 28 May. Available at: https://www.nytimes.com/2015/05/31/upshot/the-24-7-work-cultures-toll-on-families-and-gender-equality.html

Miller, G. 2008. "Women's Suffrage, Political Responsiveness, and Child Survival in American History." *Quarterly Journal of Economics* 123(3): 1287–1327.

Miller, R. L. 1998. "Women's Job Hunting in the 'Ice Age': Frozen Opportunities in Japan." *Wisconsin Journal of Law, Gender and Society* 8(2): 223–255.

———. 2003. "The Quiet Revolution: Japanese Women Working Around the Law." *Harvard Journal of Law and Gender* 26: 163–215.

Milne, P. J. 1989. "The Patriarchal Stamp of Scripture: The Implications of Structuralist Analyses for Feminist Hermeneutics." *Journal of Feminist Studies in Religion* 5(1): 17–34.

Moore, A. 2017. "Cyberstalking and Women: Facts and Statistics." ThoughtCo. Available at: https://www.thoughtco.com/cyberstalking-and-women-facts -3534322

Morrison, A., and Orlando, M. B. 1999. "Social and Economic Costs of Domestic Violence: Chile and Nicaragua." In *Too Close to Home: Domestic Violence in the Americas.* New York: Inter-American Development Bank.

Mott. L. 1849. "Asking Favors." Available at: https://www.quotemaster.org /asking+favors

Murdock, G. P. 1965. *Culture and Society.* Pittsburgh, PA: University of Pittsburg Press.

Nakakubo, H. 2007. "'Phase III' of the Japanese Equal Employment Opportunity Act." *Japan Labor Review* 4(3): 9–27.

National Center for Injury Prevention and Control. 2003. *Costs of Intimate Partner Violence Against Women in the United States.* Atlanta, GA: Centers for Disease Control and Prevention. Available at: https://www.cdc.gov/violence prevention/pdf/IPVBook-a.pdf

National Council to Reduce Violence Against Women and Their Children. 2009. *The National Council's Plan for Australia to Reduce Violence Against Women and Their Children, 2009–2021.* Available at: http://www.nasasv.org.au /National_Plan/The_Plan.pdf

Nelson, D. 2013. "Delhi Gang-Rape Victim to Haunt Attackers with 'Dying Declaration.'" *Telegraph.* 11 January. Available at: http://www.telegraph.co.uk /news/worldnews/asia/india/9796076/Delhi-gang-rape-victim-to-haunt -attackers-with-dying-declaration.html

New Family. 2017. "Marriage in the Rabbinate." Available at: http://www .newfamily.org.il/en/marriage-in-the-rabbinate/

Nordberg, J. 2014. *The Underground Girls of Kabul.* New York: Crown.

Obama, M. 2014. Remarks by the First Lady at Girls' New York: Crown. Education Conference. Available at: https://obamawhitehouse.archives.gov/the-press -office/2014/12/12/remarks-first-lady-girls-education-conference

Office of the High Commissioner for Human Rights. 2003. "The Right to Equality and Non-Discrimination in the Administration of Justice." In *Human Rights in the Administration of Justice: A Manual for Judges, Prosecutors and Lawyers.* OHCHR Professional Training Series No. 9. New York: Chapter 13, 631–679. Available at: http://www.ohchr.org/Documents/Publications/training9chap ter13en.pdf

Oglobin, C. G. 1999. "The Gender Earnings Differential in the Russian Transition Economy." *Industrial and Labor Relations Review* 52: 602–627.

Open Doors International. 2013. "Our Bodies, Their Battleground: Boko Haram and Gender-Based Violence Against Christian Women and Children in North-Eastern Nigeria since 1999." NPVRN Working Paper No. 1, Abuja-Nigeria. Available at: http://www.worldwatchmonitor.org/old-site-imgs-pdfs/3117403.pdf

Organisation for Economic Co-operation and Development (OECD). 2017. "Gender Wage Gap." Available at: https://data.oecd.org/earnwage/gender-wage -gap.htm

———. 2017. LMF1.5: "Gender Pay Gaps for Full-Time Workers and Earnings Differentials by Educational Attainment." 15 December. OECD–Social Policy Division–Directorate of Employment, Labour and Social Affairs. Available at: OECD Family database http://www.oecd.org/els/family/database.htm

Ortiz-Barreda, G., and Vives-Cases, C. 2013. "Legislation on Violence Against Women: Overview of Key Components." *Revista Panam Salud Publica* 33(1): 61–72.

Ortner, S. B. 1984. "Theory in Anthropology since the Sixties." *Comparative Studies in Society and History* 26 (1): 126–166.

Oster, E. 2005. "Hepatitis B and the Case of the Missing Women." *Journal of Political Economy* 113(61): 1163–1216.

Oster, E., Chen, G., Yu, X., and Lin, W. 2010. "Hepatitis B Does Not Explain Male-Biased Sex Ratios in China." *Economic Letters* 107: 142–144.

OXFAM. 2017. *Fight Equality, Beat Poverty.* Available at: https://www.oxfam.org .uk/get-involved/campaign-with-us/inequality-and-poverty

Palacios-López, A., and López, R. E. 2015. "The Gender Gap in Agricultural Productivity: The Role of Market Imperfections." *Journal of Development Studies* 51(9): 1175–1192. Available at: https://www.researchgate.net/publication /282990756_The_Gender_Gap_in_Agricultural_Productivity_The_Role_of _Market_Imperfections

Palermo, T., Bleck, J., and Peterman, A. 2014. "Tip of the Iceberg: Reporting and Gender-Based Violence in Developing Countries." *American Journal of Epidemiology* 179(5): 602–612.

Pan, P. 2008. *Out of Mao's Shadow: The Struggle for the Soul of a New China.* New York: Simon & Schuster.

Parent-Thirion, A., Fernández-Macías, E., Hurley, J., and Vermeylen, G. 2007. *Fourth European Working Conditions Survey.* Dublin: European Foundation for the Improvement of Living and Working Conditions. Available at: www.eurofound.europa.eu/pubdocs/2006/98/en/2/ef0698en.pdf

Parliament of Victoria. 2016. "Women's Suffrage Petition." Available at: https://www .parliament.vic.gov.au/about/the-history-of-parliament/womens-suffrage -petition

Pearce, D. 1978. "The Feminization of Poverty: Women, Work, and Welfare." *Urban and Social Change Review* 11: 28–26.

Power, K. 1995. *Veiled Desire: Augustine's Writings on Women.* London: Darton.

Preston, J. A. 1999. "Occupational Gender Segregation: Trends and Explanations." *Quarterly Review of Economics and Finance* 39(5): 611–24.

Program for International Student Assessment. 2015. OECD. Available at: https:// www.oecd.org/pisa/pisa-2015-results-in-focus.pdf

Pryor, F. 1985. "The Invention of the Plow." *Comparative Studies in Society and History* 27(4): 727–743.

Psytel. 2009. *Estimation du coût des violences conjugales en Europe.* Programme Daphné. http://www.psytel.eu/violences.php

Quisumbing, A. R., and Hallman, K. 2005. "Marriage in Transition: Evidence on Age, Education, and Assets from Six Developing Countries." In *The Changing Transitions to Adulthood in Developing Countries.* Edited by Lloyd, C. B., Behrman, J. R., Stromquist, N., and Cohen, B. Washington, DC: National Academies Press.

Quisumbing, A. R., and Malucci, J. A. 2003. "Resources at Marriage and Intra-household Allocation: Evidence from Bangladesh, Ethiopia, Indonesia, and South Africa." *Oxford Bulletin of Economics and Statistics* 65(3): 283–327.

Ramey, V. A. 2009. "Time Spent in Home Production in the 20th-Century United States: New Estimates from Old Data." *Journal of Economic History* 69(1): 1–47.

Read, D. 1994. *The Age of Urban Democracy: England 1868–1914.* London: Longman.

Ribero, R., and Sanchez , F. 2004. "Determinantes, efectos y costos de la violencia intrafamiliar en Colombia." [Determinants, Effects and Costs of Domestic Violence in Colombia]. Centro de Estudios sobre Desarrollo Economico, Universidad de los Andes. Available at: http://economia.uniandes.edu.co/es/investigaciones _y_publicaciones/cede/publicaciones/documentos_cede/2004/determinantes _efectos_y_costos_de_la_violencia_intrafamiliar_en_colombia

Ries, E. 2011. "Racism and Meritocracy." Available at: https://techcrunch.com /2011/11/19/racism-and-meritocracy/

Roberts, G. 1988. "Domestic Violence: Costing of Service Provision for Female Victims—20 Case Histories." In *Beyond These Walls: Report of the Queensland Domestic Violence Task Force to the Honourable Peter McKechnie, M.L.A., Minister for Family Services and Welfare Housing.* Edited by Queensland Domestic Task Force. Brisbane, Australia. Available at: https://violencehurts.wordpress .com/2015/06/03/family-domestic-violence-the-economic-costs-to-australia/

Rodhinson, M. L. 1918. *The Babylonian Talmud.* Available at: https://www .jewishvirtuallibrary.org/jsource/Judaism/FullTalmud.pdf

Rosenblatt, C. 2013. "Is Caring for Aging Parents Unfair to Women?" *Forbes.* 9 May. Available at: https://www.forbes.com/sites/carolynrosenblatt/2013/05/09 /is-caring-for-aging-parents-unfair-to-women/#315ab0c63e1c

Rubin, A. J. 2015. "A Thin Line of Defense against 'Honor Killings.'" *New York Times.* 3 March. https://www.nytimes.com/2015/03/03/world/asia/afghanistan -a-thin-line-of-defense-against-honor-killings.html

Rubin, A. J. 2015. "Flawed Justice After a Mob Killed an Afghan Woman." 26 December. *New York Times.* Available at: https://www.nytimes.com/2015/12 /27/world/asia/flawed-justice-after-a-mob-killed-an-afghan-woman.html

Sabic, P. 2016. "Not Just America: S&P Euro 350 Has Just 14 Companies with Female CEOs." S&P Global Market Intelligence. September. Available at: https://www.valuewalk.com/2016/09/ceo-gender-gap-sp-500/

Saez, E., and Zucman, G. 2003. "Wealth Inequality in the United States from 1913 to 1998: Evidence from Capitalized Income Tax Data." *Quarterly Journal of Economics* 18(1): 1–39.

Sasaki, M. 2002. "The Causal Effect of Family Structure on Labor Force Participation Among Japanese Married Women." *Journal of Human Resources* 37(2): 429–440.

Saul, H. 2014. "Police Officers 'Called Teenager a 'F°°°°°°' Slag' after She Made a Domestic Violence Complaint." *Independent.* 19 February. Available at: http://www.independent.co.uk/news/uk/crime/police-officers-called-teenager-a-f-slag-after-she-made-a-domestic-violence-complaint-9138957.html

Scott, L. 2013. "Low Fertility Nations Have Fewer Working Women, Not More." Available at: http://doublexeconomy.com/2013/02/07/low-fertility-nations-have-fewer-working-women-not-more

Sczesny, S., and Stahlberg, D. 2000. "Sexual Harassment over the Telephone: Occupational Risk at Call Centres." *Work and Stress: An International Journal of Work, Health and Organisations* 14(2): 121–136.

Sedgh, G., Henshaw, H., Singh, S., Ahman, E., and Shah, I. H. 2007. "Induced Abortion: Estimated Rates and Trends Worldwide." *Lancet* 370: 1338–1345.

Sen, A. 1990. "More Than 100 Million Women Are Missing." *New York Review of Books.* 20 December.

———. 1992. "Missing Women." *British Medical Journal* 304(6827): 587–588.

———. 1999. *Development as Freedom.* Oxford: Oxford University Press.

———. 2003. "Missing Women—Revisited." *British Medical Journal* 327(7427): 1297–1298.

———. 2005. "Mary, Mary, Quite Contrary!" *Feminist Economics* 11(1): 1–9.

———. 2009. "Adam Smith's Market Never Stood Alone." *Financial Times.* 11 March.

———. 2012. "The Future We Want." Outcome Document of the United Nations Conference on Sustainable Development, Rio de Janeiro, Brazil, 20–22. Available at: https://sustainabledevelopment.un.org/content/documents/733 FutureWeWant.pdf

Sen, G., George, A., and Östlin, P., eds. 2002. *Engendering International Health: The Challenge of Equity.* Cambridge, MA: MIT Press.

Shah, I., and Ahman, E. 2009. "Unsafe Abortions: Global and Regional Incidence, Trends, Consequences, and Challenges." *Journal of Obstetrics and Gynaecology Canada* 31(12): 1149–1158.

Shaikh, M. A. 2003. "Is Domestic Violence Endemic in Pakistan: Perspective from Pakistani Wives." *Pakistan Journal of Medical Sciences* 19(1): 23–28. Available at: http://www.pjms.com.pk/issues/janmar03/article03.pdf

Shears, R. 2005. "Outrage as Muslim Cleric Likens Women to 'Uncovered Meat.'" *Daily Mail*, 26 October. Available at: http://www.dailymail.co.uk/news /article-412697/Outrage-Muslim-cleric-likens-women-uncovered-meat .html

Sheeley, E. R. 2007. *Reclaiming Honor in Jordan: A National Public Opinion Survey on "Honor" Killings.* Amman, Jordan: Black Iris.

Shepard, M., and Pence, E. 1988. "The Effects of Battering on the Employment Status of Women." *Affilia* 3(2): 55–61.

Shin, K. Y. 2006. "The Politics of the Family Law Reform Movement in Contemporary Korea: A Contentious Space for Korea and the Nation." *Journal of Korean Studies* 11(1): 93–126.

Singapore Women's Charter. 1 January 2017. Available at: https://sso.agc.gov.sg /Act/WC1961

Smith, Adam. 1776. *The Wealth of Nations.* Edwin Canaan, ed. 1994. New York: Modern Library.

Smith, A. 2015. "UK Poised to Miss Target for Women Board Members." *Financial Times.* 8 March. Available at: https://www.ft.com/content/f732b724-c35a -11e4-9c27-00144feab7de

Smith, S. 2015. "ISIS Militants Subject Wives to 'Brutal,' 'Abnormal' Sexual Acts; Abused Women Say Foreign Fighters Are 'Like Monsters.'" *Christian Post.* 19 February. Available at: http://www.christianpost.com/news/isis-militants -subject-wives-to-brutal-abnormal-sexual-acts-abused-women-say-foreign -fighters-are-like-monsters-134351/

Snively, S. 1994. *The New Zealand Economic Cost of Family Violence.* Auckland: Coopers and Lybrand.

Stanko, E. A., Crisp, D., Hale, C., and Lucraft, H. 1997. *Counting the Costs: Estimating the Impact of Domestic Violence in the London Borough of Hackney.* Middlesex, UK: Brunel University.

Stark, L., Roberts, L., Wheaton, W., Acham, A., Boothby, N., and Ager, A. 2010. "Measuring Violence Against Women Amidst War and Displacement in Northern Uganda Using the 'Neighborhood Method.'" *Journal of Epidemiology and Community Health* 64(12): 1056–1061.

Statistics Canada. 2006. "Measuring Violence Against Women." Statistical Trends 2006, Ministry of Industry. Available at: https://www.statcan.gc.ca/pub/85-570 -x/85-570-x2006001-eng.htm

Stotsky, J. 2006. "Gender and Its Relevance to Macroeconomic Policy: A Survey." IMF Working Paper WP/06/233. Available at: https://www.imf.org/external /pubs/ft/wp/2006/wp06233.pdf

Subbarao, K., and Raney, L. 1995. "Social Gains from Female Education: A Cross-National Study." *Economic Development and Cultural Change* 44 (1 Oct.): 105–128. Available at: https://www.journals.uchicago.edu/doi/abs/10. 1086/452202

Summers, L. 1992. "Investing in *All* the People." World Bank Policy Research Working Paper Series 905. Available at: https://pdfs.semanticscholar.org/40e4/5c33c9d6c83c068f78ef56d70f6972e6afe1.pdf

Swamy, A., Azfar, O., Knack, S., and Lee, Y. 2001. "Gender and Corruption." *Journal of Development Economics* 64(1): 25–55.

Tallan, C., and Taitz, E. (n.d.). "Learned Women in Traditional Jewish Society." *Jewish Women: A Comprehensive Historical Encyclopedia.* 1 March 2009. Available at: Jewish Women's Archive. https://jwa.org/encyclopedia/article/learned-women-in-traditional-jewish-society

Temin, P. 1997. "Is It Kosher to Talk about Culture?" *Journal of Economic History* 57(2): 267–287.

Terzieff, J. 2002. "Pakistan's Fiery Shame: Women Die in Stove Deaths." *Women's eNews.* 27 October. Available at: http://womensenews.org/2002/10/pakistans-fiery-shame-women-die-stove-deaths/

Thakur, U. 2015. "India Doesn't Understand Its Rape Problem." *Foreign Policy.* 12 January. Available at: http://foreignpolicy.com/2015/01/12/india-rape-verma-delhi-modi/

Thibos, M., Lavin-Loucks, D., and Martin, M. 2007. *The Feminization of Poverty: Empowering Women.* J. McDonald Williams Institute and YWCA, Joint Policy Forum on the Feminization of Poverty.

Thomas, D. 1990. "Intra-Household Resource Allocation: An Inferential Approach." *Journal of Human Resources* 25(4): 635–664.

Tiefenthaler, J. 2000. "The Economics of Domestic Violence." In *Reclaiming Women's Spaces: New Perspectives on Violence Against Women and Sheltering in South Africa.* Edited by Park, Y. J., Fedler, J., and Dangor, Z. Johannesburg: Nisaa Institute for Women's Development.

Udwin, L. 2015. "Delhi Rapist Says Victim Shouldn't Have Fought Back." *BBC News Magazine.* 3 March. Available at: http://www.bbc.com/news/magazine-31698154

UNICEF. 2018. "Literacy Among Youth Is Rising, but Young Women Lag Behind." Available at: https://data.unicef.org/topic/education/literacy/

United Nations. 2010. *The World's Women 2010: Trends and Statistics.* New York: Department of Economic and Social Affairs.

———. 2013a. *The Millennium Development Goals Report 2013.* New York: http://www.un.org/millenniumgoals/pdf/report-2013/mdg-report-2013-english.pdf

———. 2013b. *World Population Prospects: The 2012 Revision, Volume 1: Comprehensive Tables.* New York: Department of Economic and Social Affairs.

———. 2015. *The World's Women 2015: Trends and Statistics.* New York: Department of Economic and Social Affairs.

United Nations Food and Agriculture Organization. "Women and Decent Work." Available at: http://www.fao.org/rural-employment/work-areas/women-and-decent-work/en/

United Nations Global Initiative to Fight Human Trafficking. 2007. "Human Trafficking: The Facts." Available at: http://www.unglobalcompact.org/docs/issues_doc/labour/Forced_labour/HUMAN_TRAFFICKING_-_THE_FACTS_-_final.pdf

United Nations Human Rights. 2010. "The Right to Water." Fact Sheet 35. Available at: http://www.ohchr.org/Documents/Publications/FactSheet35en.pdf

United Nations Population Fund. 2006. *The Human Rights of Women.* Available at: http://www.unfpa.org/rights/women.htm

United Nations Security Council. Resolution 1267. Available at: https://en.wikipedia.org/wiki/United_Nations_Security_Council_Resolution_1267.

United Nations Treaty Collection. Available at: http://treaties.un.org/Pages/ViewDetails.aspx?src=TREATY&mtdsg_no=IV-8&chapter=4&lang=en

United Nations Treaty Collection. 1999. "Optional Protocol to the Convention on the Elimination of All Forms of Discrimination Against Women." 6 October. Available at: https://treaties.un.org/Pages/ViewDetails.aspx?src=TREATY&mtdsg_no=IV-8-b&chapter=4&lang=eng

United Nations Watch. 2015. "UN: Iran Discriminates Against Women." *UN Watch.* 1 March. Available at: http://blog.unwatch.org/index.php/2015/03/01/un-iran-discriminates-against-women/

United Nations Women. 2017a. Convention on the Elimination of All Forms of Discrimination Against Women. "Declarations, Reservations and Objections to CEDAW." Available at: http://www.un.org/womenwatch/daw/cedaw/reservations-country.htm

———. 2017b. Examples of Cases Where Women Have Used the First Optional Protocol to the ICCPR to Challenge Sex Discrimination. Available at: http://www.un.org/womenwatch/daw/cedaw/protocol/cases.htm

———. 2017c. "Facts and Figures: Leadership and Political Participation: Women in Parliaments." Available at: http://www.unwomen.org/en/what-we-do/leadership-and-political-participation/facts-and-figures

United States Equal Opportunity Employment Commission. 2016. "Select Task Force on the Study of Harassment in the Workplace." June. Available at: https://www.eeoc.gov/eeoc/task_force/harassment/report.cfm

Universal Declaration of Human Rights. 1948. Available at: http://www.ohchr.org/EN/UDHR/Documents/UDHR_Translations/eng.pdf

Universal House of Justice. 1985. *The Promise of World Peace.* Baha'i World Centre. Available at: http://reference.bahai.org/en/t/uhj/PWP/pwp-3.html

VicHealth. 2004. *The Health Costs of Violence: Measuring the Burden of Disease Caused by Intimate Partner Violence: A Summary of Findings.* Victoria, Australia: Victorian Health Promotion Foundation. Available at: http://www.vichealth.vic.gov.au/assets/contentFiles/ipv.pdf

Vlassoff, C. 1990. "The Value of Sons in an Indian Village: How Widows See It." *Population Studies* 44(1): 5–20.

Walby, S. 2004. *The Cost of Domestic Violence.* London: Women and Equality Unit.

Waldron, I. 1983. "Sex Differences in Human Mortality: The Role of Genetic Factors." *Social Science and Medicine* 17(6): 321–333.

———. 1998. "Sex Differences in Infant and Early Childhood Mortality: Major Causes of Death and Possible Biological Causes." In United Nations, *Too Young to Die: Genes or Gender?* New York, 64–83.

———. 2003. "Mortality Differentials by Sex." In *Encyclopedia of Population.* Edited by Demeny, P., and McNicoll, G. New York: Macmillan, 662–665.

Waring, M. 1988. *If Women Counted: A New Feminist Economics.* New York: Harper & Row.

———. 2004. *Counting for Nothing: What Men Value and What Women Are Worth.* Toronto: University of Toronto Press.

Wei, S., and Zhang, X. 2011a. "The Competitive Saving Motive: Evidence from Rising Sex Ratios and Savings Rates in China." *Journal of Political Economy* 119(3): 511–564.

———. 2011b. "Sex Ratios, Entrepreneurship, and Economic Growth in the People's Republic of China." Cambridge, MA: National Bureau of Economic Research Working Paper No. 16800.

Weiss, A. 2014. *Interpreting Islam, Modernity, and Women's Rights in Pakistan.* New York: Palgrave Macmillan. Available at: https://books.google.fr/books?id=ExpHBQAAQBAJ&printsec=frontcover&dq=A.Weiss+interpretation+religion&hl=en&sa=X&ved=0ahUKEwim3KmZsY7aAhXpB8AKHfcSBOkQ6AEIKDAA#v=onepage&q=A.Weiss%20interpretation%20religion&f=false

Welchman, L., and Hossain, S., eds., 2005. *"Honour": Crimes, Paradigms, and Violence Against Women.* New York: Zed Books.

Winthrop, R. 2015. "Global '100-Year Gap' in Education Standards." *BBC News.* 29 April. Available at: http://www.bbc.com/news/business-32397212

Wisner, C. L., Gilmer, T. P., Saltzman, L. E., and Zink, T. M. 1999. "Intimate Partner Violence Against Women: Do Victims Cost Health Plans More?" *Journal of Family Practice* 48(6): 439–443.

Wollstonecraft, M., and Mill, J. S. 1792. *Vindication of the Rights of Woman: With Strictures on Political and Moral Subjects.* London: Joseph Johnson.

Woolcock, M. 2014. "Culture, Politics, and Development." Policy Research Working Paper 6939. Washington, DC: World Bank. Available at: http://documents.worldbank.org/curated/en/199871468335978774/Culture-politics-and-development

Woolf, V. 1973. *A Room of One's Own.* United Kingdom: Penguin Modern Classics.

———. 1938. *Three Guineas.* United Kingdom: Hogarth Press.

World Bank. 2008. *World Development Report 2008: Agriculture for Development.* Washington DC.

———. 2010. *Women, Business and the Law: Measuring Legal Gender Parity for Entrepreneurs and Workers in 128 Economies.* Washington, DC.

———. 2012. *World Development Report: Gender Equality and Development.* Washington, DC.

———. 2013. *Women, Business and the Law: Removing Restrictions to Enhance Gender Equality.* London: Bloomsbury.

———. 2014. *World Development Indicators.* Washington, DC: World Bank.

———. 2016. "Labor Force Participation Rate, Female (% of female population ages 15+) (modeled ILO estimate)." International Labour Organization, ILOSTAT database. Available at: http://data.worldbank.org/indicator/SL.TLF.CACT.FE.ZS

World Bank Group. 2015. *Women, Business and the Law 2016: Getting to Equal.* Washington, DC: World Bank.

World Economic Forum. 2016. *The Global Gender Gap Report 2017.* Available at: https://www.weforum.org/reports/the-global-gender-gap-report-2017

World Health Organization. 2005. "Alcohol, Gender and Drinking Problems: Perspectives from Low and Middle Income Countries." Available at: http://www.who.int/substance_abuse/publications/alcohol_gender_drinking_problems.pdf

———. 2010. *Nutrition Landscape Information System: Country Profile Indicators.* Available at: http://whqlibdoc.who.int/publications/2010/9789241599955_eng.pdf

World Health Organization, UNICEF, UNFPA, and World Bank. 2010. *Trends in Maternal Mortality, 1990–2008.* New York: World Health Organization. Available at: http://apps.who.int/iris/bitstream/10665/44423/1/9789241500265_eng.pdf

World Values Survey. Available at: http://www.worldvaluessurvey.org/wvs.jsp

Yale Law Women. 2014. "Quality of Life Survey: Report and Analysis." Available at: http://www.yale.edu/ylw/survey.pdf

Yu, W.-H. 2002. "Jobs for Mothers: Married Women's Labor Force Reentry and Part-Time, Temporary Employment in Japan." *Sociological Forum* 17(3): 493–523.

Zakaria, F. 1994. "Culture Is Destiny: A Conversation with Lee Kuan Yew." *Foreign Affairs* 73(2): 109–126.

Zarya, V. 2016. "The Percentage of Female CEOs in the Fortune 500 Drops to 4%." *Fortune.* 6 June. Available at: http://fortune.com/2016/06/06/women-ceos-fortune-500-2016/

Zhu, W., Lu, L., and Hesketh, T. 2009. "China's Excess Males, Sex Selective Abortion, and One Child Policy: Analysis of Data from 2005 National Intercensus Survey." *British Medical Journal* 338: b1211. Available at: https://www.bmj.com/content/338/bmj.b1211

INDEX